Packard

ASK THE MAN
WHO OWNED ONE

THE LIFE AND TIMES OF THAT PROUD CAR
THAT BECAME A WAY~OF~LIFE AMONG THE
AMERICAN GENTRY — PORTRAYED BY PITHY
ADVERTISING FROM THE GREAT MAGAZINES

A selection by
Otto A. Schroeder

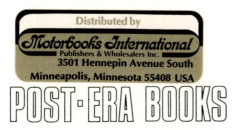

Distributed by

Motorbooks International
Publishers & Wholesalers Inc.
3501 Hennepin Avenue South
Minneapolis, Minnesota 55408 USA

POST-ERA BOOKS

Arcadia CA 91006

Nearly eighty years ago, a young woman secretary held a letter before her employer and said:

*"This man asks for more information, for literature. He says he wants to know how he can be **sure** that the car we make is a good one."*

James Ward Packard stared out of the window a few moments, then swung around toward the waiting girl.

*"Tell him that we have no literature — we aren't that big yet. But if he wants to know how good an automobile the Packard is, tell him to **ask the man who owns one.**"*

Because of its sincerity, and its sound common sense, this man's expression of perfect faith in the product bearing his name became one of the most familiar slogans in American life.

The slogan became a creed.

Foreword

In the early years of the American motor age Packard established a reputation for quality, comfort and prestige unprecedented in the industry. Its workmanship in cars, trucks, and marine and aircraft engines came to be known all over the world.

The origin of this enterprise by the Packard brothers down in Ohio, and its growth into a firm that became Detroit's proudest jewel, is a story marked by an integrity nearly unique in an industry known for cutthroat methods.

Even its radiator design reflected consistency. In the pioneer years Packard established a distinctive ox-yoke shape which it later carried over into each succeeding model.

Packard's sound business practices weathered both the early trials of an infant industry and the responsibility of a mature company in the forefront of the fine car field.

Packard engineers ventured far to make Packard cars better. The company led the way with eight cylinders-in-line, four wheel brakes, completely machined combustion chambers, noiseless axle bevel gears, automatic chassis lubrication and even steel-cored steering wheels.

The public came to respect the idea that it could save money by paying slightly more in original cost and keeping its cars longer. Packard consistently protected the investment of its owners by building cars which could, without sacrifice of comfort or prestige, be driven longer than the usual.

For an exciting generation Packard dominated the luxury production car field. A host of other well-intended automobiles, among them the Alco, Lozier, Pope Hartford and Stevens-Duryea, fell by the wayside.

Later, the Locomobile, the Peerless and the Mercer, magnificent cars all, would cease production in a continuing bow to Packard's supremacy with the gentry. Even the Winton, which years before had inspired original construction of the Packard car, failed to maintain parity.

The market for cars built without compromise ended, for all practical purposes, in 1930. As the field narrowed to minor favorites like the Pierce-Arrow, the Marmon, the Stutz, the Kissel, the Lincoln and the big Chryslers, even General Motors' most popular contender, the Cadillac, was still being outsold by Packard two-to-one.

Then the concept of greater volume entered the picture. All of Packard's accumulated skill went into its building. New tools brought even finer results than those that had developed the Packard reputation. The lighter car met with instant public approval.

Packard had begun to confuse Park Avenue with Main Street. With the introduction of the lower priced car, the tremendous obligation imposed by Packard's willingness to rest its reputation entirely upon the experience of *any Packard owner* became broader than ever before. For a while Packard seemed to be pleasing two worlds. Midst mixed product and emotion, for a generation to come, the venerable company was to forge onward. But the grand times lay behind by the closing years of the Thirties. No automobile lineage can be more clearly traced through its own promotional literature than the Packard, in whose behalf the company issued some of the most graphically elegant and expensive to produce advertising brochures ever freely distributed to the prospect for any new motor car.

The same story can be told in more cursory tones through a thoughtful and representative selection of magazine advertising, for Packard was also noted as a heavy investor in the display pages of the consumer periodicals of its era. This volume has been compiled in just such a manner, to unfold the Packard story for the novice. More detailed lore and descriptions of the full line, which encompassed superb custom models by Brunn, Dietrich, Rollston and others, is offered in the vast body of original literature. To depict this story through reproduction of the highlight pieces of this literature would require many volumes the size of this one.

Time was when the Packard truck was as prominent and respected in commerce and industry as was the passenger automobile on the avenue. Packard was one of the first companies to produce both trucks and cars. For the decade preceding the first war this proud conveyor was a familiar sight. Its heyday occurred during the war, after which its importance declined concurrently with the rise of specialty truck builders.

It has been my pleasure to have grown up with Packard in the great days. I removed and preserved these pages from various magazines beginning in the earliest days of my interest as a young boy, with an issue from 1902. Together with complementary material from J. L. Elbert, whose pursuits were similar to mine over a somewhat later calendar period, these ads have been arranged to portray the Packard story from its beginning through the years of World War II.

Only the Packard Motor Company speaks in this volume, making it a primary reference source for both enthusiast and historian. The turbulent early story is drawn from company-issued Educational Bulletins, as are a series of introductory notes which delineate model progression. For the first generation, and more, successive Packard models were marked, not by the calendar, but, by the company's policy of introducing improvements when, and as, they were developed and proven.

Post World War II ads, which chronicle the decline and fall of the Packard, are omitted from this volume. Being the most recent, they would have been the easiest to include. But, somehow, to a buff who has followed the Packard from its infancy, and basked in the reflected glory of its golden years, the postwar cars seem but faint images of those early gleaming chassis. The Packard, as I knew it, ended with the war.

As Garet Garrett, once the editor of *The Saturday Evening Post,* observed in his conclusion to *THE WILD WHEEL*:

> It was a world many people grew not to want, or wanted so little that they were unwilling to defend it. Only the strong could love it. Anyhow it is gone. The number of those who knew it is rapidly dwindling. In a little while nobody living will be able to remember it at all.
> . . . You may like it better this way. Many people do. In any case, it was not to be argued. Only this — that if *laissez faire* had not begotten the richest world that ever existed there would have been much less for the welfare state to distribute.

The Packard, the apple of my eye for thirty-five years, was the crowning symbol of that glorious age in America.

— Otto A. Schroeder
July 1974

Contents

DOWN *through the* YEARS *with* PACKARD

By
H. F.
OLMSTED
~
The First
Chapter

Ask *the* man who owns one

The first factory at Warren, O.   *W. D. Packard in an early model.*

SOME 35 or 40 years ago, among all of the beautiful, little towns in Ohio, a state noted for the character of its villages and hamlets, one of the prettiest, also one of the most somnolent was Warren. It has changed but little.

Along Warren's well-kept streets, shaded with age-old maples and elms, lived typical Ohio retired business men and farmers possessed of modest wealth and a desire to spend the rest of their years in quiet comfort away from the hurry and flurry of business. In the clear waters of the Mahoning River were black bass, and quail in the fields. Seldom did there occur anything to mar the quiet serenity of the village.

Then Came Steel

Steel had taken possession of the Mahoning valley a few miles down the stream and had made of Niles, Girard and Youngstown a district of humming activity, smoke, hard men of steel and countless restless dollars accumulating into vast riches. Warren wanted nothing of steel, or the dollars and trouble that are born of steel. It strove hard to bar manufacturing enterprises from its borders and it looked askance on innovations of any kind.

Two young men of the village cared nothing for the bass in the river, the quail in the fields, afternoon siestas, or other kindred features of normal

BACK of the metals and materials which fashion your Packard lies a history more fascinating than fiction. What of these brothers who gave the car you drive its name? Why did they enter this fearsome horseless carriage business and what path did their success trace through automotive history? To answer such questions Mr. Olmsted has compiled what might be termed the only Packardana in existence. From a variety of historical sources he draws a graphic picture of old Model A's birth in this article, the first of a series to acquaint owners with their Packard heritage.

Warren daily routine. They insisted on doing things and making things. They were brothers, J. W. and W. D. Packard.

People of the town one night were nearly startled out of their customary calm. In front of the Packard home a great light hung over the street. Nearly the whole town turned out to see it. It was Warren's first arc lamp and one of the very first hung up in a city street anywhere. The Packard boys had made it during weeks of intensive effort.

People of Warren could never tell what would be made next by the Packard brothers from the time they were youngsters. They continued a close partnership through youth and into manhood. Lehigh University gave J. W. Packard's natural mechanical genius a finishing polish and W. D. Packard developed a genius for business administration and financing. The partnership thus represented an organization of both management and manufacturing. It developed a successful company for making electric lamps and other electrical equipment, later incorporated as the Ohio Electric Company. The business prospered and the Packards were regarded as moderately wealthy.

Horseless carriages began to be thought possible and the Packard brothers conceived the idea of building one for themselves. In 1893 drawings were made for a carriage to

J. W. Packard   *Their arc lamp— an early venture.*   *W. D. Packard*

be built at the electrical shop and negotiations were opened to buy a motor from Charles King of Detroit. The industrial depression of 1893 intervened and the project was dropped for the time.

It was in 1898 that J. W. Packard took his first real vacation. He made a trip to France. Hardly had he landed in that country when he saw what was then one of Europe's best horseless carriages, a queer contraption of three wheels and an ability to keep going, sometimes for as long as a half-mile without a stop. It interested him even more than his first electric arc lamp, and he bought one to take back to Ohio with him. At home the two brothers tinkered with it for weeks and finally were able to keep it running for miles without stopping, much to the discomfiture of the whole Warren citizenry.

Another horseless carriage seemed less complicated and easier of operation to them when they had an opportunity to inspect it. They ordered one just like it and it too had to be imported from Europe.

Warren Packard, son of W. D. and active in the company today, in the motoring outfit of early days.

Saved by a Team

Some time later J. W. Packard heard that a man in Cleveland by the name of Alexander Winton had made a horseless carriage which operated rather successfully, so he hurried to Cleveland to buy one. Fourteen hours were required to get this new machine over the 50 miles of road between Cleveland and Warren. It arrived in tow of a team of horses. During the trip, J. W. Packard believed he saw many ways by which it could be improved. Further experiences with the carriage strengthened his belief that *he* could build a better one and his brother agreed.

It took months to do the job in a little shed attached to the electrical manufacturing plant. On November 6, 1899, the carriage was finished and rolled out of the shed. There was little that was complicated about it and in appearance it was greatly different from horseless carriages which had been built up to that time. It had the finished appearance of a fine horse-drawn carriage and it was noticeably lacking in a maze of wires, wheels and gadgets thought necessary then for a self-propelled vehicle. However, more important still, it ran. It climbed hills, pulled through sand and mud, and kept right on chugging its slow, deep-throated chugs from its single cylinder until the throwing of an electrical switch gave it the signal to stop, just as with its brothers of today.

The machine had several things which are almost universally used on modern automobiles. It had three speeds forward and one reverse through the sliding the belt drive. So successfully did the original Packard car work and so insistent were friends that similar vehicles be built for them, that plans were made to manufacture others.

The Packards were aided in the building of their machine by George L. Weiss of Cleveland, who was one of the organizers of the Winton Company, and by W. A. Hatcher, who had been the Winton shop superintendent. "J. W." and Hatcher took charge of the mechanical part of the job and "W. D." and Weiss looked after the financial and business ends.

A partnership was formed with Weiss on December 30, 1899, and work was started on a second car. The first sale of the new automobile company occurred January 3, 1900, when the first vehicle was purchased by George D. Kirkham for $1250.

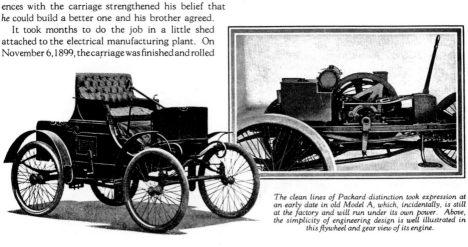

The clean lines of Packard distinction took expression at an early date in old Model A, which, incidentally, is still at the factory and will run under its own power. Above, the simplicity of engineering design is well illustrated in this flywheel and gear view of its engine.

The Second Chapter

Ask the man who owns one

© BROWN BROS.

An exhibition of easy maneuverability.

The show where Packard first exhibited.

REAL attention began to center on the work of the new automobile firm in Warren, O., when J. W. Packard and Weiss on May 21, 1900, drove the second car they had built from Warren to Cleveland by way of Ashtabula, a distance of more than 100 miles, between 10:20 A. M. and 7:15 P. M. —of the same day! Five days later they drove from Warren to Buffalo, N. Y., in 13½ hours and would have made it in less, probably, had battery trouble not slowed them up. Another trip which attracted much attention was that of A. F. Harris, of Warren, from his home to Lakewood, N. Y.

Weiss, acting as the salesman of the organization, obtained an order for a special machine from W. D. Sargent, of Chicago. It was provided with a copper-jacketed cylinder and had four speeds. Mr. Sargent obtained his carriage October 24, 1900, and paid $1750 for it. A few more of the standard machines were also built and sold.

It was decided to display one of these at an automobile show in Madison Square Garden, New York. The exhibition, held from November 5 to 10, consisted principally in the driving of carriages around a circular track

EARLY electrical ventures of the Packard brothers in Warren, O., their investigation of the horseless carriage, the building of historic Model A and formation of the first company in response to the demand of friends were described in the last issue. Continuing in this series to give owners the fascinating history back of their Packard purchase, Mr. Olmsted traces the "Quality First" standard of Packard manufacture back to the pioneer days of production problems when the famous slogan, "Ask The Man Who Owns One," was originated.

Packard

WE DO NOT WANT YOU TO THINK THAT OUR CAR CONTAINS EVERYTHING THAT IS POSSIBLE IN AN AUTOMOBILE. THERE ARE A GREAT MANY THINGS WHICH OTHER VEHICLES WILL DO WHICH THE PACKARD MOTOR CAR WILL NOT—AND WE ARE THANKFUL FOR THAT.

WE KNOW that, with the same care and attention, it will give you better satisfaction than any other automobile made. There are two ways for you to make dead sure of this:

ASK THE MAN WHO OWNS ONE

AND

BUY ONE.

From the 1902 catalog—an early printed record of the famous slogan.

in the Garden. Obstacles were placed at various points on the track and the carriages were driven· among them to demonstrate how easily they could be handled.

The "Packard carriage," as it was called, was declared to be the center of interest at the show. It was operated so successfully that orders for a special machine and two standard vehicles were taken at the track. Newspapers began giving much attention to the horseless carriage, and, early in 1901, the arrest of Alden S. McMurtry at Warren, O., on the charge of having driven his Packard 40 miles an hour in the city streets, was considered an international news item.

Enough of the cars of the new firm were operating in 1901 so that the service problem was born. Besides manufacturing the machines, J. W. Packard took care of the service end of the business and gave not only technical advice but also instructions in driving to new owners.

"Minor parts which are apt to give out on our carriage are very few," he wrote G. E. Warner, an owner at Buffalo, N. Y., in a letter dated May 3, 1901. "We would hardly know what parts to send for a reserve supply. There is not a bolt on the carriage which is not riveted; pinions, gears, etc., have never in our experience been broken."

Mr. Warner was somewhat interested in a machine having more than one cylinder and wrote J. W. Packard to inquire if the manufacture of such a carriage was contemplated.

Mr. Packard replied that he considered a single cylinder for anything less than 20 horsepower much preferable to a double or four-cylinder machine. "Ask any user of a gasoline-motor vehicle if a single cylinder does not give him trouble enough without adding another one," he added in this letter. "Your sparking and battery troubles are bound to be doubled, and two small cylinders, even if they figure out to the same capacity, are not nearly equal to one larger one, as the larger engine is much more efficient and with our system is under control."

Road Tests

During 1900 and 1901, both J. W. and W. D. Packard made frequent trips in their machine and many improvements resulted from their personal experiences on the road. The first car, and several of those which followed, were steered with a shovel-handle tiller. Sometimes the front wheels would catch in deep ruts and throw the driver out into the mud if he kept a tight hold on the steering handle. The old tiller soon gave way to a wheel, and Packard was the first car in this country to be steered with a wheel.

A 10 or 12-mile trip in a horseless carriage in those early times was a good day's work. Farmers were wont to place logs across the roads for the hapless motorist to crash against. Boards with nails in them and broken glass were strewn along the highways so thickly by farmers that a trip of 10

miles without at least one puncture was practically out of the question.

"We were constantly changing tires," said J. W. Packard; "this, too, despite the fact that in order to keep them running we were filling tires with all kinds of dope. One such mixture, designed to close up the hole in case of a puncture, I remember quite well. It was composed of glue and chicken feathers and was placed in a double-walled inner tube. It stopped a small hole, but if there happened to be a bad cut or blow-out, then car, pilot and passenger received a shower of the concoction. It was not unusual to see a car come in looking as if both it and the occupants had been through a most successful tar-and-feathering party."

The Origin

Their "long" trips over roads which would give motor cars of today a real test afforded the Packard brothers a great amount of valuable data in their unending struggle to make their car better. On the cover of the first Packard catalogue was printed the now famous slogan, Ask The Man Who Owns One, and the Packards were striving their utmost to live up to the obligation which the phrase entailed.

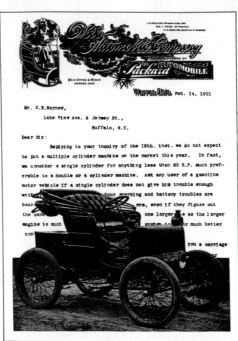

The Packard policy of proven yet advanced engineering instead of impractical ventures took form at an early date, as this letter indicates. It was borne out by Model C, pictured above, first American-built car to provide the convenience of wheel steering.

When it was decided to build the first Packard for sale, it was determined that it would have to be of the same high quality as the Packard brothers' electrical products, which were bringing them fame. They agreed that the carriage they built would have to be so good that the man who owned one would, through his enthusiasm, recommend it to his friends or to anyone wanting a machine whom he might meet. Thus, Ask The Man Who Owns One, became a creed which has lost none of its force in more than a quarter of a century.

The
Third
Chapter

Ask the man who owns one

Model F of 1902, first to use artillery wood wheels

The original Packard office building at Warren, O.

THESE early struggles into which the Packards poured a boundless enthusiasm, unlimited energy and the wizardry of a mechanical genius—J. W. Packard—gave much to the motor car of today. The automatic spark advance, now as much an accepted part of every automobile as its tires, was an original Packard patent granted February 12, 1901. The gear shift "H" slot so universally used on cars of today was another original Packard patent granted November 4, 1902.

While these are the best known devices in modern general use, there were many others. Inter-connected clutch and brake on one pedal; three-point suspension of motors; the toe rest at the side of the accelerator pedal; separating devices for the bows to prevent top material from chafing when the top was lowered; internal and external brakes on the rear wheels and many more could be added to the list.

You Use This Today

A patent granted in 1905 covered a device by which the hand control of the engine throttle could be set as desired and the foot control operated without disturbing the setting of the hand control. This also is universally used on modern motor cars. Another contribution whose pioneering dates back to early Packard days is the spiral bevel gears in the rear axle of practically every car driven today.

The men who blazed such trails in building the first Packard cars were forerunners of a new art. There was no great accumulated mass of engineering and manufacturing data to aid them. They had to work things out for themselves. It may be that

From the time the two Packard brothers startled staid Warren, O., with their arc lamp to the birth chugs of Model A, the exhibit at the first Show and the origin of the famous slogan, Mr. Olmsted has traced the Packard heritage which is that of every Packard owner today. He continues this series with an outline of pioneering contributions to the modern motor car and a description of some early manufacturing problems.

this is one of the greatest heritages handed down to the Packard of today. The pioneering spirit still persists. It is the spirit which causes the Packard organization to seek continuously to better both the car and the methods of producing it. The entire automobile industry continues to receive many benefits of the Packard inventive genius.

Nearly all of the difficulties experienced by the early Packard genius embodied in the two Packard brothers

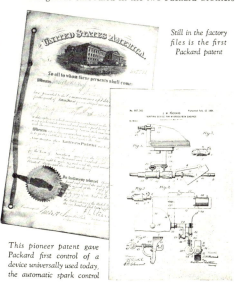

Still in the factory files is the first Packard patent

This pioneer patent gave Packard first control of a device universally used today, the automatic spark control

was due to materials used in the cars. The manufacturer who supplied them with wheels at one time refused to make any more for them because the Packards rejected so many as not meeting their strict standards. The only steel they could find which proved suitable for gears was that made for armor-piercing shells for the Navy. Gray-iron castings imported direct from France were used for the cylinders.

Pioneers in Heat-Treatment

Armor-piercing shell steel proved to be so hard that it ruined the tools and broke up the gear cutters. The machine tool builders washed their hands of the problems then presented. This forced the Packard brothers into the heat-treatment of steel, a science in which Packard was a pioneer and one which revolutionized manufacturing processes throughout the world.

"A trouble which involved both design and materials," said J. W. Packard in an interview about his experiences of the early days, "came when we put a governor on our spark. We were afraid to let the engine run too fast, so we had the spark stopped at what we thought a safe point. One of the men in Warren learned that he could move the governor and after he did so, ran circles around every other car in town. Finally he speeded up the engine too fast. The fly-wheel blew up and with it went the whole car. Another of the early troubles in design had to do with the likelihood that the wheels would deflect whenever they hit a bump. The construction was such that if one wheel were elevated much beyond the other, the whole car would swing toward the lower side. There was a constant stream of cars running into ditches or trying to climb telegraph poles as a result. We finally put in a special radius link which largely prevented this."

W. D. Packard's son, Warren, frequently was a passenger on the test trips his father and "J. W." took with the first cars. He was the proud custodian of two of the most important touring accessories: the box of ammonia-filled glass balls and a common building brick. Dogs insisted on running alongside the car and nipping the tires—until discouraged by the ammonia released when the glass balls were shattered against their noses. The brick was an emergency brake. If the car at any time stopped on a bad hill, the custodian of the brick had to jump out quickly and place it under a real wheel.

Hostile farmers, frightened horses, nail-studded boards hidden in the dust of highways and roads the best of which today would be thought all but impassable, made motoring of this pioneering period a matter of high adventure. That there might have been considerable justification for the feeling farmers held against the new fangled contraptions which rattled and coughed their alarming way along the country roads at the breath-taking speed of 15 miles an hour is indicated in Warren Packard's recollection of the first trip he made with his uncle and father. There were 10 runaways.

They Ran

However, the automobiles of the period did run. The first Packard catalog points with pride to the record of five Packard cars on an endurance trip of many different makes over a course from New York to Buffalo. Eighty-nine machines started, 44 finished and among them all five of the Packards, the catalog points out, adding that four were given "First Class Certificates." The average speed of the winners in the endurance contest was from 10 to 15 miles an hour.

Tireless efforts on the part of the Packard brothers to better the materials going into their machines and to simplify the cars themselves made of the first Packards "horseless carriages" that were outstanding. They obtained a reputation for reliability, a most important attribute in the days when "get out and get under" really and truly meant something.

A VISITOR to the Packard plant today is given transportation in one of the company "courtesy cars." Here is its forerunner, "courtesy car" of the old firm at Warren

The First Packard Store in Manhattan   W. D. Packard Leaving New York on a Run

BACK in 1900 and 1901 the "horseless carriage" or "motor wagon" was thought by the greater part of the world to be a passing fad only. Its quick death and the return of wealthy men who were playing with the new "fad" to fine horses was thought to be a matter of only a very short time.

First came the early electrical ventures of the Packard brothers in Warren, O. How Model A was built and the origin of "Ask The Man Who Owns One" then followed. Next, manufacturing problems of the past and pioneer work in patents appeared. Now Mr. Olmsted adds more background to the history heritage of every Packard owner with this chapter on the company's move to Detroit.

Michigan Stove Company and, placed in his motor boat, it worked.

Mr. Joy was looking for a machine which would start, when he and Mr. Newberry set out on their shopping expedition in New York. He had considerable doubt about his quest, for he knew the problems concerning carburetors and how little progress had been made toward meeting them.

However, even with the limited market offered in 1901 for the automobile, the machines produced by the Packard brothers operated so well that purchasers paid a premium for them. It was about this time that a sales place was opened in New York for Packard "carriages" by the firm of Adams and McMurtry.

Shopping in New York

New York was to a very considerable extent the market place for the new "horseless carriage." Because of this Henry B. Joy, of Detroit, went to New York to shop for one. He was accompanied by his brother-in-law, Truman H. Newberry, when he set out to look over the carriages offered.

Mr. Joy had always been attracted to things mechanical. Possessed of a fortune he was enabled to gratify a desire to experiment with machinery. He had owned for some time a motor boat with a gasoline motor and in a small way had manufactured gasoline motors for boats. Hence he knew some of the ills to which the gasoline engine was then subject.

Ignition and carburetion were the two things which most often tried the patience of the gasoline engine owner. Mr. Joy himself had met the ignition problem largely by fashioning what probably was the first spark plug ever to be placed in a gasoline motor. He made it from a bit of mica he obtained at the plant of the

One of the first stops was at a store where a steam carriage was on exhibit. There was no question about

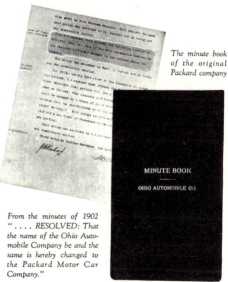

The minute book of the original Packard company

From the minutes of 1902 ".... RESOLVED: That the name of the Ohio Automobile Company be and the same is hereby changed to the Packard Motor Car Company."

a steam engine starting and the makers of this "wagon" made a big point of this. Mr. Joy had nearly made up his mind that the steam-engine-driven machine was the one he wanted. An accident, however, started him looking further and the present Packard Motor Car Company was one of the results.

Mr. Newberry was inspecting a glass tube fastened at the side of the carriage which showed the level of the water in the boiler. Suddenly it exploded almost in Mr. Newberry's face. That ended further consideration of steam-driven carriages, and the shopping continued.

The Adams and McMurtry store was the next place visited. In front of it were two of the carriages made by the Packard brothers about which Mr. Joy and Mr. Newberry had heard considerable. The two shoppers from Detroit looked them over carefully. Mr. Joy was much impressed with them, reserving however the paramount question: "Would they start?"

As he made up his mind to go in the store and consult with some one on this point, the question was answered emphatically in the affirmative. For many pieces of fire apparatus came dashing on up the street. The drivers of the waiting machines ran to their carriages. They threw on the switches and

Sometimes "endurance runs" tested the strength of farmers' horses

gave quick spins to the starting cranks at the sides. Both began their deep-throated coughing from their one cylinder and each sped away in pursuit.

Mr. Joy was satisfied. The engines in these Packard carriages did start, and more important, they started when their owners wanted them to do so. He bought one of the carriages immediately for $1200 and by paying a bonus of $100 succeeded in getting delivery. From this grew the Packard Motor Car Company.

Mr. Joy tinkered with his car as he had tinkered with his motor boat. He made frequent trips to Warren because of his deep interest in the machine and consulted with J. W. Packard on ways the engine could be improved. During one of these trips he invested $25,000 in the Packard brothers' company, then known as the Ohio Automobile Company.

J. W. Packard confided to Mr. Joy his belief that it would be possible to build and sell 200 carriages in a single year. It was agreed by both, however, that a new plant of very much greater size would be necessary. Also, additional financing would be needed.

Mr. Packard set out to interest friends in Pittsburgh or Cleveland in the proposal to build a plant and manufacture the unprecedented number of 200 machines in the first year. He was told at every hand just how ridiculous a thing the horseless carriage was and how supremely ridiculous was the idea of putting into a company enough money to build a big plant and manufacture 200 machines.

Mr. Joy and Mr. Newberry in the meantime consulted a number of friends in Detroit who already knew much about the Packard carriage through having seen it operate under their hands. They readily agreed to become investors in the company and to build a Detroit plant.

Like Mr. Joy and Mr. Newberry, they were all young men of wealth and sons of well-known Michigan pioneer families. This has had an effect of the utmost importance on the Packard Motor Car Company ever since its very inception. For Packard never has been forced by necessity to depart from its ideals. It has been able to adhere rigidly to its first adopted plan of building only the best automobile it could produce. It was organized and owned by men whose names were already well known in America.

As in every business Packard in its first two years needed more and more money. This need, however, never was so great that the large fortunes and almost unlimited credit of its organizers were not ample to meet it. In all its years of history Packard never has felt the pinch for money that has driven many a manufacturer to court ultimate disaster by sacrificing quality for quick profits.

It was on October 13, 1902, that the directors of the old Ohio Automobile Company voted to increase the capital stock to $500,000 to provide for shares to be issued to the Detroit investors. The name of the company was changed to "Packard Motor Car Company".

Mr. Newberry at the time of the early company

Mr. Joy shortly after Packard moved to Detroit

THE whole year of 1902 stands out conspicuously in the early history of Packard because of the far-reaching results of many important decisions then made. The decision for expansion of the small Warren company through Detroit capital was an outstanding one in its bearing on the young industry then struggling to get on firmer feet.

A review of the infant among the country's industries up to 1922 is most interesting.

In 1895 there were only four cars built in America. In 1899, the year of the first Packard, approximately 2500 cars were produced. In 1902, there were manufactured in round numbers about 9000 cars.

From the time that the first American automobile made its appearance in 1895 up to the close of 1902 there had been 128 automobile companies organized, which had built a total of 25,629 cars. One hundred and seven of these concerns sprung into existence during the memorable years of 1900, 1901 and 1902.

It was during this highly competitive period that the "trade in" was born. Horses, buggies and carriages were taken as part payments on new automobiles at amazing values. Even saddles and harnesses were accepted. Cheap cars were priced high enough to permit of heavy allowances. The manufacturer of one of these once told Mr. J. W. Packard he so established his prices that he "could allow a couple of thousand dollars on a second-hand wheelbarrow and still make money."

This fascinating serial first outlined the early mechanical start of the Packard brothers in Warren, O. It has traced the growth of Packard through the birth of Model A, the origin of the famous slogan, pioneer work in manufacturing and patents, and last how Detroit investors became interested in the car. Mr. Olmsted continues this history of Packard's prestige background

Competition was further heightened by reason of the fact that the market was limited. The "horseless carriage" was deemed only a plaything of the rich. It was struggling valiantly against every kind of adversity. Only men of great vision and daring could see the tremendous possibilities that lay just ahead in the business of making automobiles. Manufacturers themselves had to get out on the road with their carriages and prove they would run. Bankers looked askance at the "horseless carriage" and refused to aid with their dollars in its development. Money and men who were not afraid to use it in backing their business judgment—men with ability to see far into the future—formed the crying need of the automobile industry, infant of them all.

Above, leading home a "trade in." Below, the famous Packard "Grey Wolf," first to do a mile-a-minute

It was of particular significance that just at this time Detroit capital became interested in Packard.

The town of Warren was unsympathetic to the automobile. It was a quiet residential place and preferred to remain quiet. Mechanics imported from other places to work in the Ohio Automobile Company's plant, had difficulty in finding homes in which to live. Roads were poor but the city was inclined to feel that because they were good enough for wagons and carriages, they would have to serve for the "new-fangled" vehicles.

When production was increased from 12 cars a year to 24, the Warren bankers began to wonder where there would be sale for such a quantity. This was the state of affairs when Henry B. Joy and Truman H. Newberry interested other Packard owners and personal friends in Detroit in the possibilities of manufacturing a high-class type of car, with Detroit the center of the new automotive project.

Here is Model K, the car for which they used to get $7500!

The transmission on the rear axle as first introduced by Packard

What this car should be was a point over which there was much discussion. It was agreed however that the manufacturing ideals of J. W. and W. D. Packard established with the building of their first car must be continued, and that any machine to be built must be the best that the company could produce, sparing neither designs, materials or labor.

Some time before, while driving in Bronx Park in New York, J. W. Packard and Mr. Joy had met Charles Schmidt, former superintendent of the Mors automobile factory in France. Subsequently they found Schmidt in jail at Greenwich, Conn., where he had been arrested for running over a dog with his car. They rescued Schmidt and took him to Warren to aid in the design of a new car which would replace the single-cylinder Packard machine, built up to that time.

It was realized that the single-cylinder car, successful as it had proved among other cars of the day, was out of date. Decision was reached to build a four-cylinder machine and Schmidt went to work on it. Model K

was the result. It proved entirely too complicated and too expensive for the market then offered for horseless carriages. It was necessary to put a price of $7500 on it.

While Model K proved impractical and a start on a new model was necessary at once, the experiments and work which had been carried on in the development of Model K furnished a number of important innovations. Principal among these was the radical departure represented in placing the transmission on the rear axle. The same design also was used in building the *Grey Wolf*, one of the most famous racing cars in history. This Packard was the first automobile to put the record for one mile below one minute. Probably it had more to do than any other one machine in centering world attention on the possibilities offered by the horseless carriage.

Incidentally the *Grey Wolf* in appearance was much the same as the racing cars of today. It was beautifully streamlined and weighed less than 1500 pounds. The radiator consisted of a series of long copper tubes which extended along each side of the body. This system of radiation was used by Great Britain in building the winner of the 1927 Schneider Cup race. Elimination of the resistance offered by other radiators aided the British entry in reaching a speed of more than 300 miles an hour. The "new" radiator was much discussed.

With the design still in process for the car which the new Detroit company was to build, reorganization of the old company was completed. The first stockholders' meeting was held January 29, 1903. In this session Directors were elected as follows: J. W. Packard, W. D. Packard, Russell A. Alger, Jr., T. H. Newberry, Philip H. McMillan, Henry B. Joy, Joseph Boyer and S. D. Waldon. Stockholders in the company at the time of the first meeting were the following: J. W. Packard, W. D. Packard, P. H. McMillan, Russell A. Alger, Jr., F. M. Alger, John S. Newberry, T. H. Newberry, Robert E. Gorton, S. D. Waldon, Henry B. Joy, C. A. DuCharme and Rembrandt Peale.

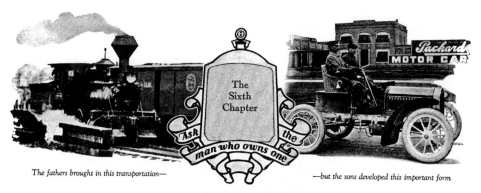

The Sixth Chapter

Ask the man who owns one

The fathers brought in this transportation—

—but the sons developed this important form

THE original Packard Motor Car Company to quite some extent was a family affair and still remains so. The McMillan, Alger, Newberry and Joy families were the moving forces in its organization and they have been principal owners and, to a large extent, directors of the company's destinies ever since.

All four families were closely related either by business or blood ties. The new motor car company was destined to bring them into even closer relationship, an harmonious association that was to steer Packard over the dangerous shoals of early days and carry it to the high place in the world of industry it

Starting with the pioneer mechanical work of the Packard brothers, this serial has traced the inception of Model A and has carried Packard history through its early engineering, manufacturing and patent work. Formation of the Detroit company followed and now Mr. Olmsted adds more interesting facts to the prestige background behind the Packard company and Packard products

The early locks at the Soo which Mr. Joy helped construct

built the first locks at Sault Ste. Marie and then turned his attention from water to rail transportation, building later the Kansas City, Fort Scott and Gulf railroad. He had much to do with the building of the Union Pacific railroad and erected the first railroad bridge across the Missouri River. With Lewis Cass and Zachariah Chandler he interested Cornelius Vanderbilt in the possibilities offered by the great but almost virgin State of Michigan. Thus he obtained for the Wolverine State its greatest need at that time: adequate railroad transportation.

R. A. Alger, Sr., Senator James Mc-Millan and John S. Newberry, Sr., were

now holds. Perhaps this had much to do with the fact, most unique in the automobile business, that Packard's organization has remained practically unchanged for more than a quarter of a century.

The Joy family had made its mark in Michigan through James F. Joy, father of Henry B. and Richard P. Joy, names now almost synonymous with Packard. James F. Joy, professor of law at Dartmouth College, had come to Michigan in 1836 when 24 years old. He

closely associated with Mr. Joy in the development of their state. In the Alger Smith Company the senior Mr. Alger was one of the great figures in the famous Michigan white pine days. He became one of the biggest lumber operators in the white pine forests of both Michigan and Canada. Later he relaxed from business enough to become Secretary of War during the administration of President McKinley. He held that post during the Spanish-American War.

Contrast the Detroit River front in 1905, shortly after Packard began production in that city,—

Senator James McMillan and John S. Newberry, Sr., were pioneers also in furnishing railroad transportation facilities to Michigan and to a great part of the rest of the country. In the early days of railroading in the United States all money that could be obtained was needed for rights of way and road construction work. So little was left for rolling stock that most of the car equipment was leased from private companies. Mr. Newberry and Mr. McMillan built large shops in Detroit and turned out thousands of freight cars which were rented to railroads on a mileage basis.

All four of these men, Joy, Alger, Newberry and McMillan, were possessed of great vision. They foresaw something of the future position Michigan was to hold in the Union and it was plain to them that Detroit would always be the State's metropolis. As they amassed large sums in their pioneer development work, they invested heavily in Detroit real estate. The Joy, McMillan and Newberry estates today are among the most important real estate owners of the city.

Just around the corner from the early Detroit building site

Something of the pioneer spirit of their fathers must have been possessed by the young men who back in 1903 went into the then hazardous business of building horseless carriages. It was needed, too, during those first two or three years. During this period of Packard's development these scions of great pioneer builders were to receive the jeers and scoffings of their friends and acquaintances, just as without doubt their fathers before them had when they fought against countless adversities toward goals that their clear vision of the future held always before them.

But the interesting thing is that as each generation had its struggles against a new idea, that new idea was based on the one theme: transportation, whether by water, rail or road; and as did the fathers succeed in their clear-headed vision so did the sons in their enterprise, which was then a novelty.

Captains Courageous

Perhaps an even stronger courage was needed by these young men for during two whole years they were assailed by the advice of men much their elders—bankers, lawyers and business men of long experience—urging them to drop "this foolish automobile business." They were told most pointedly many times that if they persisted in trying to build up a business out of anything so absurd as an automobile, they most certainly would accomplish nothing but the squandering of the fortunes for the building of which their fathers had labored so long and so hard. The son like the father bucked the wall of stern opposition on the single theme of transportation and it is a credit to family foresight that each won out in his hardy undertaking.

—with this modern skyline to whose development the automobile industry has added so much

22

The Seventh Chapter

E. F. Roberts, present Vice-President of Manufacturing (at driver's left) returns from a tough test trip

The famous Packard script became a part of Packard identity as early as the big sign before the factory

ONE QUARTER million dollars in cash went into the treasury of the newly formed Packard Motor Car Company from stock subscriptions of the Detroit investors. It seemed a huge sum of money then and was deemed ample for any needs which could possibly arise. However, those who had launched the business venture which was to mean so much, quickly learned, as hundreds of others later were to find, that an automobile factory had an absolutely insatiable appetite for dollars. Fortunately however, Packard never felt pinched for money. The public never was called upon to bear any part of the burden through skimping on the product.

Definite decision had been reached to move the plant from Warren, O., to Detroit. Quite naturally the question of a site was one for much thought. It was learned that F. B. Shipman, a real estate man, could offer a farm of 40 acres at considerably less than $1000 an acre. Several things were thought to be in favor of the property but a number of arguments could be used against it. For one thing Shipman's farm was located far from the center of the city and the price, while not excessive, was no bargain. The proposed site was located

Electrical ventures first intrigued the Packard brothers in quiet Warren, O. Then came Model A, intended for their own use. Immediately friends demanded others like it. They went into business, had interesting problems in manufacture, pioneered patents used today and soon attracted Detroit capitalists. Now Mr. Olmsted adds another chapter to this prestige history with an account of the early Detroit factory

The deed to the Detroit site, a treasured relic in the Packard files

along the Inner Belt line railroad of the Michigan Central and that was thought to be considerably in its favor. Detroit some time before had built a thoroughfare around the outside edges of the city, known as the Grand Boulevard. Shipman's property was located on this boulevard where it cut through east side cow pastures. However, the owners did not require that the frontage on the boulevard be purchased and this considerably lessened the cost.

After much discussion it was decided to buy the Shipman property. Directors of the company agreed that five acres would be ample for the factory, which was to be erected at once, and for a reserve of vacant land that would care for any possible needs which might arise in the future. It was agreed that 35 acres might be sold later and possibly at a profit.

Bricks and mortar flew fast when work was finally started on the two-story factory building. All Detroit was interested in this new structure and smiled behind its collective palms. Here was a factory of fine finished brick with arched and awninged windows in front and almost solid sheets of glass on all the other three sides, so closely were the windows spaced.

"Why try to make a factory look like anything else but a factory, and why try to light a factory with the sun?" Detroit asked. And down town, along Griswold Street which then was Detroit's banking district, heads which had shook at the idea of these popular young men having anything to do with a business so sure of failure as building automobiles, wagged vigorously.

Summed up, these indictments could be found spelling certain failure for this newly born Detroit enterprise: the horseless carriage never would amount to anything; anyone who risked his dollars in manufacturing such a silly thing was crazy; the factory was located way out in the country; money had been thrown away uselessly in putting in so many windows and in building a structure that was more like a down town store building than a manufacturing plant.

Off to Detroit

With the new factory completed, all the works in Warren were loaded into freight cars and shipped to Detroit. The handful or more of men who made up the Warren plant payroll, with one or two exceptions, also moved to Michigan. Among them were C. J. Moore, Sidney D. Waldon and E. F. Roberts.

J. W. and W. D. Packard remained in Warren, O., administering the affairs of the Packard Electric Company, a prosperous concern which they owned and which manufactured electric lamps and other electric equipment. J. W. Packard remained as president of the new Detroit company, although he left the active management to the Detroit men after the factory had been moved from Warren. H. B. Joy, as general manager, was the directing head. Directors T. H. Newberry, Philip H. McMillan and Russell A. Alger worked closely with Mr. Joy. From the start they stuck to the principle that they would only "make such a 'wagon' as they would drive themselves."

Discussing Packard's early days one afternoon at his home in Grosse Pointe, Mich., Mr. Joy frankly confessed that he had known nothing about manufacturing. "I presume in many ways I was like a babe in the woods," he said. "I didn't much like the idea of taking charge of the plant, but no one else would and having gotten my friends into the thing I felt it was up to me to take the job and do the best I could. Don't know where I ever would have landed, however, if it hadn't been for the other directors who stuck with me."

Sturdy Principles

Joy insisted that the Packard car always should be the best that the factory could build and that it always should be sold for its full list price. He was a pioneer in the idea of making materials to fixed dimensions with tolerance limits so low as to make one part fit another exactly. His fight for this idea and for the principle that Packard cars must always be of the best quality, made sledding hard in the first year of the new company. Had it not been for the courage and vision of the other directors with Joy, it would have ended in disaster in the first year.

"I used to take the blue prints from the engineering department out into the shop and tell everyone I wanted the work done exactly as the blue print said it should be. The shop superintendent, foremen and the men on the machines all had their own ideas. They did the work in accordance with their ideas rather than following the blue prints. During the first year, as a result, we threw away tons of costly material."

Losses in the factory sent any hopes of profit glimmering. Banks would loan no money to automobile factories and the men back of the Packard company had to use their personal wealth to keep the company going. The net result of the first year's operation was a loss of $200,000 on a production of 200 cars.

The early Detroit factory, "lighted by the sun," to the great amusement of the many skeptical critics

1899 - MODEL A

1899-Model A

THE FIRST Packard car appeared on the streets of Warren, Ohio, November 6, 1899. It was a one-seated model of the buggy type, equipped with wire wheels. The power unit was a single cylinder horizontal motor with a single chain drive to the rear wheel. The motor was rated at 12 brake H. P. It was the product of the genius of James W. Packard and William D. Packard, brothers, who, together with G. L. Weiss and W. A. Hatcher, organized the partnership of Packard and Weiss in July, 1899.

1900-Model B

MODEL B was the first Packard to be exhibited at Madison Square Gardens. It had the same power plant and chassis as Model A, but was equipped with a dos-a-dos seat and an improved dash. This model became quite popular, and several were manufactured and sold. It developed a maximum speed of 22 miles per hour. On September 10, 1900, capital stock of the Company was increased to $100,000 and the name was changed to the Ohio Automobile Company. J. D. Packard was elected President.

1900 - MODEL B

1901-Model C

THE OUTSTANDING improvement on Model C was the steering wheel and rigid steering post. This displaced the spade handle tiller type steering arrangement which had been used on previous models, and which was used generally by automobile manufacturers at that time. Five cars of this model entered the New York to Buffalo endurance contest, and, although but half of the 89 cars entering completed the race, all of the Packards finished among the leaders and received national recognition.

1901 - MODEL C

1902-Model F

MODEL F marked the emergence from the buggy to the automobile type. It was a four passenger model with entrance to the back seat from the rear. Wheels were of wood with 4″ herring-bone tread single tube tires. This was the first Packard to have three speeds forward and one reverse. In the Long Island fuel economy test, a model F averaged 27½ miles to the gallon. On October 13, 1902, the capital stock was increased to $500,000, and the name changed to the Packard Motor Car Company.

1902 - MODEL F

25

Our Foresight Was GOOD!

Early last fall few factories had their 1902 models designed or tested, but the 1901 Model PACKARD was so satisfactory, and we had so much confidence in the ability of The Ohio Automobile Company to produce the best American Gasoline Car, that we placed a large order for early delivery.

12 H.-P. PACKARD

A good many of them are now in the hands of satisfied customers. A few are ready for immediate delivery. They will not last long after the many PACKARD enthusiasts learn of it. No machine in this or any other country is more graceful or powerful. It is a machine that satisfies the most critical. YOU ARE INVITED TO INSPECT AND RIDE IN IT.

The Adams-McMurtry Co.

317 West 59th St.   **NEW YORK**

Ask *the* MAN who OWNS ONE.

"Like a chip on his shoulder
every Packard Owner
carries his Packard Car."

Ready to defend it enthusiastically, aggressively against
attacks. BECAUSE—clearly
convinced, by all tests, of its
invincible reliability, ease of
operation and simplicity.

He "Stands By" His Car—
Its defense "rests on him."

*Price $2500.00
Seats 5 People*

Write Dept. P for Illustrated Booklet

Packard Motor Car Company, Warren, Ohio

PACKARD

PACKARD

The Car Ahead

With the same care and attention, the **PACKARD MOTOR CAR** will give you better satisfaction than any other made.

This is not mere advertising talk, but the verdict of hundreds of satisfied users.

IT HAS MADE

100 miles without stop on 3⅔ gallons of gasoline; 244 miles in 13 hours without stopping the engine; 500-mile contests winning 9 first-class certificates and 2 gold medals; 2500 miles with absolutely no adjustments or repairs. 16,000 miles without a hitch or breakdown.

It is so designed and constructed that every bearing is instantly accessible for inspection or adjustment.

It carries gasoline sufficient for 250 miles, oil for two days and water for four weeks. It will climb any grade upon which the rear wheels can secure traction and will travel 30 miles per hour upon the level.

"Ask the Man Who Owns One"

And write Dept. P for new illustrated catalog.

The price of the car ready for the road is $2500.00. " Licensed Manufacturers under Selden Patents."

PACKARD MOTOR CAR COMPANY, Warren, Ohio

1903-Model K

PRIOR TO model K, all Packard cars offered to the public were equipped with single cylinder motors. Model K was one of the first four cylinder American cars on the market. The motor which was located up in front under a hood developed approximately 26 H. P. Limousines and other closed bodies were first offered by Packard on this model. On September 5, 1903, the directors of the Packard Motor Car Company decided to move the factory from Warren, Ohio, to Detroit.

1904 - MODEL L

1904-Model L

PACKARD RADIATOR lines and the Packard hub cap came in 1904 with model L. This car embodied many of the fundamental principles which are found on current models, such as rear wheel transmission, progressive gear shift, and the automatic governor. The Grey Wolf broke the American one mile record 13 times in two days, and won the 1,000 mile non-stop run at Grosse Pointe track August 6, 1904. Model L was the first car built on a production basis in the Packard Detroit factory.

The PACKARD ride our agent will give you, if you will send us your name, will convince you of the superiority of the Four-cylinder PACKARD over other motor cars — superiority in strength and power, in comparative light weight, in speed, in smooth, quiet running, in hill climbing powers — in fact, in every point of importance in automobile construction.

Model "L," 1904, Four-cylinder Packard, 22 horsepower, price $3,000. Other models at $1,500. to $10,000.

Send for illustrated descriptive literature and name of nearest agent.

PACKARD MOTOR CAR CO., Dept. G, DETROIT, MICH.

Member Association of Licensed Automobile Manufacturers.

New York Agents — Packard Car Co. of New York, 317 W. 59th St., New York City

1905 - MODEL N

1905-Model N

THE ENTRANCE to the tonneau by means of side
doors came with model N. Other features
which differed from model L were a longer
wheel base and a 28 H. P. engine made by increasing the cylinder bore. The first enclosed
bodies built in Packard shops were made for
this model. The wheel base was 106". The
price of the standard touring was $3,500 as
compared with $7,500 for model K. This
model developed a speed of 45 miles per hour.
Approximately 500 model N cars were built
in 1905.

"Probably the most scientific long-distance
test of an automobile that has ever been
made was that of a standard Packard
Touring Car on the Grosse Pointe mile
race track at Detroit when the machine was driven around
the oval 1000 times without stopping the motor in 29
hours, 53 minutes, 37 3/5 seconds."—*Editorial Comment,
Scientific American, Oct. 8, 1904.*

This test was made with a standard four cylinder Packard car, and
with the 17 first-class certificates and 5 gold medals won by other
standard Packard cars in open competition makes such a consistent
record for uniform running and absolute reliability as stands unparalleled.

Price (with standard Equipment) **$3,500.00, f. o. b. Detroit.**

For our new catalogue and name of the nearest Packard dealer, address

Packard Motor Car Co., Dept. E

Member A. L. A. M.   **Detroit, Mich.**   New York Branch, 1540 Broadway.

In presenting the
Packard Gasoline Motor
Truck we offer a vehicle for commercial
purposes the design of which is based upon
experiments extending over a period of two years
with different constructions of business wagons.

This particular type of car has seen almost every kind of commercial service during all of an exceptionally severe winter, and is now offered in full confidence that it is worthy to bear the Packard name into new fields.

Normal load capacity, 1½ tons. Speed range, 1 to 15 miles per hour. Price of chassis complete ready for body, $2,500 f. o. b. factory. Body designs and quotations submitted upon application. Record of tests in different lines of business sent on request.

PacKard Motor Car Company, Dept. E

Member A. L. A. M.   **Detroit, Mich.**   New York Branch
1540 Broadway

The car that has been consistently successful in the past can be depended upon to be more successful in the future.

Each successive model has added to the Packard record for endurance and reliability and that unequaled smoothness of running.

The latest model, the New Packard 24, upon which will be concentrated every thought and every facility of the Packard factory during the coming season, has already proven itself to be the best thing we have ever turned out. On June 8th the first car of this model made the run of three hundred miles from Detroit to Chicago in the total elapsed time of 12½ hours, running time 11 hours, carrying five to six passengers. After a night's rest in Chicago the car made the return journey on the following day, June 9th. This severe test of six hundred miles was made without repairs or replacement except to tires.

Price with Standard Equipment, $4,000.00, f. o. b. Detroit. For our catalog and name of nearest Packard dealer, address

Packard Motor Car Co., Dept. E
Detroit, Mich.

Member Association
Licensed Automobile Manufacturers

New York Branch
1540 Broadway

1906 - MODEL S

1906-Model S

MODEL S, better known as the Packard 24 was built on a 119″ wheel base chassis and developed 24 H. P. Semi-elliptic springs displaced the platform type, used up to this time. Magneto ignition also made its appearance with this model. The carburetor was improved by the addition of the auxiliary air valve, and a hot water jacket. About 700 Packard 24's were built. Model S was offered in seven body types at prices ranging from $4,000 to $5,325.

The constant development of a single type of car year after year has enabled the Packard Company to work out methods, machines and special appliances to make every detail of that car better than it has ever been made before and better than it could possibly be made under any other conditions.

Packard Motor Car Co., Dept. B

Detroit, Mich.

Mch. 1906.

The man who visits the Packard plant sees every modern mechanical device that is applicable; sees a thousand minds concentrated on a single type of car; feels the Packard spirit of perfection; then knows why the Packard stands in a class by itself.

Packard Motor Car Co., Dept. F
Detroit, Mich.

Member Association
Licensed Automobile Manufacturers

New York Branch
1540 Broadway

1907-30

1907-30

THE FAMOUS model Thirty was first built in
1907 and continued with refinements over a
period of five years. Its four cylinder motor
developed 30 H. P. The body was longer, lower
and larger than that of model 24. The standard wheel base was 123½″. Four experimental
cars with model 30 motors participated in a
50,000 mile road test before this car was offered
to the public. Six body types were designed
and built in Packard shops for this model.

MOUNT VERNON

Through ten years of consistent progress can be traced the unwavering pursuit of Perfection to its culmination in the

"PACKARD 30"

An American Product Worthy of America

Price (in standard colors and equipment) - - $4,200 f. o. b. Factory
Special Colors, Upholstery and Equipment, Extra.

Packard Motor Car Co., Dept. E

Member Association
Licensed Automobile Manufacturers

Detroit, Mich.

New York Branch
1540 Broadway

39

WINDSOR CASTLE

"ASK THE MAN WHO OWNS ONE"

PACKARD MOTOR CAR CO.
DETROIT, MICH.

1908-30

1908-30

THE WHEEL housing of the second series was
cut into the side of the tonneau to allow the use
of 36″ wheels in combination with a lower and
more comfortable body. In 1908 a touring car
of this series was driven from Los Angeles to
New York, a distance of 3,693.08 miles in 25
days, 5 hours and 25 minutes running time,
which was considered a real record. The price
of the standard touring was $4,200. In 1908
the Packard Motor Car Company boasted 10
acres of floor space.

Packard "THIRTY" 1908

FOR the season of 1908, the Packard Motor Car Company continues its time-tried policy of devoting its great factory to the production of motor cars of one model — a new Packard "Thirty." In its most notable form this is a touring car, and also is furnished as a runabout, limousine, and landaulet, or equipped with cape cart or Victoria top. Capable, modish in design and luxurious in appointment, the car is a Packard throughout, with improved detail and refined construction. The price of the touring car, in standard finish and equipment, is $4,200.00, f. o. b. Detroit.

Packard Motor Car Company
Detroit, Michigan

1909-30

1909-30

PACKARD CALLED its 1909 Thirty the masterpiece of the largest exclusive motor car factory
in the world. In that year the number of
Packard employes had grown approximately
to 2,500. This was the first Packard to be
equipped with the cellular type radiator. The
extra lever for reverse gear which was introduced in 1904 on model L was replaced on this
Thirty by the improved style which controlled
both advanced and reverse positions. Head-
lights became standard equipment in 1909.

Packard "Thirty" with Limousine Body

"ASK
THE MAN
WHO OWNS
ONE"

Packard Motor Car Company
Detroit, Michigan

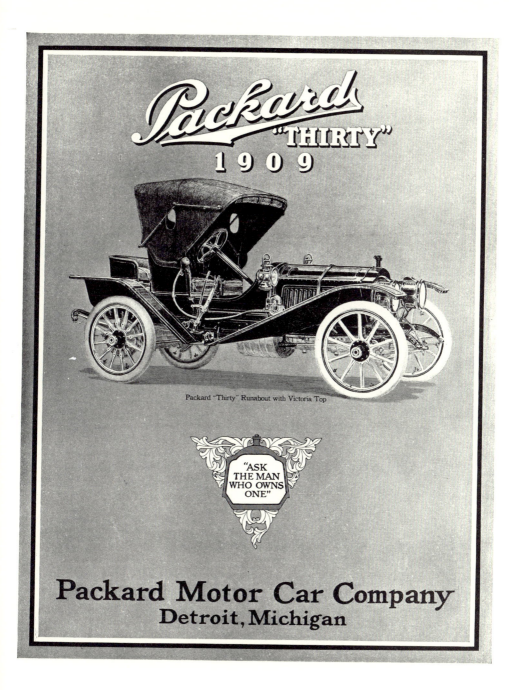

Packard "Thirty" Runabout with Victoria Top

"ASK THE MAN WHO OWNS ONE"

Packard Motor Car Company
Detroit, Michigan

46

1909 - MODEL 18

1909-18

THE PACKARD Eighteen was first offered in 1909 as a companion to the heavier and more powerful Thirty. It was built along the same lines as the Packard Thirty, except that it was equipped with an 18 H. P. motor and a close coupled body. The wheelbase of the Eighteen was 112 inches, which was 11½ inches shorter than the standard Thirty wheelbase. The standard open car of the Packard Eighteen type sold for $3,200 which was a thousand dollars less than the Packard Thirty.

Packard

"EIGHTEEN" 1909

THE TOWN CAR

As a Landaulet

Also supplied as a
limousine, runabout
and with open body

"BUILT
ENTIRELY IN
THE PACKARD
SHOPS"

Packard Motor Car Company
Detroit, Michigan

1910 - MODEL 30

1910-30

THE PACKARD dry plate clutch made its appearance on the 1910 Thirty and has been a feature of all Packard cars and trucks built since its introduction. Shock absorbers were also added as standard equipment. The front fenders were redesigned to give a more graceful appearance to the body. In 1910 Packard had 58 dealers with branches in New York and Philadelphia. There were 3270 cars produced in 1910 which was three times the production of 1907.

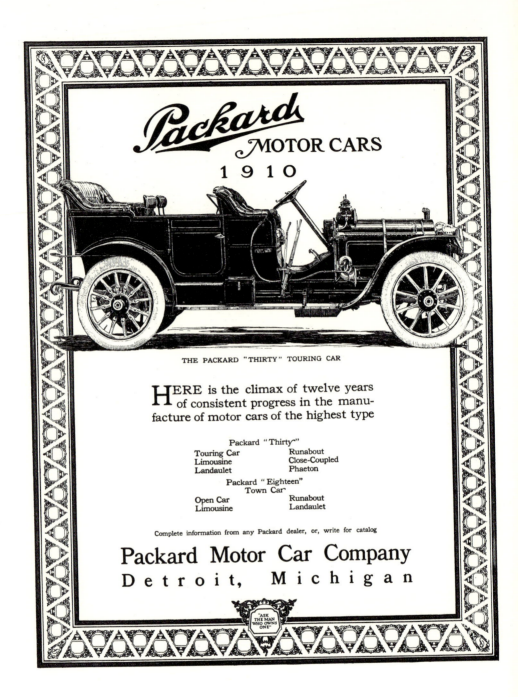

THE PACKARD "THIRTY" TOURING CAR

Hᴇʀᴇ is the climax of twelve years of consistent progress in the manufacture of motor cars of the highest type

Packard "Thirty"

Touring Car	Runabout
Limousine	Close-Coupled
Landaulet	Phaeton

Packard "Eighteen"
Town Car

Open Car	Runabout
Limousine	Landaulet

Complete information from any Packard dealer, or, write for catalog

Packard Motor Car Company
Detroit, Michigan

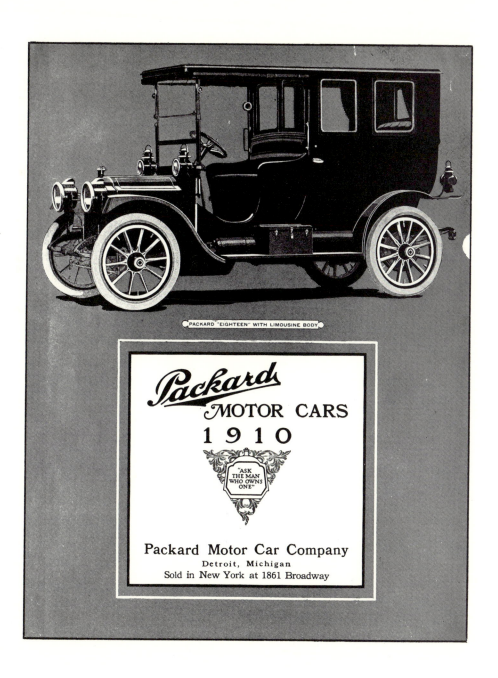

PACKARD "EIGHTEEN" WITH LIMOUSINE BODY

Packard
MOTOR CARS
1910

"ASK
THE MAN
WHO OWNS
ONE"

Packard Motor Car Company
Detroit, Michigan
Sold in New York at 1861 Broadway

51

1911 - MODEL 30

1911-30

"FORE" DOORS improved the 1911 Thirty body
lines and resulted in important changes in
Packard body designs. The Packard cape cart
top first appeared in 1911. Other refinements
made this Thirty outstanding for its attrac-
tiveness. From 1903 to 1911 the growth of the
factory was healthy and continuous. In 1911
there were 6,000 employees and the factory
was using 33 acres of floor space. There were
1,884 Packard Thirty models built that year.

1911 PACKARD "THIRTY" TOURING CAR
Standard equipment includes top

Packard
MOTOR CARS

"ASK
THE MAN
WHO OWNS
ONE"

1911 COMPLETE LINE OF CARS WITH FORE-DOOR BODIES

Built entirely in the Packard shops. One
quality; two sizes—the Packard "Thirty"
and the Packard "Eighteen" Town Car

TOURING CAR   CLOSE-COUPLED
RUNABOUT   COUPÉ   PHAETON
LIMOUSINE   LANDAULET

Forty-eight page catalog mailed on request
Full information from any Packard dealer

PACKARD MOTOR CAR COMPANY
DETROIT, MICHIGAN

A S K   T H E   M A N   **Packard** MOTOR TRUCKS   *W H O   O W N S   O N E*

Shows Its Fitness to Meet the Supreme Test

PACKARD THREE-TON TRUCK OVER-RIDES THE BARRIERS FROM COAST
TO COAST WITH A RECORD UNMARRED BY MECHANICAL REPLACEMENT

THREE thousand, eight hundred and eighty miles, straight across the country
from New York to San Francisco, in forty-six and one-half days, total elapsed
time, without a single replacement of a defective part, without a mechanical
breakdown and without the assistance of any power except the motor in the car—this
is the unique and unparalleled record made by the Packard three-ton truck. W. T. Fish-
leigh, of the Packard engineering staff, who accompanied the truck, sends this statement:

"Not a mechanical part has been changed since leaving New York City. Our replacement record is perfect except for tires. The motor was taken down in plain view of a
crowd in Cuyler Lee's show room in San Francisco to convince everyone that the
truck was as good as the day it left the factory."

Packard Motor Car Company, Detroit, Michigan

Packard

The first motor truck to cross the continent entirely under
its own power. Left New York July 8th; reached San
Francisco August 24th.   Carried a 3-ton load all the way.

This is a remarkable demonstration of the stamina and capability of the Packard
truck under every conceivable condition of hauling.   The trip is one that has been
accomplished by only a very few automobiles.   The venture has been regarded as
virtually out of the question for a heavy truck.

It was easily within the ability of the Packard truck because both Packard
trucks and Packard cars are built to surmount difficulties much greater than they
encounter in actual service.

Their margin of efficiency is your margin of safety in purchasing Packards for
whatever purpose.

The Packard 3-ton truck is used in 137 lines of trade and in 205 cities.
Dealers with Packard standard Service Depots in 104 different cities.

Packard Motor Car Company, Detroit, Michigan

Packard truck with special equipment for handling large loads of lumber

Ask the man who owns one

Packard

MOTOR TRUCKS

331 companies in 93 lines of business have purchased Packard trucks. 48 per cent of all Packard trucks sold have been purchased by companies who have repeated their first orders for one or more additional trucks.

Packard Motor Car Company Detroit

1911 - MODEL 18

1911-18

THE 1911 Packard Eighteen body models were also of the fore door type. Standard equipment included two gas head lights, two oil side lamps and an oil rear lamp. The Packard Eighteen motor had a 4$\frac{1}{16}$" bore and 5$\frac{1}{8}$" stroke. Tires were 34" x 4" front and rear. Standard open car painting was Packard blue striped with Packard grey. A large variety of upholstering materials were offered optional on enclosed bodies for this model.

Ask the man who owns one

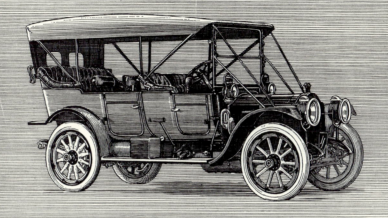

MOTOR CARS

1911

PACKARD MOTOR CAR COMPANY · DETROIT

1912-30

THE 1912 Packard Thirty was the last of the four cylinder Packards. During this year the six cylinder car was introduced. The Packard headlight igniter and combination oil and electric side and rear lamps were furnished in 1912 as standard equipment. On the later cars of this model the windshield was attached to the body instead of being integral with the top and removable when the top was lowered.

1912-18

IN 1912 eight body types were offered on the Packard Six chassis with the Packard Eighteen motor. The standard wheelbase was 112″ with a runabout chassis 108″. Dome lights and toilet cases were offered as standard equipment. The two compartment enclosed bodies were equipped with speaking tubes, buzzers, hat and parcel carriers. Sales for the first six months of 1912 exceeded sales for the entire preceding year.

1912-48

IN 1912 the first Packard Six was introduced. It was called the 1912 Six Forty-Eight. Equipped with a six cylinder vertical type water cooled motor with 4½″ bore and 5½″ stroke, it developed 48 H. P. The wheel base of the standard chassis was 133″. The Phaeton had a 139″ wheelbase, and the runabout 121½″ wheelbase. This model was offered in twelve body types at prices ranging from $5,000 to $6,550.

Packard
MOTOR CARS
1912

THE Packard is the prevailing car at every touring center because it is a being of fibre and sinew. To such qualities has been added the unusual touch of elegance that gives the Packard its distinction in the motor car parade

According to the registrations published in the Paris edition of the New York Herald, 53 per cent of all the cars driven by American tourists in Europe, from April 1 to July 1, were Packards and there were over three times as many Packards as cars of any other make.

Since 1907 the management of the Hotel Elton (Waterbury, Conn.) has kept a register for the use of touring automobilists. Every tourist is registered who has stopped there in the last four years. It is interesting to note that the three leading cars represented have stood in the same ratio for the last four years.—*New York Herald.*

The registrations at the Elton, as published in the New York Herald, show that among sixty-six makes 14 per cent of all cars were Packards and that there were nearly twice as many Packards as cars of any other make.

Ask the man who owns one

Packard Motor Car Company, Detroit, Michigan

The 1912 Packard "Six" Phaeton

THE DOMINANT "SIX"

The greatest piece of machinery that ever went upon the highways and the most luxurious carriage

Fastest getaway

60 miles an hour in 30 seconds from a standing start.

Best hill-climber

At all speeds and regardless of road conditions.

Power without noise

The Packard "Six" motor makes the least noise, whether running fast or throttled down—yet its power is amazing:

Six cylinders—Bore, 4½ inches; stroke, 5½ inches
Horsepower, by standard A. L. A. M. rating . . 48
Actual horsepower under brake test 74

Easiest large car to drive

The Packard "Six" Touring Car, with a wheelbase of 133 inches, will turn around in a street 44 feet wide.

Smoothest starting and stopping

The clutch always engages without jerk. The brakes provide the maximum safety with the minimum effort.

Safest investment

Packard cars have the highest second-hand value.

The smoothest running motor and the easiest riding car, even at speeds from 60 to 70 miles an hour

These things have been made possible in the Packard "Six" by the cumulative experience of an unrivaled organization which for more than a decade has devoted its entire efforts to the building of motor cars exclusively of the highest type. Packard "Six" cars, including bodies, are built entirely in the Packard shops, which comprise 37 acres of floor space.

THERE ARE MORE THAN ONE THOUSAND
1912 PACKARD "SIX" CARS ON THE ROAD
Ask the man who owns one

All Packard cars are sold at the published prices
A square deal and Packard Service for every patron

Any kind of a demonstration on any kind of a road by any Packard dealer

32-PAGE CATALOG UPON REQUEST

Packard Motor Car Company, Detroit, Michigan

1913 - MODEL 48

1913-48

THIS CAR commonly called the Two Forty-Eight did not differ much from the first series Six. It was also offered in 10 body styles, but the longer wheelbase was eliminated. Complete force feed lubrication displaced the combination splash and force feed system used on all Packard Eighteen and Thirty cars. This Packard Six motor was famed for its simplicity and efficiency, and set new standards in the automobile industry.

1913 - MODEL 38

1913-38

SIMULTANEOUSLY WITH the development of the Forty-Eight, the Engineering Department was writing specifications for a lighter six cylinder car to fill the niche made by the Packard Eighteen. This was the Thirty-Eight, the first Packard to be equipped with the electric starter. It introduced the centralized control feature with lighting, ignition and carburetor controls on the steering column. Left hand drive first became standard on this model.

THE ANSWER

In the make-up of the Packard "38" carriage are more features directly appealing to the owner and driver than ever before have been embodied in any one motor vehicle

Left Drive
Avoids the necessity of stepping into the street. This result in connection with other far reaching improvements.

Electric Self-Starter
Easily and simply operated from a driving position.

Centralized Control
Complete mastery of the car from the driver's seat. A compact arrangement at the finger tips operated with the slightest effort.

Electric Lighting
Controlling switches at the centralized control board.

Magneto Ignition
A high tension dual ignition system independent of the self-starting battery and motor generator. Insures Packard efficiency at all speeds.

Hydraulic Governor
Enabling the novice to drive with the assurance of an expert. Prevents "stalling" the motor in crowded traffic; prevents racing the motor when "declutching"; affords agreeable uniformity of road speeds without requiring skillful use of the accelerator pedal.

Short Turning Radius
The Packard "38" turns in a circle forty-one and one-half feet in diameter.

Six-Cylinders Perfected
Flexible, efficient, silent, giving motion with no sense of exerted power.

Dry Plate Clutch
Proof against "burning leather" surfaces and certain of engagement without "grabbing."

Forced Feed Oiling
Especially desirable for "sixes." An auxiliary system feeds oil directly to the cylinder walls and is automatically regulated for different power requirements.

Six-Inch Depth of Frame
Proof against sagging. Prevents possibility of body distortion, body squeaks and cramping of doors.

Size of Crank Shaft
The diameter of the crank shaft is 2⅛ inches. Ample size of bearings insures maximum period of service without refitting.

The sum of these essentials is to be found in no other car. This comprehensive solution, in one motor carriage, of all the chief problems of recent years, compels the consideration of the critical patron

Demonstration on any kind of road
Color catalog mailed upon request

Packard Motor Car Company, Detroit

PACKARD

ASK THE MAN WHO OWNS ONE

The New Packard "38" Limousine in London

From the etching by E. Horter

The Packard Landaulet at Monte Carlo.   From the etching by E. Horter.

MANY American buyers of foreign cars have been influenced largely by habit. But invariably their first purchase of a Packard has shown them the superior worth of the American-made car. In large proportion they have been converted because they have realized in the Packard an expression of their own thought and taste, coupled with the superlative quality in performance on the road.

PACKARD MOTOR CAR COMPANY
DETROIT

68

PACKARD

ASK THE MAN WHO OWNS ONE

Packard "48" Phaeton Roomy — *From the etching by F. H....*

PACKARD

ASK THE MAN WHO OWNS ONE

The Packard Phaeton-Runabout in Paris

1914-48

ALL OF THE new features introduced by the first Thirty-Eight were incorporated in the 1914 Forty-Eight. Of the 20 body types offered, nine were closed, seven had canopy or cape cart tops, and the remaining four were open bodies without tops. The cabette, a body specially designed for women, and the imperial coupe, for four passengers were new and exclusive designs. The 1914 Forty-Eight motor developed 82 H. P. by actual tests.

1914 - MODEL 48

1914 - MODEL 238

1914-448

THE FOUR Forty-Eight motor was noted for its clean design. All ignition wiring was carried in conduits. Enclosed bodies were beautified. The rounded corners on the sedan and limousine tops made their appearance and set new body styles. A disappearing rumble seat for runabouts was first offered on the Four Forty-Eight. Tire sizes were standardized, and made interchangeable, previous models having been equipped with 36″ x 4½″ front, and 37″ x 5″ rear.

1914 - MODEL 338

1914-238

THE CURVED tooth beveled driving gear developed by Packard and now in universal use made the second series Thirty-Eight famous. The spare tire carrier was moved from the left front side to the rear. The one man top was first introduced on the Two Thirty-Eight. Cylinders were cast in blocks of three instead of two, as in former sixes. It had electric side lights as well as head lights, with dimmers an integral part of the head lamps.

1914 - MODEL 448

1914-338

THE THREE Thirty-Eight was in reality only a new series of the Two Thirty-Eight improved to the last word. The ambition of the Packard engineers was to make this and its companion, the Five Forty-Eight, the easiest riding and the most luxurious cars on the road. The price range of the Three Thirty-Eight was $3,100 to $5,150, with the Five Forty-Eight $1,000 more for each model. The Five Forty-Eight earned the title "Boss of the Road."

72

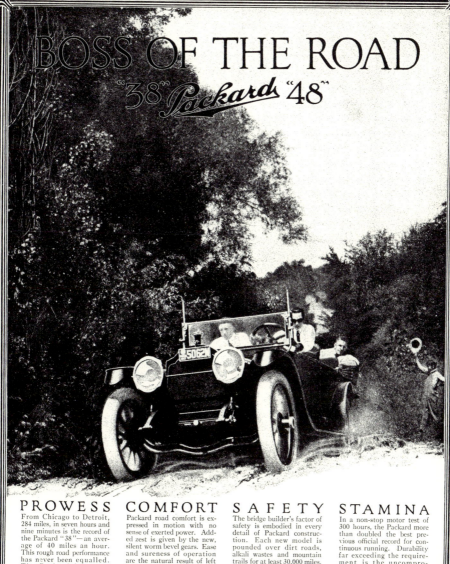

BOSS OF THE ROAD
"38" *Packard* "48"

PROWESS

From Chicago to Detroit, 284 miles, in seven hours and nine minutes is the record of the Packard "38"—an average of 40 miles an hour. This rough road performance has never been equalled. The Packard has more speed than you can use.

COMFORT

Packard road comfort is expressed in motion with no sense of exerted power. Added zest is given by the new, silent worm bevel gears. Ease and sureness of operation are the natural result of left drive, electric self starter and centralized control board.

SAFETY

The bridge builder's factor of safety is embodied in every detail of Packard construction. Each new model is pounded over dirt roads, alkali wastes and mountain trails for at least 30,000 miles. That is one reason why your family is safest in a Packard.

STAMINA

In a non-stop motor test of 300 hours, the Packard more than doubled the best previous official record for continuous running. Durability far exceeding the requirement is the uncompromising standard to which every Packard is built.

Ask the man who owns one

PACKARD MOTOR CAR COMPANY · DETROIT · MICHIGAN

TWIN SIX - FIRST SERIES

Twin Six—First Series

THE FIRST Twin Six was a product of 1915. Its motor was of the "V" type with twelve cylinders arranged six on a side at an included angle of 60 degrees. Cylinders were cast in blocks of six. The first series motor did not have a removable cylinder head. The bore was 3″ and the stroke 5″. Horsepower was 43.2 S. A. E. Rating. Nine body types used on the Five Forty-Eight were offered on the Twin Six chassis. It weighed 500 pounds less than the Five Forty-Eight chassis.

INNUMERABLE REFINE-
MENTS DISTINGUISH THE

Packard
"TWIN-SIX"

A TWELVE-CYLINDER CAR
that recasts every motor car standard

GREATER RANGE OF ABILITY ON HIGH GEAR
MORE MILES PER GALLON OF GASOLINE

Faster pick-up	Shorter wheelbase	Reduced weight
Unequalled hill-climbing	Perfect accessibility	Shorter turning radius
Lower up-keep	Greater speed	Low, graceful lines

Inspect the car itself at any Packard store and arrange for a convincing ride. You owe yourself this remarkable opportunity to revise your ideas of motor car design, performance and values.

The 1-35—Wheelbase 135 inches. Thirteen styles of open and closed bodies. Price, with any open body, f.o.b. Detroit, $2,950.

The 1-25 Wheelbase 125 inches. Nine styles of open and enclosed bodies. Price, with any open body, f.o.b. Detroit, $2,600.

PACKARD MOTOR CAR COMPANY, DETROIT, MICH.

Contributor to Lincoln Highway

The Motor of the

"TWIN-SIX"

IT HAS TWELVE CYLINDERS, each of 3-inch bore by 5-inch stroke, arranged in twin sets of six, at an angle of 60 degrees.

It yields the most even torque obtainable in a gasoline motor and thereby provides the greatest flexibility of action possible in a motor car.

It has the vibrationless balance of the "Six," plus the greater activity that results from reducing the weight of reciprocating parts one-half and doubling the number of impulses per revolution.

It makes possible a shorter, lighter car, with shorter turning radius, without sacrificing any of that roominess, comfort and luxuriousness, in both open and enclosed bodies, to which Packard owners have become accustomed.

It makes the new Packard master of every situation, whether that situation demands the softest, smoothest, quickest action in town car usage or the fastest getaway and greatest speed in all road driving.

It is shorter and more compact than a "Six" of equal power, yet it

increases activity,	**cuts down up-keep,**
reduces weight,	**saves gasoline,**
eliminates vibration,	**gives longer service,**
provides perfect accessibility of all parts.	

Ask any Packard dealer to let you drive the car yourself. The experience will revise your present ideas of motor-car sufficiency. The printed matter which is now ready for distribution, upon request, details not only the many features of the "Twin-Six" motor, but also those innumerable car improvements that you naturally would expect in a Packard of new design.

The I-35—Wheelbase 135 inches. Thirteen styles of open and enclosed bodies. Price, with any open body, f. o. b. Detroit, $2,950.
The I-25—Wheelbase 125 inches. Nine styles of open and enclosed bodies. Price, with any open body, f. o. b. Detroit, $2,600.

PACKARD MOTOR CAR COMPANY, DETROIT, MICHIGAN
Contributor to Lincoln Highway

The Packard 1-35 Phaeton

ANNOUNCING
THE

Packard

"TWIN-SIX"

By a rapidity of pick-up, a range of high-gear activity, an ease of hill-climbing and a sureness of sustained speed we have never before seen combined in any motor car—

The ABSOLUTE MASTER *of every situation*

By a smoothness of action and a nicety of control at all speeds we have never before seen combined in any motor car—

The PERFECT SERVANT *of every driver*

The combination of this sum of efficiency with compelling refinement RECASTS EVERY STANDARD OF MOTOR CARS AND MOTOR CAR ACCOMPLISHMENT

Arrange with any Packard dealer for a demonstration on the road and in traffic. IT WILL ANTIQUATE ALL YOUR PREVIOUS IDEAS OF MOTOR CAR SUFFICIENCY

CHASSIS IN TWO LENGTHS—The 1-35, which has a wheelbase of 135 inches, and is fitted with any of the familiar Packard 3-38 bodies—The 1-25, which has a wheelbase of 125 inches and is fitted with correspondingly shorter bodies. The 1-25 will be announced in the subsequent advertisement.

SEND FOR PRINTED MATTER ILLUSTRATING AND DESCRIBING THE TWIN-SIX, TWELVE CYLINDER MOTOR, AS WELL AS THE MANY IMPROVEMENTS IN CHASSIS AND BODY

PACKARD MOTOR CAR COMPANY—DETROIT

Contributor to Lincoln Highway

"A PAIR OF SIXES"

Packard

3·38 AND 5·48

MADE IN AMERICA

The Salon Brougham   The Coupe

Packard supremacy has become an institution. Car standards change from year to year—but the discriminating buyer is always sure of the Packard. It is his constant criterion.

Packard dominance is perennial, and this season it is more pronounced than usual.

The new Packard Sixes—"3-38" and "5-48"—reveal a sweeping readjustment of values as applied to road ability, comfort and elegance in motor cars.

Ask the man who owns one

PACKARD MOTOR CAR COMPANY
DETROIT · MICHIGAN

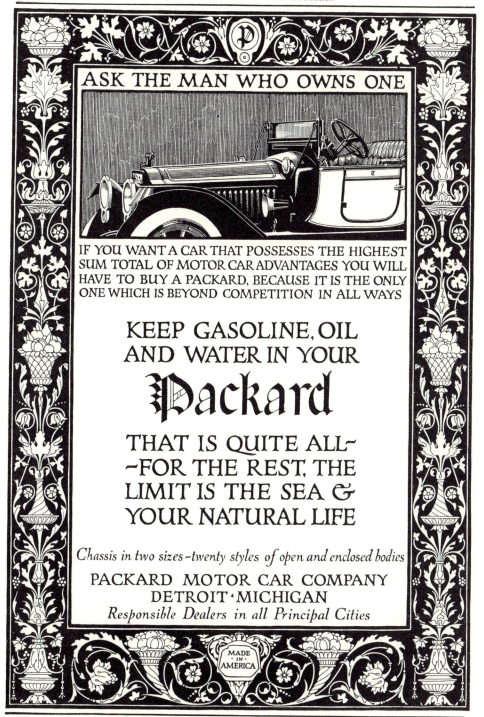

ASK THE MAN WHO OWNS ONE

IF YOU WANT A CAR THAT POSSESSES THE HIGHEST
SUM TOTAL OF MOTOR CAR ADVANTAGES YOU WILL
HAVE TO BUY A PACKARD, BECAUSE IT IS THE ONLY
ONE WHICH IS BEYOND COMPETITION IN ALL WAYS

KEEP GASOLINE, OIL
AND WATER IN YOUR

Packard

THAT IS QUITE ALL~
~FOR THE REST, THE
LIMIT IS THE SEA &
YOUR NATURAL LIFE

Chassis in two sizes~twenty styles of open and enclosed bodies

PACKARD MOTOR CAR COMPANY
DETROIT·MICHIGAN
Responsible Dealers in all Principal Cities

MADE
IN
AMERICA

DELCO

ELECTRIC CRANKING LIGHTING IGNITION

24,000 sparks a minute.

That is the requirement of the new twelve cylinder, high speed Packard motor.

Delco Ignition is meeting the requirement

It is a significant fact that the two gasoline engines requiring the highest speed ignition ever built—the Cadillac high speed eight and the Packard Twin Six have both adopted the Delco Ignition.

**The Dayton Engineering Laboratories Co.,
Dayton, Ohio**

DELCO-IGNITION
BUILT-FOR-THE
NEW-PACKARD
TWIN-SIX

Packard
TWIN-SIX

IN PLAIN SPEECH, that car is best which will start quickest, control easiest, ride smoothest and run longest. To obtain this result, the PACKARD MOTOR CAR COMPANY a year ago created the *twelve-cylinder engine*, and provided in the *PACKARD TWIN-SIX* greater safety, smoother action, longer wear—with the elegance of a really fine carriage. By its performance in the hands of more than 6000 owners, this latest Packard has made the twelve-cylinder car the world's standard of automobile sufficiency and value. *Thirteen styles of open and enclosed bodies. Prices, with any open body, f. o. b. Detroit — The 1-35, $3150.00; the 1-25, $2750.00*

ASK THE MAN WHO OWNS ONE

Ask the man who owns one

EVERY SUPERIORITY
of the PACKARD TWIN-SIX *has been* <u>*Verified at the Hands of Owners*</u>

EVERY day adds to the long roll of men at the wheel who know by experience just why this car has shattered all traditions—who have found its stark bone and sinew to be a compact combination of stealth and strength, fusing power with silence, activity with control, speed with security — who have learned that its twelve-cylinder engine is the eventual power for every particular service. ¶ A new thrill awaits you, a new experience in luxurious travel, in your first Packard Twin-Six demonstration. *Arrange for it now.*

PACKARD MOTOR CAR COMPANY, DETROIT

Builders, also, of PACKARD *Chainless Motor Trucks*

TWIN-SIX

Twin Six—Second Series

THIS TWIN was offered in September, 1916. Body types were lower with more flowing lines. The cylinder head of the motor was made removable. The shelf on the rear fender, a feature since 1904, dropped to follow the curve of the wheel. Much attention was given to the interior furnishings and accessories. Disappearing folding seats for Seven Passenger cars were designed. The touring car of this series was offered at $3,050 as compared to $2,600 for the first Twin.

Steady! It's smoothest—surest—evenest power which the *refined* Twin-six gives to the new Packard

Air-men travel the most treacherous of all roads.

They must have *dependable, continuous* power—with energy-wasting vibrations canceled.

Therefore—

The Twin-six type of motor is the dominant equipment of the modern aëroplane.

In sky-flight and track-flight, in America and Europe, in peace and war, in the automobile and the aëroplane—this motor is *the modern* and the most efficient power plant.

Man's fiercest tests—in history's great motor epoch—have culminated in the Twin-six.

And Packard, ever leading, leads here.

Eight thousand of the first model Packard Twin-sixes were too few to satisfy the demand of fore-seeing buyers.

Both the demand and supply are now immensely greater. An early order will insure an early delivery for you. Prices, for the open cars—2-25, $2,865 and 2-35, $3,265—f. o. b. Detroit.

Ask the man who owns one

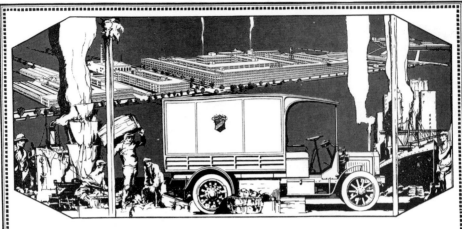

Hauling Problems Now are Simplified—the Introduction of PACKARD Light Service Motor Trucks Insures Dividend-Earning Delivery for Every Branch of Traffic

THEY are true Packards all the way through—of the same quality and stamina as the 10,000 Packard heavy trucks now serving successfully in more than 200 lines of trade. Their construction embodies every efficiency principle learned in the ten years the Packard Motor Car Company has been engaged in truck manufacture. And they are guaranteed by the $25,000,000 investment in the Packard factory—a mile-long plant employing 12,300 workmen.

They are built throughout in that factory—within the 51 acres of floor space where, also, are made Packard Twin-Six Cars and Packard Heavy Service Trucks. It is the only place in which a Packard can be made—because assembled units will not make Packard vehicles.

These Light Service Packard Trucks are built in two sizes, rated respectively at 1 to 1¼ tons and 1½ to 1¾ tons. They provide the speed, ease of operation, activity in traffic, reserve power and permanent economy of maintenance necessary to make light delivery a source of greater profit—qualities to be found only in a vehicle built as these are built.

They are sold with the backing of a world-wide service organization as truly and essentially Packard as the institution of their origin—the institution upon which was conferred the HIGHEST AWARD for MOTOR VEHICLES at the Panama-Pacific International Exposition.

There are seven sizes, altogether, in the Packard commercial line, ranging from 1 to 6½ tons' capacity, inclusive. All sizes are of the same advanced chainless design. In sending for catalogue, please specify the kind of hauling.

PACKARD MOTOR CAR COMPANY, DETROIT

Ask the man who owns one

Packard

The "little fellow"—as well as the big business man—finds Packard silent, chainless trucks the cheapest to own and operate. Built in seven sizes, with fifty body types to choose from, the Packard line *alone* offers the one economical truck for every hauling task. Shock-proof design makes them ten year investments. Their improved motors get more power, even from low-test gasolines. Worm-drive uses all this power, cuts up-keep, saves wear and tear. Fitness! Economy! Ask the man who owns one.

Packard
TRUCKS

Packard
TRUCKS

Bridge the gap to new and bigger fields of business—to a wider circle of customers—with a *dependable* Packard. A sure delivery short-cut, saving in both time and cost. Let us show you how the *new series* of silent, chainless Packards will save *for you*. Built by the Packard Motor Car Co., Detroit. Ask the man who owns one.

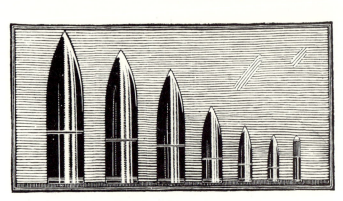

Seven sizes! The right ammunition—*the right motor truck*—are important factors in the winning

It's range—and speed—and carrying power—that win "the great drives" in battles for business.

You can't compete without the right ammunition.

Your hauling may require burly six-tonners of great capacity—or a battery of nimble, far-reaching one-ton delivery units. On your selection depends your fighting efficiency.

Seven sizes Packard offers—seven sturdy models—one to six and one-half tons—with bodies for all purposes—at prices from $2200 to $4550.

There is a Packard truck for your every trucking need—a full line to standardize on—obviating a troublesome "mixture of cars."

Make sure of the right truck—in quality—in size—in price. Enlist the aid of our specialists at Detroit or the local branch.

Ask the man who owns one

CHAINLESS TRUCKS

PACKARD TRUCKS

Where the flag goes, there Packard trucks back our fighting men

More than twelve hundred Packards have been bought by the United States Government.

Army, navy, marine and aviation corps—their efficiency and striking force will be supported by Packard endurance and pulling power.

Proved out by Pershing's expedition on the roadless, burning deserts of Mexico—and on the battlefronts of Europe—Packard ability to conquer desperate road conditions has been radically increased.

The four-speed, silent, chainless Packards are setting new standards of economy and dependability in every hauling field.

Built in seven sizes by the Packard Motor Car Company, Detroit. *Ask the man who owns one.*

Packard

And here now is a new fulfilment of a *great idea*—an idea that won in an unprecedented way

Up—up to still higher levels the Twin-six advances—time tested by nearly eight thousand exultant owners.

Fine has been *re-fined*—by an added year's development.

And the new series 2–25 and 2–35 are here announced.

A *transcendent* Packard—unchanged in essentials—enriched in details—fixes new standards of usefulness and luxury.

To better the best Packard--has been the aim—and the inspiration—of the day's work.

How well we have succeeded is told in the fact that our *three-fold* output has not kept pace with the ascending demand.

Changes?

A little lower body—with lines more flowing—refinements of the mechanism—and removable cylinder heads!

But—you must see the new car itself, to appreciate the significance of the unmatched success of the Twin-six idea—and what these newer developments mean for you. Prices—open cars—$2865–$3265, f. o. b. Detroit.

Ask the man who owns one

Quick blade and a strong one—an agile car and a powerful one—insurance both for the owner's *safety* and unquestioned prestige

Again—the old armorer's splendid tradition of exquisite production lives.

Jeweled rapiers from Damascus, combined matchless service-ability with unmatched beauty.

The spirit of the old painstaking craftsmanship survives in Packard production.

Distinction for the stateliest occasions—grace of line, refinement of finish, the assurance of correctness that ever marks the equipment of discriminating folk.

Added, all, to the balanced strength of a chassis as flawless as a Damascus sword, and the economical power of the Twin-six motor, quick and mighty to meet any crisis of the city street or the country highway.

Spring's coming—and there are many Packard styles to select from. Guard against disappointment in your choice—now.

Ask the man who owns one

TWIN-6

Year 'round—and everywhere—this *luxurious* enclosed Packard is yours for the most exacting and satisfying service

This winter—for sheltered comfort, health insurance, travel independence. Next spring and summer—for all these, coupled with the joys of far-range *country touring*.

Protection from cold and snow, from dust, and wind and rain.

Plus the deep satisfaction which comes from knowing that, go where you please, you carry with you the atmosphere of refined and substantial elegance.

The surplus power of the silent twelve-cylinder engine gives to the enclosed Packard the velvety action—the wide range—the road mastery—of the Twin-six touring car.

And the unmatched riding comfort of the Packard body has been enhanced by new and marked improvements.

Until you have experienced at first hand this rich harmony of power and beauty, you cannot appreciate all that it means in sumptuous ease—for you.

Twenty-one styles of open and enclosed Twin-sixes for your choice. Cars are now on display at all branches.

Ask the man who owns one

TWIN-6

Economy! Cheapest power is that which makes best use of Nature's resources. With the gliding drive of a full-rigged ship—plus a speed no craft ever had—the twelve agile and powerful cylinders of the Packard motor will carry you anywhere in greatest security and comfort—at least possible cost. The economical use of gasoline is one of the major advantages of the Twin-six. ꙮ There are twenty and more Packard styles. Prices, open cars, three thousand fifty and thirty-five hundred dollars, at Detroit. ꙮ ꙮ Packard Motor Car Company.

A s k   t h e   m a n   w h o   o w n s   o n e

Packard
TWIN-6

$5000⁰⁰

for the best examples of Truck Operating Efficiency

Attention is called to the following announcement recently made by the Council of National Defense:

"The Council of National Defense has given its formal approval to all measures designed to facilitate the use of the motor truck in transportation wherever it can be utilized. It is urging all communities as far as possible to adapt the motor truck to their local needs and encourage its use in any way to help existing transportation problems."

To promote maximum results in motor transportation, the Packard Motor Car Company offers a total of $5,000 in awards to owners and drivers for greatest efficiency in hauling. The awards will be based on certified records of Packard truck operation over a period of three months, beginning June 1. Best results are obtained through full loads, careful routing and proper maintenance of the trucks. To win the awards records must be kept in accordance with the National Standard Truck Cost System. Full particulars will be furnished by us or any Packard dealer. Every Packard truck owner and driver is invited to compete for the awards.

EFFICIENT HAULING is now a patriotic duty. It will release railway cars for government use.

Ask the man who owns one

PACKARD MOTOR CAR COMPANY, *Detroit, Mich.*

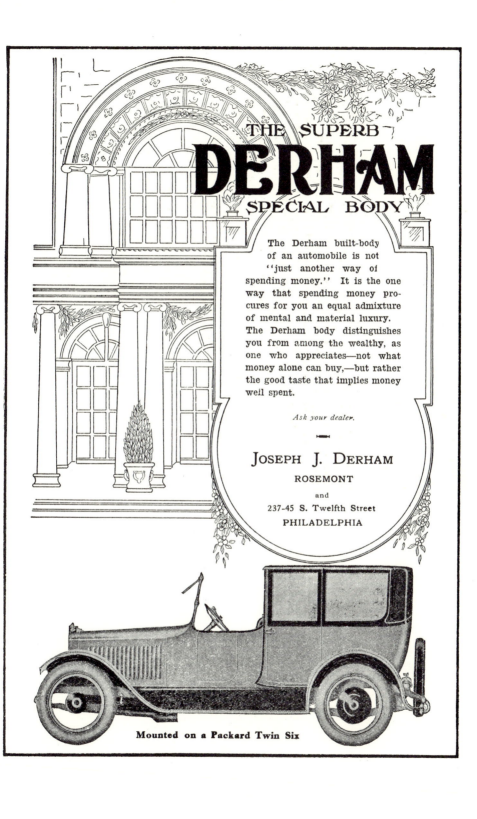

THE SUPERB
DERHAM
SPECIAL BODY

The Derham built-body of an automobile is not "just another way of spending money." It is the one way that spending money procures for you an equal admixture of mental and material luxury. The Derham body distinguishes you from among the wealthy, as one who appreciates—not what money alone can buy,—but rather the good taste that implies money well spent.

Ask your dealer.

JOSEPH J. DERHAM

ROSEMONT

and

237-45 S. Twelfth Street

PHILADELPHIA

Mounted on a Packard Twin Six

TWIN SIX - THIRD SERIES

Twin Six—Third Series

In August, 1917, the third series Twin Six arrived. Within two years its fame had become world wide. The fuelizer, a Packard invention, first appeared on the third series Twin Six engine. This motor did not undergo any perceptible changes after 1917, until it was finally superseded by the Packard Eight. The high pressure lubricating system and the thermostatic cooling controls were perfected on Twin Six motors.

A new creation! A more beautiful Packard is here announced. Now—a remarkable accomplishment in *body designing* matches the achievement of the epoch-making Twin-six motor. And thereby is rounded out the smartest and *most efficient* motor carriage we have ever built. Branches and dealers today have ready for your inspection models in the new, *third* series—3-25 and 3-35. Open car prices are $3450 and $3850 at Detroit.

Packard
TWIN SIX

"ASK THE MAN WHO OWNS ONE."

ARMY PACKARDS RUN *on* SCHEDULE FROM *the* LAKES TO *the* SEA

PERSHING needed trucks "over there." Railroad traffic congestion was at its height. The Government said, "Move them under their own power."

It is 542 miles overland from Detroit to Baltimore. The first trucks fought their way through state-wide stretches of unbroken snow. They crossed two mountain ranges.

And since then hundreds of "Packards for Pershing" have rolled into Baltimore. They carry war material and run on schedule.

It is now an every-day job. During the next few weeks many hundreds of Army Packards will be delivered by the cross-country route.

Packard trucks have proved their stamina on every battle front in Europe. Their performance in war gives graphic evidence of their enduring quality which established their leadership in commercial use.

Packard silent chainless trucks are building profits for their owners in 200 lines of trade. Backed by country-wide Packard service.

PACKARD MOTOR CAR COMPANY

A s k   t h e   m a n   who   o w n s   o n e

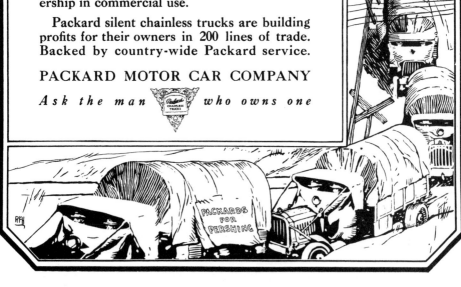

PACKARD TRUCKS

Priority freight! No rail embargo can halt shipments by Packard trucks.

"You must wait your turn" is the order of the railroad war board to all lines of business not directly supplying army and navy needs.

Acute freight congestion is here.

Tonnage handled has been increased twenty per cent over 1916. But the volume offered has increased still more. Hence the decision to hold up ordinary traffic and give priority to government shipments and civilian necessities.

With winter adding further to the blockade, thoughtful business men have turned to Packard *direct transportation* as the most certain means of moving their materials and goods on schedule.

And thousands of Packard trucks are proving their ability every day to carry full loads any distance, through any weather, *cheaply—safely—on time.*

Silent, chainless drive and four-speed transmission make them masters of every road—and *economize* on gasoline, tires and upkeep expense. Write Packard Motor Car Company, Detroit, for information. *Ask the man who owns one.*

Packard

Executives going to a conference in their company's Packard. Hundreds of Corporations have standardized on Packard on an economy basis—high mileage per dollar of investment and low running cost over a term of years.

Does the Car Buyer *Want* the Facts

THE late Joseph Choate used to say that lawyers would go out of business if men were not so bent on making the same old mistakes the same old way.

No one need — or *can* — make the old mistakes in selecting his motor car, if he will look for *transportation facts* instead of "features" and "talking points."

The strong Packard opinion which he finds on every hand does not express itself in technical details or costly luxury — but in such everyday words as *economy, comfort, ability,* and *lasting value.*

LET a man figure on keeping his Packard from *six* to *ten years*— and he has a material saving in *investment* as against the car that must be traded in every two or three years.

Think of the *stability* of the Packard design! His Packard always a "new model."

His gasoline mileage will be from nine to thirteen, depending on road conditions. Oil mileage, 700 or more to the gallon. Tires properly cared for, ten thousand to sixteen thousand miles.

The steel in his Packard is worth more than twice as much as the steel in the ordinary car.

The moving parts in the Twin-Six engine are better balanced than in any other automobile engine. Consequently there is less vibration and less wear on bearings.

WHEN a man buys a motor car he knows pretty well what sort of transportation he expects it to deliver.

Economy does not lie in the direction of temporary make - shifts or compromises.

Packard first-class transportation will give him a definite and permanent advance in his way of traveling. It will cost him less per passenger mile during his whole motoring experience — than even second-class transportation.

"Ask the Man *Who Owns One"*

PACKARD MOTOR CAR COMPANY, *Detroit*

8274 passengers in cars of 31 different makes drove up before this Opera House entrance one evening last month. Many of them are traveling in second-class comfort, not realizing that they pay first-class prices for it.

Does it Really Cost any more to Travel First Class

YOU will often hear people say, with an air of resignation, how much they would rather ride in a Packard, if they could only afford it.

Putting the Packard owner in a *class apart,* with special comforts and privileges—assuming that he pays more for his motoring than they do.

A GREAT many people would be less resigned to their own inconveniences of travel, if they knew how *little* the Packard owner pays for the comfort they speak of.

Packard Transportation never costs a passenger more than second-class transportation—and often *less.*

The *gasoline mileage* of the Packard is from 10 to 14, according to road conditions. The *oil mileage,* 1,000 to the gallon. *Tires,* properly cared for, 10,000 to 16,000 miles.

The Packard exclusive *heat-treating* process adds greatly to the strength of the steel, reducing repairs and depreciation.

The longer life and greater used value of the Packard more than takes

care of the difference in initial investment.

FOR twenty years the Packard Company has been studying motor cars from the standpoint of *Transportation Experts.* Time after time it has proved that trying to save on the initial investment costs a man more in the long run than buying a Packard.

Transportation facts are not a matter of compromise, but *absolute*— as the Packard Transportation Experts can show any man who really *wants* the facts.

"Ask the Man *Who Owns One"*

PACKARD MOTOR CAR COMPANY, *Detroit*

For sound, practical reasons and the best use of your money, why not make an attempt to verify the facts before deciding whether you will spend two or three thousand dollars for an ordinary automobile, or invest in a Twin Six Packard with all that a Packard can give you.

Transportation facts are established

A LEADING transportation expert has said that most automobiles are built on theory and bought on personal opinion.

Transportation is now a science. It is a science that applies to your own car whether it carries you across the Continent or merely from your home to your office or serves your family or friends in their daily activities.

It would astonish the average car owner to see a scientific test of his car in its relation to the whole question of transportation.

We say the *whole question* because advantages are claimed and economies cited for certain parts of a car or special phases of the question.

It is only by treating the problem *as a whole* that we get the facts.

For example a man may have his eye filled by economy of gasoline and tires, and he may throw away more on engine tinkering than he saves on both these items.

He may get speed at the cost of vibration that racks and wrecks his car.

He may get lightness at the expense of safety or dragging weight at a heavy upkeep charge.

If he gets power when he wants it he may have to pay for it when he doesn't use it.

While passenger cars were bought as luxuries alone, it was difficult to get consideration for the facts.

Just as today the average automobile for family use is a compromise from the standpoint of scientific transportation; its advantage in one direction offset by loss in another.

When corporations buy Packard cars for the transport of their executives, there is something for the average car buyer to think about.

That is the result of expert analysis of all the factors. It is a matter of business.

When will the purchase of the family car be regarded as a business transaction?

The Packard people are transportation experts; they can tell you more on this subject than any other organization in the world. You can ask them to discuss your car problem without obligation.

It is to your interest and profit to do so.

Ask the Man Who Owns One

PACKARD MOTOR CAR COMPANY, Detroit

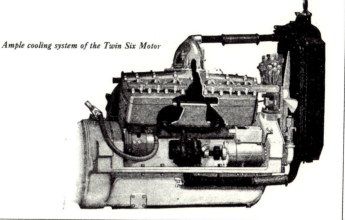
Ample cooling system of the Twin Six Motor

HERE is a scientific principle many a motorist overlooks. No matter how fast or how slow you want to go, you cannot go right unless your car has reserve power —rightly applied. Until a man has driven the Packard Twin Six he will never know exactly what that means.

Low Cost of Packard Reserve Power

WITH everybody reading about motors, talking about motors, swapping motor experiences, you might suppose that the basic facts of motor engineering would be generally known by this time.

Yet even such a fundamental principle as the economic value of reserve power is not understood by one motorist in ten.

Some car owners take years to wake up to what it is costing them to compromise in the matter of power. Why should a man have to wear out one car after another before he learns that it costs more to operate a car of limited reserve power rather than one of high reserve power?

The man who has been through it all knows that the very reason why the Packard is good for 75 miles an hour is the reason why 25 miles an hour, day after day, costs less from the Packard than from the car of low reserve power.

In the Packard—the power is there— in reserve. It costs you nothing unless you use it. You call on it when you want it—and not unless you do want it.

The Packard Twin Six Engine is a motor of *live moving parts*. Power is used only in moving the car—not in excess, merely to keep the engine turning over.

The basic design of the Packard Twin Six Motor has been wonderfully justified during the past few years of both peace and war work, so that any changes that may be made from time to time will be merely in the nature of refinements.

The Packard people are transportation experts. They have more to tell you on this subject than any other organization in the world. You can ask them to discuss your car problem without obligation. It is to your interest and profit to do so.

"Ask the Man Who Owns One"

PACKARD MOTOR CAR COMPANY, *Detroit*

105

Simplicity and Accessibility, attributes of Twin-Six Engineering

MOTOR CAR SAFETY *depends* *on* RIGHT ENGINEERING

A STUDY of the causes of motor car mishaps will show that in nine cases out of ten they are as much the fault of the car as of the driver.

In planning for the safety of a man and his family, Packard Engineering never compromises with chance. Even if every one of the 6,000,000 motor car drivers in this country were always careful and thoughtful — there would still be accidents.

The greatest possible care will not help a man if his car fails.

Safety is the first and foremost consideration in Packard Engineering. There is a sound, practical engineering reason for every factor of safety in the Packard car.

Consider the security afforded by the high reserve power of the Packard Twin-Six — the stored-up energy which responds instantly in an emergency, but costs nothing when it is not in use.

The Packard is the safest car in the world to handle in traffic. From less than two miles an hour on high, it will pick up in a few blocks to more than a mile a minute. Its perfect balance — its ease of control — make it stop or start without effort.

The Packard car is built to withstand extraordinary strain. The Packard engine is built to deliver extraordinary power. Yet a Packard habitually runs on less power and in no way sacrifices strength to secure lightness.

Its weight is scientifically adjusted to its power. It stays on the road when lighter cars show a tendency to leave it.

To the man who has any regard at all for himself or his family, Packard safety is priceless.

The Packard people are transportation experts; they have more to tell you on this subject than any other organization in the world. You can ask them to discuss your car problem without obligation. It is to your interest and profit to do so.

"Ask the Man Who Owns One"

PACKARD MOTOR CAR COMPANY, - - *Detroit*

Who is the Judge of Good Taste

 A GREAT designer once said: "Good taste comes of wisdom and intuition." What about the design of the average motor car? Is it born of artistic genius or a desire to be different?

It is a question for the motor car buyer to consider. How soon will his car be out of date?

Packard answers the question at once. Packard design is fundamental with the car—not grafted onto it.

Lines may change, and have. But the *character* of the Packard has not changed for sixteen years.

At the Packard plant the first principle of distinction is quality. Hand-buffed, whole-hide leather for upholstery, instead of machine buffed "splits." Double thick material for tops. Nickeled bronze fittings, designed and made as jewelry might be. Coach work by craftsmen rather than body building by machines.

In the *London Daily Mail* recently an Englishman paid a tribute to the Packard method of building high grade cars. He wrote: "It is for America an expensive car, but, compared with the same class of car at home, it is decidedly cheaper."

The fact of the matter is this: If the Twin-Six were built in Europe with European methods it would be higher priced than even the most expensive European car.

PACKARD MOTOR CAR COMPANY · Detroit

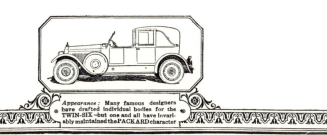

Appearance: Many famous designers have drafted individual bodies for the TWIN-SIX—but one and all have invariably maintained the PACKARD character

Packard scores another

The "FUEL-IZER"

Makes Any Gasoline a Perfect Fuel

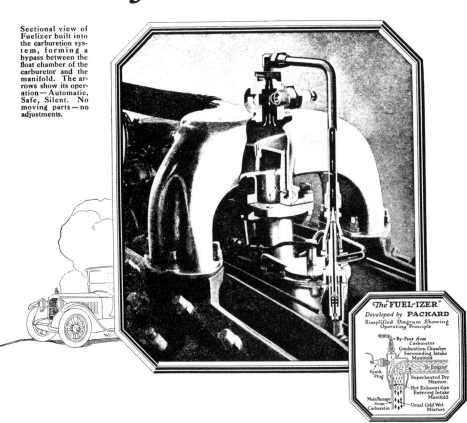

Sectional view of Fuelizer built into the carburetion system, forming a bypass between the float chamber of the carburetor and the manifold. The arrows show its operation—Automatic, Safe, Silent. No moving parts—no adjustments.

The "FUEL-IZER"
Developed by **PACKARD**
Simplified Diagram Showing Operating Principle

By-Pass *from* Carburetor
Combustion Chamber Surrounding Intake Manifold
Spark Plug
To Engine
Superheated Dry Mixture.
Hot Exhaust Gas Entering Intake Manifold.
Main Passage *from* Carburetor
Usual Cold Wet Mixture

PACKARD MOTOR CAR

Engineering Triumph

This Marvelous Achievement Standard Equipment on every new Packard Car ~ Simple, Positive, Automatic ~ Gives Packard owners Freedom from Carbon troubles, Spark Plug fouling, Cold Weather Starting troubles ~ and Protects Oil from dangerous dilution

Part of cylinder head—motor without Fuelizer. The best designed motors known show such carbonizing in a few thousand miles.

Part of cylinder head. Motor equipped with Fuelizer. Mirror surface of cylinder head unchanged after 5000 miles.

Motor completely packed with snow. Temperature of air was 11° above zero. Seldom is a motor in actual service so thoroughly chilled.

Motor started instantaneously. The Fuelizer rapidly thawed its way through snow. Perfect response to throttle attained in 10 seconds.

WITH the development and perfecting of the "Fuelizer"—Packard Engineering again demonstrates its faculty for going to the heart of a problem and getting *practical results.*

The Fuelizer achieves *perfect combustion* of all grades of gasoline.

It makes starting as quick and sure in winter as in summer.

It makes available the power in any grade fuel more quickly.

It does away with carbon fouling of combustion chamber, crankcase, valves and spark plugs.

It does away with the dilution of lubricating oil in the crankcase—removing the main cause of premature wear on engine bearings and scoring of cylinder walls, and preventing sticky valve guides and valve stems.

* * *

Small wonder that the Fuelizer proved the sensation of the recent annual meeting of the Society of Automotive Engineers!

Every motor engineer had known for years that the proper application of *heat* will break up "wet" mixture.

How to apply the heat has always been the problem—now solved by the Fuelizer.

The Packard Fuelizer not only applies the *right degree* of heat at the *right place*—

But more important still—it applies the heat at the *right time* —when the *engine* is *cold* at starting; and maintains an ideal heat—*not overheat*—under all running conditions.

* * *

These illustrations tell, better than many words, how the Fuelizer does its wonderful work.

A small part of the mixture is drawn into the Fuelizer and exploded into *hot gas* by the spark plug.

This hot gas is drawn down through the Fuelizer heating manifold into the "wet" mixture in the main manifold. It heats up and breaks the "wet" mixture into a dry vapor, which explodes *completely* in the cylinders. No time lost in "warming up!"

The Fuelizer has raised the manifold temperature from 33° to an ideal temperature (120° or over) in less than forty-three seconds—2° a second!

Tests made last winter at 5° below Zero showed that the engine is able to pull on *high gear* almost immediately.

During the months of testing after the perfecting of the Fuelizer, not one single case developed of foul spark-plug or valve, combustion chamber wall or piston rings. Nor was there any dilution of oil.

Winter or *summer,* the Fuelizer revolutionizes motoring—reducing repair bills—lengthening the useful life of a motor.

A Packard achievement. *Exclusively* Packard — now *standard equipment* with every new Packard Car.

In every way a development worthy of the long established Packard tradition of *practical transportation service* to the owner of a Packard Car.

Oil tests without Fuelizer showed lubricating oil diluted with over 7 ounces deposit of kerosene in 4 hours of idling. With Fuelizer, no dilution.

Left—Valve from Fuelizer-equipped motor after 6200 miles. *Right*—Typical carbonized valve from motor without Fuelizer. Note burning of metal.

Any car without Fuelizer if started after idling exhausts mist of unburned gasoline and wasted oil.

Packard Car with Fuelizer starts instantaneously. Invisible exhaust after idling or when starting indicates perfect combustion.

"Ask the Man Who Owns One"

COMPANY, Detroit, Mich., U.S.A.

Who Pays for all the Discarded Cars

 OW many car owners are still running the cars they bought five years ago—or three years—or even two? As an individual, the motorist can no doubt afford the cost of replacing his car every couple of years.

As a business man, can he afford the enormous depreciation in value—the thousands of hours of skilled workmanship; the iron, steel, aluminum, fine wood and leather, discarded year after year?

As business men, car owners must be interested in Packard *unified engineering*—the balancing of one part against another, matching power with ample strength—the basis of true economy and long life.

In the Packard search for materials of *permanent value*. For example, Packard second growth

hickory for wheels. Seasoned a year and a half. 6000 lbs. breaking test to the spoke.

In Packard *heat-treating* of steel—the finest plant and process of its kind today.

In Packard *inspection*—an inspector to every twenty workmen, and every Packard supervised from start to finish.

These things make the difference between a motor car that can go around the world if necessary and a car tied to the apron-strings of a garage mechanic.

Between a car so well designed that wear is taken up by a few simple replacements and one whose parts wear beyond replacement.

Your typical Packard owner makes the present serve the future; and sees clearly what each dollar is going to *do for him* before he spends it.

PACKARD MOTOR CAR COMPANY, *Detroit*

The Fuelizer—the latest Packard achievement, making any gasoline a perfect fuel.

How Many Buyers Can Judge *Value?*

NEARLY every man has his visions of finding the ideal motor car. He anticipates the true mastery of the roads at last, and the prestige of being *right* at every point of his motoring.

For the man who wants the Packard qualities in his motoring, only the Packard Car will do. While if his taste and sense of values are not up to the Packard, some other car will do.

The Packard Twin-Six really is as true and fine as anyone ever assumed any car to be.

It occupies, alone and sufficient, the place it has made for itself. It stands aloof equally from the car that obviously can be no better than it looks, and from the car that strives to look better than it is.

The dominant place of the Packard is not a thing of chance. For twenty-one years the Packard has been delivering *intrinsic value*—the soundest value a motor car has ever given.

During the War, inspecting officers spoke of the Packard plant as a manufacturing marvel. The only automobile plant in the world to produce high-grade cars on a quantity basis.

Why this tremendous plant investment? Simply to produce a car of Packard grade at a price within reason. If built by piecemeal methods the Packard would be the highest priced car in the world.

PACKARD MOTOR CAR COMPANY ⸴ DETROIT

Performance: THE TWIN-SIX ENGINE—
More reserve power at all car speeds
than any other stock car engine built

The Traffic Jam in Any City will show Twenty-five Makes of Cars—no two alike. New Models today, perhaps—but what of Tomorrow?

Who Dictates the Changes in Motor Car Design

EVERY now and then it occurs to some one to ask, "What happens to all the old Packards? Not those of eight or ten years ago, now running as taxicabs, but the in-between models—'15 and '16 and. along there?"

A perfectly natural question, considering how accustomed people are to perpetual change in motor car design.

EITHER there is something sound and fundamental in motor car design—or there is not.

The Packard Company believes that design is fundamental when it is governed by established standards of good taste and engineering, and not by passing fancies.

IT is gratifying to know that this belief is shared by more than five thousand Packard owners, who have owned Packards continuously for sixteen years.

Once create a motor car design that is fundamental and it will satisfy people of good taste as long as the car lasts.

THE Packard car is designed to last as long as fine workmanship, sound engineering and the highest grade of materials can make it.

And that is why Packards are always "new models."

And why the Packard owner's investment never suffers from sudden changes of "fashion," dictated by some one over whom he has no control.

"Ask the Man *Who Owns One"*

PACKARD MOTOR CAR COMPANY, *Detroit*

The "tight-squeeze"—An hourly occurrence on every crossing and on every crowded street, with cars of fifty different makes— more or less under the driver's control

How Can the Motorist Save Himself from the "Other Fellow"

NEW YORK CITY recorded over three thousand motor car collisions last year in Manhattan Island alone.

Effective traffic regulation depends on each *individual driver* having his car under *positive control.*

If every driver could be as *sure* of his car as the Packard owner, there would be less congestion, and only the *careless* driver would get into "accidents."

THE Packard people believe that first-class transportation must deliver Safety, Ability, Comfort, Economy and Enduring Value to the highest degree.

Were the Packard to choose from the best sources of commercial parts' makers—we feel certain that these necessary features would not measure up to the present high standard maintained in the Packard car.

You are absolutely sure to get them by starting with *unified engineering* in the Packard manner.

Controlling parts by specifications and tests—through casting, forging, machining, heat-treating, finishing and inspection.

Paying 12 cents a pound for your steel, instead of taking a chance with steel at 6 cents.

You will be led straight to the Twin-Six Engine, with its sure and flexible power, and the greatest range of ability in high gear.

To gears heat-treated through and through—not merely case-hardened.

To clutch, brakes, universal and bearings that give you the safety of positive control—Packard designed for the Packard car.

IT makes little difference whether the other fellow is to blame, or merely subject to the whims and weaknesses of his car.

The Packard owner has all the chances of the road discounted, because he is sure of what his Packard will do.

He is riding in first-class safety and first-class comfort. It costs him less *all around than riding* second class!

"Ask the Man *Who Owns One"*

PACKARD MOTOR CAR COMPANY, *Detroit*

THE SINGLE-SIX—116

The Single-Six-116

BY 1920 changing traffic conditions caused through increasing popularity of the automobile called for a car which would retain the flexibility always so characteristic of Packard motors and match it with a hitherto unheard of maneuverability. The answer was the 116 Single-Six, so named as companion car to the bigger Twin-Six. The 116 was conceived before the Great War in anticipation of the potential demand for something new: a quality product in the light car field.

Announcing
Packard "Single Six"

The 10-Year Car

WE have always made large cars designed for maximum speed, great power, and all the roominess that goes with a long wheelbase. The ultimate development has been the Twin Six, which has firmly established itself in the regard of the public, and which we have been producing and marketing for a number of years.

Packard reputation for motor cars rests solidly upon the *Twin Six,* and it always will!

Packard

But there has for years been an insistent demand for another car to supplement the Twin Six: a car of shorter wheelbase and lighter weight, a general-purpose car of great maneuverability in traffic, one that would park in a short space at the curb.

And the demand was that this light car should give unusual gasoline mileage and tire mileage, and finally, that it should be designed and built Packard-wise, and therefore be able to keep out of the repair shop longest and to require least attention from its owner or driver.

We thought it over and studied the problem for a good many years, during all of which we were accumulating experience in the design and production of the highest possible grade of car.

We have at various times during the past ten years designed a light-weight companion to our larger cars, but were never entirely satisfied with our efforts.

Then the war broke out, in 1914, and believing that America would inevitably become involved, we turned our attention to designing airplane engines, and from then to the close of the war had a thoroughly successful experience in designing and man-

ufacturing airplane motors, which, as you know, must give the greatest power with the least possible weight.

* * *

We learned a great deal through this experience that was applicable to the automobile, and towards the close of the war we felt we were finally well equipped by experience to design the light-weight car.

Meanwhile, with a constantly growing talk of congestion in traffic, and increasing cost of gasoline, tires and other supplies, the demand for the light car became more and more insistent.

* * *

We have taken several years for the development and perfection of this new Packard, but we believe we have accomplished what we set out to do, and take now a pride in announcing that the Packard Single Six will soon be ready. It will be manufactured alongside the Twin Six and by the same matured and experienced organization.

The new car is of five-passenger capacity and will be offered in Touring, Runabout, Coupé and Brougham or Sedan.

The motor has six cylinders, 3⅜" bore by 4½" stroke. It is therefore of medium size, and despite its light weight is very sturdily built.

It is equipped with the Fuelizer.

The *Single Six* motor is new throughout but it is not experimental.

It includes every principle of good engineering that our experience has shown to make for maximum power, coupled with silent operation and freedom from annoying troubles. We have failed of our intentions if we have not produced a motor that will run longer and require less attention than any other.

Our chassis design is very simple and clean. Its light weight, together with its unusually efficient motor, result in a very economical car.

As an instance of this, in our test driving in cross-country runs we have made over twenty miles to the gallon of gasoline. Of course, in congested city driving the mileage will not be so high.

Average tire mileage can be expected to exceed 15,000 miles. In our extensive experimental driving of this new car we have had some tires in fair condition at the end of 25,000 miles.

It is an agreeable car to operate, having the easiest possible steering, the lightest clutch action, the shortest turning radius, and, we believe, all those qualities that you would like to have in a light-weight car for general purposes.

The workmanship and finish are Packard throughout.

Packard

The greatest obtainable luxury, the maximum power, and the ultimate in road-ability must always be found in the large car. That is the field in which the Packard Twin Six will always be dominant.

In this new car we have not attempted to compete in that field, but rather to produce an active, easily operated, high-grade, light car, with all the elements of efficiency, economy of operation and, above all, long life.

There are Packard cars today, designed years ago, that are nearing the half-million mark in miles traveled.

The new Single Six is also, we confidently believe, a TEN-YEAR CAR.

The price of the Touring Car is $3640 at Detroit.

PACKARD MOTOR CAR COMPANY, *Detroit*

PACKARD

PACKARD CARS REPRESENT THE FOREMOST ADVANCE OF THE ART

THERE has never been a pause in the development of the Packard Car. Steadily, it has been refined, improved, enhanced without stint. Just as the old one-cylinder Packard represented the highest state of the art then, so do Twin-Six and Single-Six Packards represent the foremost advance of the art now. There is only one way to realize true Packard performance, and that is to drive the Packard Car.

PACKARD MOTOR CAR COMPANY · DETROIT

The Packard Twin-Six Touring
$6000 *at Detroit*

The Packard Single-Six Touring
$2975 *at Detroit*

Ask the man who owns one

PACKARD

THIS IS THE PACKARD SINGLE-SIX COUPE

WE SOUGHT in the Packard Single-Six to build the finest car of its kind. We strove to link the refinement, comfort and long life of traditional Packard quality to the economical advantages of moderate size. If you have driven the Single-Six you will say we have been successful. We are confident its value exceeds anything previously offered the public in a motor car.

PACKARD MOTOR CAR COMPANY · DETROIT

The Packard Twin-Six Touring
$6000 *at Detroit*

The Packard Single-Six Touring
$2975 *at Detroit*

Ask the man who owns one

PACKARD

THE Packard Truck does so many different kinds of hauling at a profit because in every case it is exactly the right truck for the job.

It has the great advantage of being rated accurately to the actual conditions of service, by Packard transportation engineers. It works as a part of a fixed plan for securing better hauling at lower cost —a plan based on careful analysis of the best means of loading, hauling, and delivering its particular freight.

Packard transportation engineers, for example, studied the hauling problem of The Germania Mills, Holyoke, Massachusetts. They demonstrated that a Packard Truck equipped with special van body would do away with costly crating and boxing of goods for rail shipment. That Packard today is running on regular schedule between Holyoke and New York, effecting a substantial saving over its owner's previous transportation.

Every Packard owner also has the benefit of nationwide service facilities established to keep the Packard Truck at the highest possible level of operating efficiency.

PACKARD MOTOR CAR COMPANY · DETROIT

Ask the man who owns one

The Packard Truck goes on the job with every certainty
of doing better hauling at lower cost.

It is correctly designed for powerful, economical performance. It is built throughout of the strongest tested
materials, destined to last for years in the hardest service.
Moreover, it is rated to its work by a method that con-
siders every condition of road and load. The hauling records
of more than two hundred lines of business testify today
to the economy and earning power of the Packard Truck.

PACKARD

ASK THE
MAN WHO
OWNS
ONE

THE SINGLE-SIX—126

The Single-Six-126

THE 7-BEARING crankshaft construction and simple design pioneered by Packard in the 116 proved the greatest innovation in the light car class. Public demand, however, insisted upon greater body room with a motor correspondingly larger. In May, 1922, these features were incorporated in the 126 Single-Six which still retained the 116 virtues of economy, simplicity and long life. It was offered with two wheelbases, 126″ and 133″, in five and seven passenger models, open and enclosed.

The Literary Digest for April 22, 1922

PACKARD

-a new, a larger, a more beautiful

Single - Six

With the advent of this new Packard, we believe that a definite turning-point has been reached in the manufacture of the better motor cars.

Packard resourcefulness in producing motor carriages of incomparable charm, and brilliant, dashing performance, has, in this instance, surpassed itself.

But—something infinitely more important and impressive has also been accomplished.

The new Packard conveys an instant and vivid conviction of value so very great as to be almost epochal.

We are sure that this group of eight inimitable cars will compel you to comparisons which are certain to give the new Packard a position of overwhelming advantage.

Packard dealers are prepared to demonstrate these new cars

The price of the new Single-Six five passenger touring is $2485 at Detroit
The new price of the Twin-Six touring is $3850 at Detroit

Packard Motor Car Company · Detroit · Motor Cars and Motor Trucks

A S K   T H E   M A N   W H O   O W N S   O N E

PACKARD

SEVEN PASSENGER TOURING

–a new, a larger, a more beautiful

Single - Six

With the advent of this new Packard, we believe that a definite turning-point has been reached in the manufacture of the better motor cars.

Packard resourcefulness in producing motor carriages of incomparable charm, and brilliant, dashing performance, has, in this instance, surpassed itself.

But—something infinitely more important and impressive has also been accomplished.

The new Packard conveys an instant and vivid conviction of value so very great as to be almost epochal.

We are sure that this group of eight inimitable cars will compel you to comparisons which are certain to give the new Packard a position of overwhelming advantage.

Packard dealers are prepared to demonstrate these new cars

The price of the new Single-Six five passenger touring is $2485 at Detroit
The new price of the Twin-Six touring is $3850 at Detroit

Packard Motor Car Company · Detroit · Motor Cars and Motor Trucks

ASK   THE   MAN   WHO   OWNS   ONE

REPUTATION

The man who builds and the man who buys are both beneficiaries of a good reputation. To the one it is a continuous spur and an incentive—to the other the strongest of all guarantees that what he buys is worthy. ⊘ We sometimes speak of winning a reputation as though that were the final goal. The truth is contrary to this. Reputation is a reward, to be sure, but it is really the beginning, not the end of endeavor. It should not be the signal for a let-down, but, rather, a reminder that the standards which won recognition can never again be lowered. From him who gives much—much is forever after expected. ⊘ Reputation is never completely earned—it is always *being* earned. It is a reward—but in a much more profound sense it is a *continuing responsibility*. ⊘ That which is mediocre may deteriorate and no great harm be done. That which has been accorded a good reputation is forever forbidden to drop below its own best. It must ceaselessly strive for higher standards. If your name means much to your public—you are doubly bound to keep faith. You have formed a habit of high aspiration which you cannot abandon—and out of that habit created a reputation which you dare not disown without drawing down disaster. ⊘ There is an iron tyranny which compels men who do good work to go on doing good work. The name of that beneficent tyranny is reputation. There is an inflexible law which binds men who build well, to go on building well. The name of that benevolent law is reputation. There is an insurance which infallibly protects those whose reason for buying is that they believe in a thing and in its maker. The name of that kindly insurance is reputation. ⊘ Choose without fear that which the generality of men join you in approving. There is no higher incentive in human endeavor than the reward of reputation—and no greater responsibility than the responsibility which reputation compels all of us to assume. Out of that reward and out of that responsibility come the very best of which the heart and mind and soul of man are capable.

President, Packard Motor Car Company

PACKARD

To speak of the Twin-Six is to speak of something that is singular—something that stands apart and alone.

It is quite literally true that there is no other car like it—no luxury such as Twin-Six owners enjoy.

Things they would not ask or expect from any other motor car are their daily portion with the Twin-Six.

It is not surprising that the very term Twin-Six has established itself in modern literature as the synonym for the ultimate in motoring.

It is not surprising because the term is simply the reflection and expression of a fact—a fact which transports the owner into an exclusive world of his own.

The price of the Twin-Six touring is $3850 at Detroit
The price of the Single-Six five passenger touring is $2485 at Detroit

The Single-Six conveys an immediate conviction of very great, and very unusual, value. Packard Trucks are known for their durability and low ton-mile cost.

TWIN·SIX

ASK THE MAN WHO OWNS ONE

TWIN-SIX CUSTOM-BUILT LIMOUSINE

Trust Your Own Thoughts of
PACKARD

In your own mind you instinctively award a high place to Packard.

The *thought* of Packard comes first, and instantly, when the finest cars are discussed.

The *name* of Packard leaps to your lips when you are seeking a synonym for the best.

These instincts, intuitions and impressions of yours can be trusted.

They can be trusted because they are *true*—and because your mental process in regard to Packard is the almost universal process.

Packard has passed into the inner life of the nation and taken a permanent place in literature as symbolic of pre-eminence.

Nothing that we might say of Packard could possibly compare with this spontaneous, almost unconscious, and wellnigh unanimous tribute.

Trust your own thoughts of Packard— they will lead you to unalloyed satisfaction.

Five-Passenger Touring, $2485; Seven-Passenger Touring, $2685; Runabout, $2485; Sport Model, $2650; Coupe, $3175; Five-Passenger Sedan, $3275; Seven-Passenger Sedan, $3525; Five-Passenger Sedan Limousine, $3325; Seven-Passenger Sedan Limousine, $3575; at Detroit

ASK THE MAN WHO OWNS ONE

The
SINGLE-SIX
SEVEN-PASSENGER SEDAN
LIMOUSINE

PACKARD

It is evident that most people award to Packard a special, peculiar and preferential place in their minds.

They apparently concede to Packard, in other words, certain broad and definite superiorities not always admitted of others.

Thus, we are confident that the vast majority of American motorists place Packard unqualifiedly first in point of manufacturing precision.

The Packard suggests itself as a type and model of the very best in American engineering and design, whenever the question arises for discussion.

This attitude of complete acceptance is proven daily in scores of instances throughout the country by the *manner* in which the Packard is bought.

The worth, and merit, and value of the Packard—its beauty, power and assured mechanical excellence--are taken for granted by the purchaser.

This attitude is very unusual.

It is a safe attitude for any prospective Packard owner to assume. It is an asset peculiar to Packard and constitutes one powerful reason for the expectation that Packard high-quality will always be maintained.

Five-Passenger Touring, $2485; Seven-Passenger Touring, $2685; Runabout, $2485; Sport Model, $2650; Coupe, $3175; Five-Passenger Sedan, $3275; Seven-Passenger Sedan, $3525; Five-Passenger Sedan Limousine, $3325; Seven-Passenger Sedan Limousine, $3575; at Detroit

The
SINGLE-SIX
FOUR-PASSENGER COUPÉ

With the advent of the Single-Six, Packard brought about a complete reversal of fine-car manufacture.

Instead of limited production, Packard now applies the sound principles of larger production, and its resulting economies, to a car of the very highest quality.

Instead of high manufacturing costs, and lower values in the product, it accomplishes lower manufacturing costs, and far higher values in the product.

It is safe to say that no plant in the world, producing a car of Packard's quality, could go farther in this direction.

The Packard organization is skilled and experienced in the finest kind of work. Packard precision-machine equipment is not excelled.

Working to the high Packard standard of excellence, but on a basis of costs now analyzed and budgeted almost to the penny, Packard is enabled to embody in the Single-Six a height of value hitherto unattained in the field of fine cars.

Five-Passenger Touring, $2485; Seven-Passenger Touring, $2685; Runabout, $2485; Sport Model, $2650; Coupé, $3175; Five-Passenger Sedan, $3275; Seven-Passenger Sedan, $3525; Five-Passenger Sedan Limousine, $3325; Seven-Passenger Sedan Limousine, $3575; at Detroit

The Packard Twin-Six provides a quality of motoring beyond which it is not possible to go. Truck users know there is profit in hauling with Packard Trucks. All Packard upkeep is made still more economical by Packard standardized service

PACKARD

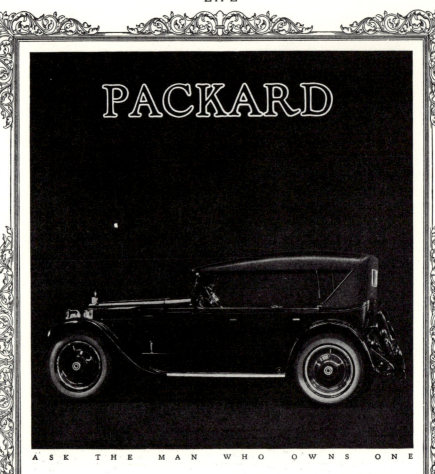

PACKARD

A S K T H E M A N W H O O W N S O N E

Because it was a Packard the soundness of Single-Six engineering was accepted from the first as a foregone conclusion.

It can be judged now, however, both by time and by numbers— thousands of Single-Sixes having been in the hands of owners for more than two years.

Its history may be summed up at this moment as one of individual instances of deep satisfaction, multiplied by thousands.

Never in Packard history was the familiar advice: Ask the Man Who Owns One, more pertinent— never was the answer surer than it is in the case of the Single-Six.

Single-Six Touring Car, Five-Passenger, $2485—Sport Model, shown above, $2650—at Detroit
Furnished in twelve popular body types, open and enclosed

Can You Afford to Overlook These Proofs of Packard Leadership?

Packard's extraordinary beauty and brilliance you can see at a glance.

Packard prestige, and the distinction attaching to Packard ownership, you already know.

The wonderful riding comfort, the wealth of power, the ease of handling, will be apparent in a demonstrating ride in a Single-Six.

Fortunately, also, a widespread personal experience with Packard is available to guide you in selecting your next car wisely.

From Packard owners you can learn why the Single-Six is good for many years of satisfaction.

Their records of operating costs will also show 16 to 20 miles per gallon of gas, and 15,000 to 20,000 miles from a set of tires.

You will find them proud in the possession of cars which seldom need service, and happy in their experience with Packard standardized service when mechanical attention is required.

The satisfaction of thousands of Packard owners explains why the Single-Six is the pre-eminently outstanding quality six today.

Four-wheel service brakes; 2 additional rear wheel brakes—a total of 6—on all Packard cars

PACKARD SINGLE·SIX

ASK THE MAN WHO OWNS ONE

THE SINGLE-EIGHT—136

The Single-Eight-136

By June, 1923, the Twin-Six had reigned supreme for eight years, but it lacked the simplicity and lighter weight demanded by new motoring tastes about which much had been learned with the Single-Six. Thus, the Single-Eight was created as successor to the Twin-Six. It has its power and flexibility with greater economy, an eight-in-line motor, 9-bearing crankshaft, ingenious arrangement of crankshaft throws and 4-wheel brakes—first on any American production car as standard equipment.

THE PACKARD SIX—226

The Packard Six-226

Again modern traffic conditions demanded better motoring control. In December, 1923 the 226 Packard Six was announced. Together with its inherent economy features it had 4-wheel brakes—first experimented with in 1919—built-in stop signal, windshield cleaner and ball bearing steering knuckles. Some 40,-000 Packard Six owners were proving the need of a flat rate service system and Packard Standardized Service Operations and Charges were then perfected on a nation-wide basis.

130

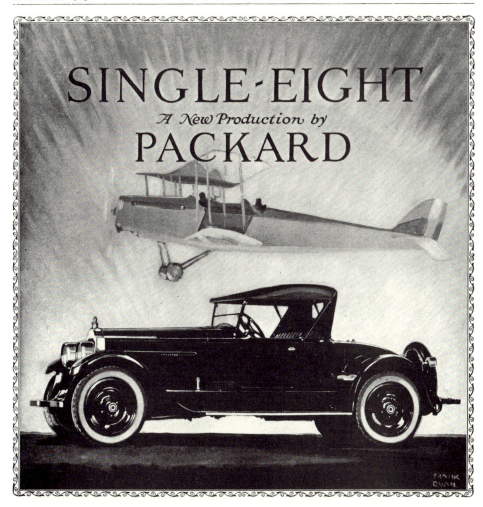

SINGLE-EIGHT
A New Production by
PACKARD

The striking thing about the Single-Eight is that it does the things which are vital, in a more positive, effective way, than they have ever been done before.

These striking contributions to safer, surer, smoother motoring, are not hidden refinements, but very definite qualities quickly discernible.

It is not just a generalization but a fact, that in comfort acceleration, flexibility, brake-action, steering and ease of control, the Single-Eight has gone far beyond previous practice.

The instant and enthusiastic acceptance of these facts renders it certain that the Single-Eight will dominate its own particular field just as unmistakably as does its companion car—the Packard Single-Six.

Furnished in Nine Distinguished Body Types, Open and Enclosed, at Prices Ranging from $3650 to $4950—at Detroit
Packard Single-Six Furnished in Eleven Popular Body Types, Open and Enclosed

PACKARD
SINGLE·SIX

It has to be a pretty good Yankee car that can overcome my initial prejudice; but when after doing that it contrives to fill me with an uncontrollable lust for possession, then I can assure you it is something right out of the common rut.

The Single-Six Packard costs (*in England*) something under nine hundred pounds, and is, in my humble opinion, as near being the very best car in the world as makes no difference. This is heavy praise, I know, but it can't be helped—I must speak as I find.

If I had leisure and one of these cars, I would like to drive it round Coventry and Birmingham and Manchester, and other places where motors are mostly made, and take British managing directors out for a run, just to show them, you understand.

The plain fact is that this is a car in which I simply cannot find a fault.

It is as docile as an angel, but goes like the very devil. It is supremely well sprung, it is uncannily silent, it is a miser on petrol, it steers no heavier than a wisp of cigarette smoke, it climbs like a chamois— in short, it just does anything that it should, and does most things a good deal better than you would think possible.

Mind you it is not one of these undergeared contraptions, for without any fuss or flurry it will do its modest seventy on the level, nor has it got a huge engine, yet it will do White Hill, Henley, with four up, at a minimum of twenty-five miles an hour. The Hindhead brings it down to about fifty-five! The Single-Six is, of course, not to be confused with the Twin-Six.

Yes, believe me, people, the six-cylinder Packard is a very wonderful car indeed. I wish it were made in this country, and I can't for the life of me see why it shouldn't be, though owing to the higher cost of raw material over here it would naturally come out more expensive.

I heartily wish the Packard were British.

It is easily amongst the first half-dozen best cars in the world, at a figure which has hitherto been associated with, comparatively speaking, mediocrity.

—Reprinted from The Tatler, London, England; issue of April 11, 1923

Why Owners are Enthusiastic

The announcement of the Packard Straight-Eight was followed by a buyer demand greatly exceeding production.

It became necessary almost immediately for Packard dealers to set delivery dates three and four months after orders.

Only now has Packard been able to build the Straight-Eight in sufficient quantity to meet demand.

The great public success of the Straight-Eight was no surprise—

Because this type was Packard's selection for its high-powered car, after 24 years of fine car engineering, and after building and testing all known types of multi-cylinder motors;

Because Packard's reputation for building only the best assured its instant and enthusiastic reception.

Now, however, Straight-Eight drivers know from experience that this new Packard surpasses all other cars, both domestic and foreign.

This endorsement of the Straight-Eight exceeds any claim Packard has ever made.

Owners tell us the Packard Straight-Eight gives more in performance than any other car, and in addition—

"Unequalled smoothness of power flow;

"Ability in acceleration which no other type of multi-cylinder car can equal;

"Accessibility of parts which readily explains why Packard no longer builds V-type motors;

"Simplicity which no comparable car can claim;

"The easiest control of any car on the road."

Exclusive Packard four-wheel brakes contain no more parts than ordinary two-wheel brakes. They operate with exceptional ease and efficiency.

You will, of course, want to ride in and drive the Straight-Eight.

A demonstration will immediately show you why this new Packard is so successful.

> ### Study These Reasons for Straight-Eight Success
>
> *Exclusive Packard Fuelizer which speeds up acceleration, shortens the warming-up period, reduces carbonization of spark plugs and valves, contributes to fuel economy and lessens crankcase dilution; heavy crankshaft with nine bearings, insuring maximum motor rigidity and durability; new design of steering gear which reduces friction to the minimum and automatically straightens the car out of a turn; three-fold lighting system; extreme depth of frame which gives unusual rigidity, tends to prevent squeaks and rattles and preserves alignment of doors and windows; beauty of finish and upholstery; completeness of equipment.*

PACKARD STRAIGHT-EIGHT

THE PACKARD-SIX—326

The Packard Six-326

THE 326 was a continuation of the 116, 126 and 226 idea with increased power, heavier frame and such long life protection features as the chassis lubricator and oil rectifier. Complete equipment was made standard, manufacturing quality raised and closed models reduced to equal open car prices. Public appreciation of this value was immediate. In 1925 Packard Six sales were double those of 1924. The Phaeton was the first American car to introduce a swanky English Burbank top built for easy folding.

THE PACKARD EIGHT—236

The Packard Eight-236

THE DESIGN of the Packard Eight was so advanced at its inception that two years of its success found but few changes necessary. In 1925 ease of maintenance was added to the 236 Packard Eight by incorporating such improvements as the chassis lubricator and oil rectifier. The two wheelbase lengths, 136″ and 143″, were continued and the Phaeton, like its younger brother the Six Phaeton, smacked of English smartness from its polished wood bowed Burbank top to its trig glove case.

ONLY
PACKARD
CAN BUILD A
PACKARD

Your 1925 Packard

The Packard you buy today will not look out of date in 1935

unless Packard is successful in doing

that which others have been **unable** to do —

improve on Packard lines.

If the industry, competing within itself, has been unable to improve on Packard lines

but rather, has appropriated them,

then, Packard has set an enduring style.

And, in an enduring style your motor car investment is best protected.

Only Packard can build a Packard. Ask the man who owns one.

S U P R E M E

The beauty of the Packard Eight is but an indication cf the incomparable quality of its performance.

Here is luxurious riding in a sense and to a degree well worth your while to know.

In power and flexibility, the Packard Eight is more agile and eager and unhampered than seems possible for a mechanical thing to be.

Yet with all its power and flexibility and effort-less speed, it handles so easily and smoothly as never to suggest strain or sense of effort. It responds to a touch—yet it unfailingly holds the road.

Beyond compare, and without a peer, the Packard Eight appeals irresistibly to those who want the finest motor car in the world.

Packard Eight and Packard Six both furnished in ten body types, open and enclosed. Packard's extremely liberal time-payment plan makes possible the immediate enjoyment of a Packard—purchasing out of income instead of capital.

P A C K A R D   E I G H T

THE CAR MEN ARE WAITING FOR

No greater tribute can be paid to a motor car than this—that men will wait weeks and even months to get one.

With all this company's experience in judging motor car markets it had no idea that the demand for the Packard Eight would be as great as it has proved to be.

There has never been a day during the past year when men were not waiting for their Packard Eights.

And today, despite the fact that months ago production was increased over the original estimate, men are still waiting for their cars.

Remember—you never see people lined up in front of the ticket window of a poor show.

Packard Eight and Packard Six both furnished in ten body types, open and enclosed. Packard's extremely liberal time-payment plan makes possible the immediate enjoyment of a Packard—purchasing out of income instead of capital

THE PACKARD SIX—426

The Packard Six—426

POPULARITY OF the Packard Six continued during 1926 and even grew greater with the 426 and its increased power which had been brought about by the new Packard Turbo head. Increased compression and turbulence in the combustion chamber brought surprising results to add to the comfort, beauty and long life features which were built into the new Packards. It was in 1926 also that the now famous Packard hypoid gears for the rear axle were introduced, also the single plate clutch.

THE PACKARD EIGHT—343

The Packard Eight—336-343

THE POWER of the Packard Eight was increased greatly by the new Turbo head and through an increase in cylinder bores from $3\frac{3}{8}$ to $3\frac{1}{2}$. Wheelbases of this luxurious Packard were 136 and 143 inches. This car also marked the start of a new system of manifolding and carburetion which Packard carried forward to further successful development. Engines of the 336 and 343 were finished in nickel, enamel and polished aluminum. Packard sales mounted to 33,000 in 1926.

ASIA

How Often Do You Buy A War Tax?

EACH time you buy a motor car you pay for five things in which you never can take a ride.

These are: war tax—freight charge—factory's profit—dealer's profit—salesman's commission.

Once every five years or more is often enough to afford yourself the luxury of such purchases.

Those who buy the Packard Six expect, on the average, to keep their cars more than five years, spending the minimum in war tax and other outside charges.

Packard encourages its owners in keeping their cars, through retaining the beauty of Packard lines and in announcing no yearly models. It is now more than ten years since Packard offered yearly models.

The most recent evidence of Packard's interest in its owners is the chassis lubricator and motor oil rectifier, found only in Packard cars. Together they double the life of the car.

The Packard Six Five-passenger Sedan is illustrated—$2585 at Detroit. Packard Six and Packard Eight both are furnished in nine body types, four open and five enclosed. Packard distributers and dealers welcome the buyer who prefers to purchase his Packard out of income instead of capital.

A S K　T H E　M A N　WHO　OWNS　ONE

A New Measure of Fine Car Excellence

THOSE who had owned Packard cars for years were convinced that the Twin Six was the ultimate Packard. They did not believe it was possible to improve upon it.

But now these veteran Packard owners are buying new series Packard Eight cars.

And they say that the Packard Eight has qualities they had never learned to expect in any car.

The new Packard Eight cars give their owners:

Wider, more comfortable and luxurious bodies which retain all of the traditional Packard grace and beauty;

More and still smoother power combined with a new ease of control and freedom from gear shifting;

An unusual economy of operation;

And, best of all, the new improvements —the chassis lubricator and the motor oil rectifier which double the life of the car. More, they emancipate Packard owners from the drudgery of constant oiling and greasing operations. On the new Packards proper lubrication is almost automatic.

The owners of Packard Eight cars have had to revise their ideas of how good a fine car can be.

The Packard Eight Seven-passenger Sedan Limousine is illustrated—$5100 at Detroit. Packard Eight and Packard Six both are furnished in nine body types, four open and five enclosed. Packard distributers and dealers welcome the buyer who prefers to purchase his Packard out of income instead of capital.

PACKARD

ASK THE MAN WHO OWNS ONE

THE AMBASSADORS' CHOICE

Those who are selected to represent this country at the courts of the great capitals must in turn select the things which will be in keeping with the importance of their missions.

Ten prominent diplomats have recently chosen Packard cars as affording that distinction so necessary to their activities.

In England, a Packard Six has appeared at the Court of Saint James's; while in France, an Eight has stood, an object of beauty, at the gates of the Palais de l'Elysée.

In either Six or Eight is found the full measure of Packard beauty, Packard distinction and Packard dependability.

PACKARD

Ask The Man Who Owns One

PACKARD

THE Navy and Army together have honored Packard with orders for new aircraft engines totaling nearly four million dollars. The new motors, proven supreme by exacting government tests, are a tribute not only to Packard leadership in power plant engineering but also to the vision and sympathetic cooperation of those men who bear the responsibility of our national defense. ≈ ≈ Packard's motor building supremacy is as available to the private citizen as to the United States government —in the Packard Six and the Packard Eight. ≈ *Ask The Man Who Owns One.*

Color , Nature abounds in beautiful and harmonious color combinations. The birds, the flowers, the sunset skies, set perfect examples—and point the way to brilliant color schemes all in perfect taste.

Yet what artistry is required in the selection of shades and tones to satisfy the modern vogue for color in motor cars! Packard has a special Board of Color made up of men of long experience and artistic judgment. These men create the standard color combinations which charm the eye in such wide variety on today's Packard Six. And they advise on the special re-

quirements of those who buy the Packard Eight.

Whether Six or Eight is your choice you may be as sure of the charm and good taste of the Packard's color scheme as you are of its lasting beauty. For Packard lavishes as much care and effort on the unusual processes which preserve the car's color and finish as upon the selection of the shades which will appeal to Packard's discriminating clientele.

Nothing finer is offered anywhere in the world than the enduring brilliance of Packard cars —long in life and long in beauty of lines and finish.

PACKARD
ASK THE MAN WHO OWNS ONE

144

"The supreme combination of all that is fine in motor cars."

Grace ⸱ It is not surprising that Packard cars have eleven times won international beauty contests abroad. For their slim, graceful, flowing lines are so universally admired and frankly imitated that they have set an enduring style in motor car design.

But the fleet grace of Packard lines is truly appropriate only to the car which created them. For grace is more than a thing of external appearance. Grace is beauty in motion.

The grace of the Packard is symbolic of the car's supreme performance—its smooth, rapid acceleration—the ease with which it reaches and maintains unsurpassed speeds—the comfort of its luxuriously roomy interior.

The improved Packards, while retaining the traditional Packard lines, have an added refinement of beauty and a new range of performance which only those who drive them can fully appreciate.

P A C K A R D

Printed in the United States, by ANDREW H. KELLOGG CO.

The Restful Car

"The supreme combination of all that is fine in motor cars."

Charm · That women of wealth and social position the world over have shown so pronounced a preference for Packard cars is a tribute to Packard's grace and beauty.

There is an irresistible charm in the simple dignity of Packard lines — a slender, thoroughbred appearance as appealing to the man of affairs as to the woman of fashion. But the real secret of Packard's universal attraction goes beyond the design and proportions which have been so widely imitated.

The prestige reflected by a genera-

tion of distinguished owners; the reputation achieved through more than a quarter century of engineering leadership, the luxurious fineness in every detail of body and chassis; the super-power of the smooth and silent motor, its alert response on hill or crowded boulevard—

These qualities all contribute to that charm which leads the discriminating man or woman to Packard ownership.

ASK THE MAN WHO OWNS ONE

PACKARD

Before men learned acid plating in the 15th century, precious metals were dissolved in mercury and applied as a liquid, the quicksilver then being evaporated in a furnace

THE life of many Packard parts today is enormously increased by the heavy plating of special alloys which protects them from wear and weather while adding to the gleaming beauty of the car.

Plating was for ages a purely ornamental art. First thin plates of gold or silver were soldered or riveted to the baser metal. Hence the name.

But through the centuries men learned better ways of coating one metal with another—and other reasons than mere appearance for doing so. The process became an industrial art involving many sciences.

In this process as in scores of other details of design and manufacture Packard spares neither pains nor expense in its effort to surpass current standards.

Packard's most valuable asset is its reputation for creating the best built as well as the most beautiful of cars. And in its effort to deserve and perpetuate this reputation, Packard never forgets that long life is an important attribute of true quality.

PACKARD

ASK THE MAN WHO OWNS ONE

Packard cars are priced from $2275 to $4550. Individual custom models from $5200 to $8970, at Detroit

147

*"The supreme combination of
all that is fine in motor cars."*

Safety ,, Packard cars are designed by the recognized leaders in automotive engineering.

They are built to the highest precision standards, in a factory which experts travel half way around the world to see and study.

Packard owners know they may place the fullest confidence in their cars. Their own experience serves only to impress the reputation which Packard has borne for more than a quarter of a century.

No matter what the demand of the moment, distinguished appearance at the opera door or brute power on a grinding grade, the Packard may be depended upon—always.

Talent, experience, facilities—these combine to produce motor vehicles unsurpassed in performance, in beauty and comfort, and in safety.

PACKARD

A S K   T H E   M A N   W H O   O W N S   O N E

"The supreme combination of all that is fine in motor cars."

Distinction ⸱ A man or a motor may gain notoriety, even popularity, almost over night — and lose them just as quickly. But distinction comes only with time and a long series of notable achievements.

The distinction which Packard cars enjoy is the result of more than a generation of leadership in engineering and in body design — a quarter century of patronage by an illustrious clientele.

Pride in Packard ownership is natural, and few would care to change the famous lines which proclaim their cars

as Packards. But there are those who wish an individual distinction. To them Packard offers the masterpieces of the foremost body designers and unlimited choice in color combinations, upholstery and the refinements of equipment.

Thus those who would add the final touch of luxury and personality to supreme comfort, beauty and distinction, can gratify their ultimate desire in a custom-built Packard.

ASK THE MAN WHO OWNS ONE

PACKARD

*"The supreme combination of
all that is fine in motor cars."*

Beauty · · It has been said that "beauty is in the eye of the beholder". And yet, while tastes differ, there are some things the beauty of which is agreed upon the world around.

The graceful proportions and distinguished simplicity of Packard design seem to command universal admiration. At home, they long ago established a style which other manufacturers sincerely flattered by imitation. Abroad, both the Packard Six and the Packard Eight have time after time won first award in International Car Beauty Contests—being acclaimed by foreign judges as superior in grace and beauty to the finest custom designs of their own countrymen!

The improved Packard retains the famous lines which have been characteristically Packard for a decade—with refinements of detail which provide still more alluring appearance and luxurious comfort. Its aristocratic beauty is in keeping with the Improved Packard's unrivaled mechanical performance.

PACKARD

ASK THE MAN WHO OWNS ONE

"The supreme combination of
all that is fine in motor cars."

Prestige • • The Packard owner, however high his station, mentions his car with a certain satisfaction—knowing that his choice proclaims discriminating taste as well as a sound judgment of fine things.

For the Packard is one of the world's few fine cars universally approved by the enthusiastic owners of other famous makes.

Recognized everywhere as supremely typifying America's genius for perfection in things mechanical, Packard cars go further in possessing to a marked degree that subtle attribute—prestige.

Packard prestige, sensed if not defined by every Packard owner, is reflected in the car's aristocratic beauty, its distinction, its luxury and comfort, its superb performance – unexcelled in traffic or on the open road.

PACKARD

ASK THE MAN WHO OWNS ONE

ASK THE MAN
WHO OWNS ONE

"The supreme combination of all that is fine in motor cars"

ℒEADERSHIP ⸱ Packard's position in the vanguard of automotive progress has been consistently maintained for twenty-seven years.

Packard leadership is the result of a deliberate intent backed from the first by means more than adequate to permit engineering research and the highest degree of precision manufacture.

For a generation Packard has been the great automotive laboratory from which have come many of the most important developments

in the evolution of the modern car.

Today, Packard-powered planes, surviving gruelling military and naval tests; Packard-engined racing boats, champions of their class; Packard cars, outstanding as the most imitated cars in the world; proclaim Packard leadership on land, in the air, and on the water.

And Packard owners, themselves leaders in every field of human endeavor, know that their cars cannot but reflect a compliment upon their taste and judgment.

PACKARD

"The supreme combination of all that is fine in motor cars"

BALANCE

What Packard means by "balance" in a motor car goes far beyond the mechanical balance of parts which assures silent, vibrationless operation. Packard's clientele takes that for granted.

The balance in which Packard takes pride is that perfect balance of desirable qualities which led one enthusiastic owner to write that his Packard was *"the supreme combination of all that is fine in motor cars."*

Packard's deliberate aim for twenty-seven years has been to develop a car of all-around excellence—not a car famous merely for one out-standing trait but of acknowledged superiority in all. Those who own Packard cars know how well Packard has succeeded.

Whatever you may expect from a motor car the Packard will provide to an unusual degree. Beauty, smartness and distinction recognized and imitated the world around. Speed unsurpassed by any but racing cars. Roominess and comfort which are proverbial. Low operating cost and long life which make Packard ownership a real economy. It is the *balanced excellence* of the Packard which makes it so universally admired and desired.

PACKARD

ASK THE MAN WHO OWNS ONE

153

THE PACKARD SIX—526

The Packard Six—526

THIS CAR represented many refinements over previous Packard Sixes but perhaps its greatest distinction was in appearance. It was hailed as one of the most beautiful cars Packard had ever produced and mechanically it had been brought up to a high degree of perfection. The lighting switch appeared on the steering wheel in place of the spark lever for the first time in this car. Much attention was given to cylinder lubrication. Oil was sprayed on the cylinder walls automatically when the engine was choked and there was an oil filter installed.

THE PACKARD EIGHT—443

The Packard Eight—436-443

IN THIS car began the long sleek lines that have added so much to Packard beauty. It was the 443 which started a long procession of triumphs in the beauty contests of Europe. The motor developed 105 horse power which gave the car a remarkable ability on the road. The 443 was the motor car which made of coast-to-coast journeys prosaic, uneventful trips. It brought use of motor cars for long trips into popular favor.

Designers of the late 18th century
made the elaborate sedan chairs of
that period beautiful in line and
artistic in color and embellishment

The New Packard Six Convertible Coupe

PACKARD body designers deserve the international reputation the beauty of their work has won for them. The graceful and distinctive simplicity of Packard bodies is everywhere admired and frequently copied.

And now Packard designers have created another worthy addition to the line of standard models—the Packard Six 2-passenger convertible coupe.

Here is the very car for combined sport and business use—and for the younger generation which so admires the runabout type.

With top up and windows closed the convertible coupe provides a snug, warm enclosed car for winter or wet-weather driving, with more than enough room for two.

With top down and windows lowered into the doors, the car becomes a smart roadster. The fully upholstered folding seat, which fits flush within the rear deck, also provides room for two.

This beautiful two-purpose car priced at but $2425 at the factory is giving new impetus to the Packard Six conquest of the fine car market.

Packard cars are priced from $2275 to $4550. Individual custom models from $5200 to $8970, at Detroit.

PACKARD
ASK THE MAN WHO OWNS ONE

The most splendid period of English furniture has been called Chippendale after the greatest of English cabinetmakers

THE MASTER cabinetmakers of the 18th century left their names permanently attached to distinct and original styles. Modern furniture still reflects the genius of Chippendale, Adam, Hepplewhite, Sheraton.

Within the graceful, characteristic Packard lines lies the workmanship of modern masters of woodworking. Their expert craftsmanship is no less exacting because it remains hidden from the eye.

For Packard bodies, whose sturdy framework is of fine hardwood, must be as long lived as Packard chassis. Packard beauty must endure under years of stress and strain unknown to workmen of the past.

And Packard beauty is enduring in another sense also. For Packard, in twenty-seven years, has created a lasting style in motor car design which like the work of the old cabinetmakers has been much flattered by imitation.

PACKARD

ASK THE MAN WHO OWNS ONE

PACKARD EIGHT PRICES REDUCED

PACKARD'S own Custom Eight cars have been reduced in price as follows:

MODEL	OLD PRICE	NEW PRICE	REDUCTION
Seven Pass. Sedan Limousine	$5250	$4550	$700
Seven Passenger Sedan . .	5150	4450	700
Two Pass. Convertible Coupe	4950	4250	700
Two Passenger Coupe . .	4800	4150	650
Five Passenger Club Sedan .	4950	4450	500
Four Passenger Coupe . .	4950	4450	500

The Packard factories are busy to capacity—busier than ever before in nearly thirty years of fine motor car building and at a season of the year when activity is least expected. It is but good business for Packard to share its prosperity with those who buy its products. Therefore the new prices.

There has been no change in quality. Each car is identical with those Packard has been building. The new prices continue to include complete custom equipment and unlimited paint and upholstery options costing hundreds of dollars extra on many other cars. This, together with the substantial price reductions, gives the Packard Eight an important first cost advantage.

The lower prices make it possible for many additional thousands to step up to the possession of America's finest and most modern car.

(Prices do not include freight and Government tax)

Packard Motor Car Company, Detroit, Michigan

PACKARD

ASK THE MAN WHO OWNS ONE

Repoussé, the ancient art of raising designs upon metal by hammering from the back, was extensively used in ornamenting early bronze armour

THE famed beauty and grace of today's Packard reflect far more than the ability of Packard body designers. Graceful lines, conceived by artists, are possible in the finished car through the modern perfection of tools and methods for the pressing of metal.

It seems but a few years ago when every Packard body was individually hammered out by wasteful hand work —the same method of beating flat metal sheets into useful and ornamental forms which has been practiced since the earliest times.

Today, great presses, some of them exerting a thousand tons of force, mold Packard body panels, fenders and other parts from sheets of special steel. The costly dies instantly form more beautiful and accurate shapes than weeks of the most expert labor could possibly produce.

Packard is proud of the large part it has played in the development of metalworking tools which contribute so much to Packard beauty and long life— and aid in making Packard ownership available to additional thousands.

Packard cars are now priced from $2275 to $4550. Individual custom models from $3875 to $8725, at Detroit

P A C K A R D

A S K   T H E   M A N   W H O   O W N S   O N E

*The skill of the medieval
swordsmiths was an heritage
from generations at the forge*

PACKARD crankshafts, gears, axles—and all of the many forgings so vital in upholding the Packard reputation for performance and long life—are fashioned with supreme skill and the most modern of precision equipment.

Batteries of huge drop forges, with their costly dies, shape selected steels into Packard parts with a speed and exactness unknown to the craft but yesterday. For while the forging of metal is as old as

history, only with the perfection of modern tools—in which Packard has long held leadership—has drop forging reached its highest development.

Every Packard part must conform to Packard's inflexible standards. Fine materials, fine craftsmen, fine tools—these are factors which for nearly thirty years have made the Packard the favored car of the world's first families.

Packard cars are now priced from $2275 to $4550. Individual custom models from $3875 to $8725, at Detroit

P A C K A R D

A S K   T H E   M A N   W H O   O W N S   O N E

Some of the world's most famous upholstery and hangings were produced at the Hotel des Gobelins under the patronage of Louis XIV.

PACKARD requires in upholstery all that modern science can add to the ancient art of textile weaving. Skilled specialists select the finest fabrics from the looms of Europe and America. Quality first, then beauty of color and design are considered.

From the whole world of materials open to its choice Packard has selected the most beautiful, durable and appro-

priate broadcloths, silks and velours. These are immediately available. From them the Packard Eight buyer may choose with the assurance that they represent not only perfect workmanship but exquisite taste.

For those desiring the individuality of custom bodies and special upholstery, Packard quickly procures tapestry, needlepoint— any fabric which the most exacting buyer wishes.

PACKARD

ASK THE MAN WHO OWNS ONE

The methods used in heat treating metals in the early days of automobile manufacture were still those of the Dark Ages

PACKARD has made the heat treating of parts—annealing, tempering or hardening to fit them for their special functions—an exact and charted science.

Before Packard began its pioneering research, heat treating, as a process distinct from forging, was almost unknown. For centuries smiths had tempered steel while forging it—gauging heat by the color of the glowing metal and quenching their handiwork in a cooling bath of oil or water.

Today, the modern Packard furnaces are regulated by the most sensitive of pyrometers—quenching baths are prescribed by accurate and recorded formulas. Specific reactions and unvarying results are known in advance—the quality standards of Packard parts have been made certain.

The Packard car is a tribute to the metallurgical and manufacturing, as well as the engineering progress in which Packard has led. It has well earned its acknowledged leadership in quality, performance and long life.

28

Packard cars are priced from $2275 to $4550. Individual custom models from $3875 to $8725, at Detroit

P A C K A R D
A S K   T H E   M A N   W H O   O W N S   O N E

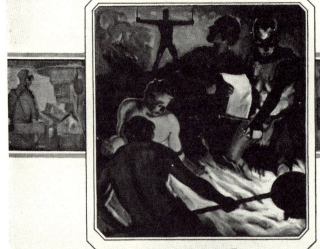

One of the wonders of the ancient world was the
bronze statue of the sun-god Helios, 105 feet high, cast
in 280 B. C. and known as the Colossus of Rhodes

PACKARD quality begins with the raw metal. It is melted and mixed and cast by Packard's own craftsmen, who practice with modern exactness an art that was ancient when the Christian era dawned.

In one of the world's most modern foundries Packard precision parts first take form under scientific control.

Every detail of temperature and the blending and pouring of metals into the intricate moulds is carefully checked.

For perfect castings are the first step in precision manufacture. And Packard standards are as exacting in the unseen water chambers cast within cylinder walls as in the lacquered finish of a brilliant body or the fine adjustment of a crank shaft balance.

From the drawing boards of world-famous engineers to the beautiful and luxurious finished vehicle, Packard exercises complete control of quality. The Packard's reputation as the best built car in the world is jealously protected. Dependable performance and long life are the result.

Packard cars are priced from $2275 to $4550. Individual custom models from $5200 to $8970, at Detroit

P A C K A R D
ASK THE MAN WHO OWNS ONE

162

The elaborate figure-heads of famous
American clipper ships were not cut
from solid timber, but built up of fitted
pieces—then carved to final form

PACKARD'S characteristic lines have set the standard for an entire school of automobile design.

First an achievement of independent, creative designing, then refined and developed through the years, Packard lines—though frequently imitated—have never been surpassed in grace and distinction.

This is not accident. The continued refinement of Packard lines, while retaining all their familiar and distinctive characteristics, is today the object of as careful thought and study as was their original conception.

When improvements are contemplated, Packard artisans construct from the drawings a full-sized body of fine wood. Under the eyes of the designers it is then reshaped until each line and curve is artistically correct, each panel, door and window properly proportioned—the whole a perfect model for a new interpretation of Packard beauty.

It is such faithful consecration to an ideal—typical of every phase of Packard design and manufacture—that has established Packard beauty and distinction as supreme among all fine cars.

Packard cars are priced from $2275 to $4550. Individual custom models from $3875 to $8725, at Detroit

PACKARD

ASK   THE   MAN   WHO   OWNS   ONE

163

The Emperor of the French was noted for his rigid standards in the inspection of his crack regiments

PRECISION is strictly interpreted at the Packard factory where artisans, trained through the years to one high ideal, are both painstaking and skilled.

Packard's inspection system, as highly organized as an army intelligence service, guards constantly against error—human or mechanical. For high inspection standards are the first requirement of undeviating quality.

Packard inspectors are ruthless. Their orders are to condemn the slightest offending part without compromise or mercy. Yet their primary duty is not the rejection of faulty work, but rather its prevention.

Inspection begins with the raw material and extends to the finished car. No part, however small, escapes careful, scientific comparison with its required standards. Not a car is released from the factory until it has passed the most rigid tests.

Thus Packard insures the laboriously earned and invaluable reputation enjoyed by the Packard Six and the Packard Eight.

Packard cars are priced from $2275 to $4550. Individual custom models from $3875 to $8725, at Detroit

PACKARD

ASK THE MAN WHO OWNS ONE

PACKARD IDENTITY
WILL ENDURE

RECENTLY there has been a great deal of discussion in the press regarding combinations and mergers of motor car companies. Most of these rumors and newspaper articles have mentioned Packard as one of the companies to be combined or merged.

Our position has been and is, that we will not merge or consolidate with anyone. We have made our own way from the beginning. We have created a position for ourselves and a reputation that is distinctive and unique. We do not intend to surrender either.

The personnel of the company from the beginning was made up of men who knew and loved fine things, mechanically and artistically. So the company was born to occupy the fine car field. Its reputation has been made in this field, so it is natural that we should feel that we can serve the public best by confining our efforts and development to it.

The history of fine things throughout the world shows that they are produced by men and organizations that have no other thought, no other ambition, and no other ideals.

We do not build to a price and we do not cater to the world. Our clientele knows us well and we know them. They are discriminating and we try never to lose sight of that fact. We know that the single standard of high quality will produce better motor cars than were we to attempt to secure the business of the world by building to all the pocketbooks in it. The public has appreciated our single standard of quality ideals and we shall stick to them.

We are not opposed to expansion. On the contrary, we realize its advantages. We shall continue to seek expansion as the merit of our product, the improvement of our facilities, and our service to the public may warrant. We may even from time to time expand by the absorption of other desirable companies. We will expand in any way that will enable us to best serve the public and win its favor.

But, very definitely, we do not intend to lose our identity through any merger, combination, or consolidation, now or hereafter.

Alvan Macauley
President

PACKARD MOTOR CAR COMPANY, DETROIT

The consummate art with which the old
masters mixed and applied their pigments
is attested by the color values and the
character still retained by their paintings

THE mixing and application of colors is an art as old as man's love of beauty. Yet within the past five years we have found better and more permanent lacquers and finishes than were discovered in the previous five thousand.

Packard, for example, now paints and finishes a body in a far more beautiful and enduring way than was possible with the materials and methods of yesterday—and in less than half the time. For Packard anticipated the modern vogue of color by investing over a million dollars in new and highly advanced equipment.

In a central mixing room Packard artists prepare the color lacquers in all their unlimited hues. Nearly ten miles of special piping then convey the liquid colors to the spray booths where expert finishers apply them to Packard bodies—artistically and permanently—by the most modern of scientific processes.

Thus Packard achieves the beauty of finish which continues and endures throughout the unusually long life of the Packard car.

Packard cars are priced from $2275 to $4550. Individual custom models from $3875 to $8725, at Detroit

PACKARD
ASK THE MAN WHO OWNS ONE

The Dietrich Convertible Sedan

CULTURED women instinctively recognize and appreciate fine work—whether it be the decorator's, the modiste's or the motor car designer's.

The preference such women have shown for Packard cars—not in a few large centers only but in every section of the Union—is a tribute to three particularly well recognized Packard qualities, beauty, prestige and long life.

For women wish the family car and particularly their own private cars to reflect good taste and discrimination inside and out, to possess a distinguished reputation and, withal, to be of good quality and lasting service.

Woman recognizes a Packard—either Six or Eight—to be something more than a mere utility. She sees it also as a work of art. Here is necessary transportation made luxurious—and clothed with beauty.

The very needlework, and there is much of it hidden in the soft upholstery of a Packard interior, reflects the pride which Packard women take in aiding to produce the best built car in the world.

PACKARD
ASK THE MAN WHO OWNS ONE

ASK
THE MAN
WHO
OWNS ONE

ACHIEVEMENT

NAPOLEON, in the nineteenth century, with all the wealth of Europe in his hands, could command no better personal transportation than Alexander 2200 years before.

But men were rapidly approaching the time when the accumulated skill and knowledge of countless generations would combine to produce a new civilization through machine power. The first Packard, containing many original features still in use to-day, was built in the same century that witnessed Waterloo!

Today, after nearly thirty years of research, experience and improvement, Packard cars come as near to the ideal of perfection in personal transportation as seems likely to be reached until some new discovery revolutionizes land travel. Possible refinements are found with less and less frequency. Packard design is tending to standardize in vehicles whose outstanding beauty, performance and prestige are recognized in every section of the globe.

Packard engineering leadership alone could not produce that thing of beauty, grace and power which so fully answers the demands of modern men—which stands, a masterpiece of combined art and science, before your door.

In the Packard organization today are combined the knowledge and skill of more than a hundred separate and distinct arts, professions, crafts and trades—each reaching its highest development in its contribution to Packard superiority, all uniting to make the Packard car the supreme expression of modern transportation.

The original painting reproduced on the opposite page hangs in the Board Room of the Packard Motor Car Company

PACKARD

The Packard Eight—626

THIS CAR, introduced in 1928, marked Packard's change from six to eight-cylinder engines for its smaller cars. Steering wheel whip and front wheel shimmy, introduced to automobiles through low pressure tires and two conditions which caused the entire industry much concern, were overcome in the 626 and its companion cars with a new trunnion spring bracket applied to the left front spring. It became one of the most important developments of years in the industry. Mechanical snubbers to check spring rebound were replaced with hydraulic shock absorbers in this car also. Popularity won by Packard cars throughout the world grew apace with the Packard Sixth Series cars. How well the public reacted to the new cars might be indicated by unprecedented sales of 48,119.

PACKARD

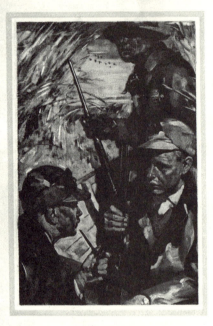

❝ my experience is that the best is always the cheapest in the long run—in any line—clothes, automobiles, or shotguns. If you keep a Packard, say four years, it won't cost you any more than your present car. You buy two cars now to my one, pay as much depreciation as I do and then don't have the car you want. And I'll bet you a good dinner that the expenses of running my Packard, gas, oil, repairs, and so on, aren't a bit more than you are paying.

Illustrated above is the Packard Eight 633
Seven-Passenger Sedan

28

PACKARD

Each Packard is built to the exacting requirements of the world's most discriminating clientele

Packard, like its patrons, demands and selects only the best the world provides.

Discriminating taste, experience, exact knowledge and scientific equipment, combine to aid in the selection of the diverse materials which Packard craftsmanship finally molds into the modern miracle of luxurious transportation.

There are artists in other fields than color, form and fabric. Packard has also its connois-seurs in steel, in bronze, in aluminum, in wood, in a score of other highly specialized departments. These men pick Packard materials with a fine appreciation of their responsibilities in upholding a priceless reputation.

Fine workmanship demands and deserves the best of materials. In things unseen as in things seen, a Packard must measure up to the one standard of quality which Packard knows— the highest.

ASK   THE   MAN   WHO   OWNS   ONE

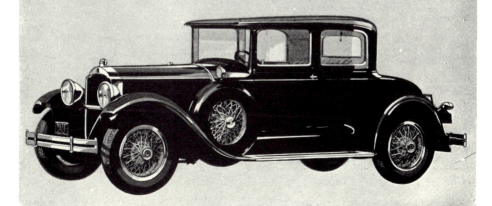

THE PACKARD EIGHT—645

The Packard Eight—640 and 645

THE "BIG" Packard grew to wheelbases of 140 and 145 inches in these two great Packards. They represented truly the height of motoring luxury among all automobiles of their period. Gar Wood in 1928, with two 1100 horse power Packard engines in his Miss America VII, won the Harmsworth race and established a new world's speed record on the water of 92.8 miles an hour.

PACKARD

The Emperor Justinian codified and restated the principles of Roman law and conduct

Packard enjoys a priceless reputation in the fine car field. It has been earned not alone by the unchanging quality of Packard cars, but as largely by the established Packard principles of doing business.

"Packard principles" is not a mere phrase. These principles—settled rules of action in public relations—have existed in substance since the founding of the Packard company. As early as 1909 they were put in writing, and in 1925 carefully codified, simply stated and published for the benefit of the nation-wide Packard organization and its growing clientele.

Today these fixed principles guide every Packard man, from chief executive to humblest employee, in courteous, dependable and just dealings with appreciative customers. For Packard reputation is not only a reward—but a continuing responsibility. No Packard man is allowed to forget the significance of Packard's slogan—

ASK   THE   MAN   WHO   OWNS   ONE

PACKARD

James Monroe, in his famous doctrine, formulated America's lasting policy of independent action and freedom from outside interference

From its inception the Packard company has been independent—free to follow its own policies in seeking its chosen destiny.

In 30 years there have been no entangling alliances—there has been no interference from outside influence, no change of purpose. And Packard's world-supremacy is the result.

Packard has achieved for its product an outstanding and unchallenged leadership in the fine car field. This has been its sole aim. The beauty and originality of Packard design, the superiority of Packard engineering, the superb performance of Packard cars could only be achieved through such singleness of purpose.

That Packard independence of policy and action will continue, that Packard has the means and the intention to remain supreme, is assured by its chief executive: "We have made our own way from the beginning. We have created a position for ourselves and a reputation that is distinctive and unique. We do not intend to surrender either."

ASK THE MAN WHO OWNS ONE

PACKARD

Only men of cultured background, sterling character and ripe experience merit ambassadorships from our nation to the world powers

Packard dealers are ambassadors of good will to the court of public opinion. They are chosen with utmost care by the Packard management. Character and courtesy, responsibility and integrity are among the first requirements.

And so Packard service—sales service to new customers and maintenance service to owners—is of high and dependable quality. Uniform, too, for Packard has developed a standardized practice for the guidance of dealers which insures a high character of service operations throughout the entire Union, and at fair and established rates.

Packard dealers subscribe wholeheartedly to the factory policy of "principle before profit." They interpret that policy in just and honorable dealings with their customers—in new car, in used car, and in service transactions *equally*. This Packard owners everywhere know and appreciate.

A S K   T H E   M A N   W H O   O W N S   O N E

THE PACKARD EIGHT—726

The Packard Eight—726
and 733

BODY LINES of the Seventh Series Packards took on added beauty through a new moulding and window reveal treatment. Non-shatterable glass was installed throughout in these cars and many refinements and improvements were added. Important among these was a new four-speed transmission. Packard made further engineering history in 1929 by building and flying the first aircraft Diesel engine.

You are Paying for a Packard
Why not Own One?

SIXTY-EIGHT per cent of those who buy the Packard Standard Eight give up other makes of cars—thousands in the ten to fifteen hundred dollar class. These new owners quickly learn—

That it costs no more to operate and maintain a Packard than their old cars —*cars costing even a thousand dollars less.*

And that it costs no more to own a Packard because Packard owners keep their cars nearly twice as long and drive them nearly twice as far as the lower-priced cars they trade in.

Those who buy on the payment plan find—

That they keep their cars several times as long as it takes to pay for them—a relief to those who have made monthly payments every other year on other cars.

And that on the average, the value of their used car equals or exceeds the down payment on the new cars—leaving each small monthly payment the largest cash outlay in the having of a Packard.

Country-wide records indicate that ninety-six out of every hundred who buy Packard cars never leave the Packard family but continue to buy Packard cars—proof that "Ask The Man Who Owns One" means just what it says.

The chances are that you are paying as much or more for your present motoring as it would cost you to own a Packard. The Packard dealer in your community can quickly show you, with pencil and paper.

Why not let him examine your used car and tell you how easily you may have a luxurious new Packard Eight? You will be under no obligation in giving him an opportunity to serve you.

PACKARD MOTOR CAR COMPANY
DETROIT   ·   ·   ·   MICHIGAN

ASK   THE   MAN   WHO   OWNS   ONE

THE *New* PACKARD EIGHTS

Built in three complete and luxurious lines - at three distinct ranges of price

The new series Packard Straight Eights are outstandingly more advanced, more beautiful, more comfortable and convenient than any Packard cars in history. ↗ ↗ They embody all the engineering improvements and the enriched luxury which the world naturally expects from Packard. ↗ ↗ Three complete lines of cars are included in the new series. They cover the entire fine car field—and dominate it! ↗ ↗ Whether you desire the supreme luxury of custom designed coach work—fitted, trimmed and upholstered according to your personal tastes—or the comfort, beauty and distinction of a Packard in the usual full measure, you will find among the new series Packard Eights a car to meet your exact requirements.

THE DE LUXE EIGHT The Packard Eight De Luxe with its 145½-inch wheelbase is the largest, roomiest and most perfectly appointed car which Packard has ever produced. It is practically an individual custom creation, for fittings, appointments, and upholstery—as well as colors and trim—are usually the individual specifications of the purchasers.

The Packard Eight De Luxe, with its eleven superb models, literally provides the supreme degree of luxury in motor car transportation.

Prices at the factory range from $4585 for the Roadster to $5350 for the Seven-Passenger Sedan-Limousine. The finest masterpieces of the world's most famous individual custom-body builders are also available to order at prices up to $10,000.

THE CUSTOM EIGHT For those who desire the power and speed of the De Luxe engine, Packard also provides the Custom Eight. Built on a chassis of 140½-inch wheelbase, it is powered with the same motor—the famous Packard Straight Eight, with its nine-bearing crankshaft, improved and developed to new standards of performance.

Save for the Packard Eight De Luxe, today's Packard Custom Eight is truly the world's finest motor car—in brilliance of performance, in grace and beauty of design and in distinction of appearance.

Prices at the factory range from $3190 for the Roadster to $3885 for the Seven-Passenger Sedan-Limousine. A wide choice in color and upholstery is available for any of the eleven beautiful body types.

THE STANDARD EIGHT The Packard Standard Eight is a smaller edition of the larger and costlier Packard cars. It is provided for those who desire the luxury and distinction of Packard transportation in cars of modified wheelbase and at more moderate price.

Eleven distinguished models are available in the Standard Eight line—each one a Packard through and through, powerful, smooth and fleet. Nothing to provide for the comfort and convenience of owners has been omitted from these splendid new Packard cars.

Prices at the factory—including a wide choice of colors—range from $2375 for the Five-Passenger Sedan of 127½-inch wheelbase to $2775 for the Seven-Passenger Sedan-Limousine with wheelbase of 134½ inches.

All new series Packard Eight cars include the new, inside, adjustable sun visors, adjustable driver's seat and steering gear, newly perfected shatter-proof glass, dashboard lockers and new beauties of fixtures and upholstery. All provide the improved powerplant with its new four-speed transmission and still further refined straight-eight engine.

We cordially invite you to see the new series Packard cars—and to drive the model of your choice. Your Packard dealer will welcome your visit—and will gladly show you, with pencil and paper, how you can enjoy the luxury and distinction of Packard transportation, very likely at no greater expense than you are paying for your present motoring.

PACKARD MOTOR CAR COMPANY ↗ ↗ DETROIT, MICHIGAN

ASK THE MAN WHO OWNS ONE

You are Paying for a Packard
Why not Own One?

The important thing to consider in purchasing a car is the cost of *owning*—not the cost of *buying*.

Operation and maintenance costs are not less because first cost is less. Even if first cost is twice as much, final cost is no greater if the car is driven twice as long. Analyze ownership costs in the light of these facts and you will find that you can enjoy the luxury of Packard transportation—at no greater expense than for cars priced down to half as much.

PHILADELPHIA RECORDS PROVE IT

Gasoline, oil and tire costs as between a Packard Standard Eight and any other car *down to half its price* are substantially the same throughout the entire country.

It costs no more to garage the Packard, and but little more for license and insurance. Upkeep and repairs for the Packard are usually less because of quality manufacture and the protection of built-in precision by centralized "instant" chassis lubrication.

The somewhat higher first cost of the Packard Standard Eight over ordinary cars is completely offset by the fact that Packard cars are built to provide and *do* provide many extra thousands of miles of luxurious and trouble-free transportation.

Even in Philadelphia, for example, where there are many of great wealth who can afford to buy cars frequently, the average life of Packard cars turned in to Packard dealers is half again longer than that of the lower priced cars turned in.

Philadelphia owners are proving that their Packard transportation is no more expensive than that afforded by cars of less prestige.

More and more Philadelphia motorists are discovering that Packard ownership involves no higher costs. Three out of every five purchasers of Packard Standard Eights in Philadelphia give up other makes of cars to join the ranks of Packard owners.

And once in the Packard family, they usually remain, for Philadelphia records show that only 7 out of every 100 Packard owners ever change to other transportation.

What is true in Philadelphia is true throughout the entire United States. Packard owners keep their cars far longer—secure in the knowledge that Packard has never depreciated cars in service by frequent and radical changes in the characteristic beauty of Packard design.

The Packard dealer in your own city will gladly show you with pencil and paper how the costs of Packard ownership compare with your present motoring costs.

Figure with him and you will find that you can enjoy the luxury and distinction of Packard transportation at no greater cost.

PACKARD MOTOR CAR COMPANY
DETROIT   -   -   -   MICHIGAN

ASK
THE MAN
WHO OWNS
ONE

The blooded camels of Arabia's merchant princes were swift and strong and luxuriously equipped

LUXURIOUS   TRANSPORTATION

THE Packard Standard Eight Five-Passenger Sedan is but one of the eleven distinguished models now offered in the Standard Eight line. It embodies the beauty and luxury which the fine car buyer has learned to associate with the name Packard.

Built on the popular 126-inch wheelbase chassis, and newly refined and improved, it differs from the famous Custom and DeLuxe Eights only in size,

power and the degree of individuality available in color, upholstery and appointments. The handsome and roomy bodies, like those of the Custom and DeLuxe models, are designed and produced entirely in the Packard factory.

The same excellence of engineering, the same expert craftsmanship, found in the larger and higher-priced Packards, produce the Standard Eight Sedan. In com-

fort, beauty and distinction, in ease of handling and brilliance of performance, this popular model is every inch a Packard —luxurious, smooth and fleet.

Since its introduction the Packard Standard Eight has been a conquest car —has won new thousands to Packard ownership. It is literally true that two out of every three Standard Eight buyers *give up other makes of cars.*

ASK   THE   MAN   WHO   OWNS   ONE

PACKARD

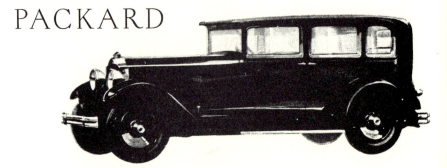

YOU ARE PAYING FOR A PACKARD
WHY NOT OWN ONE?

The important thing to consider in purchasing a car is the cost of *owning*—not the cost of *buying*.

Operation and maintenance costs are not less because first cost is less. And even if first cost is twice as much, final cost is no greater if the car is driven twice as long. Analyze ownership costs in the light of these facts and you will find that you can enjoy the luxury of Packard transportation—at no greater expense than for cars priced down to half as much.

PROVED BY OWNERS IN KANSAS CITY

Seven out of ten who buy Packard Standard Eights in Kansas City give up other makes of cars to do so.

They have discovered that driving and upkeep expenses for a Packard are practically the same as for any other car down to half its price.

And they have learned that the higher first cost of a Packard is completely offset by the fact that a Packard can be, *and usually is,* driven far longer than a lower priced car. As a matter of record, Packard cars turned in to Packard dealers in Kansas City have been driven on the average *twice as long,* lacking thirteen weeks, as other makes taken in.

Let us examine ownership costs more in detail, as between a Packard Standard Eight and a twelve to fifteen hundred dollar car. They are no different in Kansas City, comparatively speaking, than in any other American or Canadian city.

Gas, oil and tires—the principal operating costs—figure virtually the same for each car. Garage cost is the same. License and insurance are a few dollars higher for the Packard—but Packard upkeep expense is lower. Packard cars, because of quality manufacture and the protection of centralized chassis lubrication,

seldom need repairs. If they do, Packard simplicity permits quick and easy work, at a minimum of repair expense.

Depreciation is the major cost of car ownership. And simple arithmetic proves that net depreciation on a Packard is no greater than on a car priced at half as much, if the Packard is driven twice as long.

If you have been buying and trading in a twelve to fifteen hundred dollar car every eighteen months or two years, the chances are you have been paying for a Packard without realizing it. Why not, then, enjoy the luxury and distinction of Packard transportation?

Once a member of the Packard family, your satisfaction will be complete and permanent—if ownership records are indicative. In Kansas City, for example, less than eight out of every hundred Packard owners have ever changed to other makes of cars *for any reason.*

Let your Packard dealer show you how easily you may have a distinguished Packard Eight. He will gladly accept your present car as cash, and arrange the balance so that you may purchase out of income, if you prefer.

PACKARD MOTOR CAR COMPANY
DETROIT · MICHIGAN

ASK THE MAN WHO OWNS ONE

THE PACKARD EIGHT—745

The Packard Eight—740 and 745

THESE WERE more beautiful and more luxurious than any cars Packard had ever before built in all its history. Together with the other models of the Seventh Series, they had such refinements as adjustable steering gears, adjustable driving seats and adjustable inside sun visors. Those most convenient lockers built into the instrument boards of cars made their first appearance in the Seventh Series Packards. Packard created an individual custom body shop of its own to build a line of custom bodies for the 740 and 745. The year 1929 was Packard's biggest in sales and profits.

Luxurious Transportation

In the "gay" nineties of the last century a privately owned Hansom Cab was a mark of social distinction—the last word in vehicular elegance, both here and abroad

ʕ   ʕ   ʕ

PACKARD builds three complete lines of luxurious straight-eights— at three distinct ranges of price.

The Eight De Luxe lists from $4585 to $5350 at the factory; the Custom Eight from $3190 to $3885; and the Standard Eight from $2425 to $2885. Each is a Packard in every sense that thirty years of leadership has given to that famous name.

It is natural that the Packard Standard Eight should be the most popular car Packard has ever designed. A smaller Packard than the costlier Custom and De Luxe models, it still is a large and powerful car with its 90 horsepower motor and chassis lengths of 127½ and 134½ inches. Literally it has won new thousands to Packard ownership.

But as the demand for the Standard Eight has increased Packard has continued to think first in terms of quality. The factory knows no other way.

On Packard Avenue, the main thoroughfare within the Packard plant, hangs a great, permanent sign which reads "Quality First." Unseen by the public, it is a constant reminder to all Packard men, from chief executive to humble apprentice, that Packard's sole aim is the building of quality motor

cars for a world clientele of means and discrimination.

Packard quality has brought its just reward in increased business. But Packard is interested in quantity manufacture only so far as quality standards can be strictly maintained.

Each Packard car, from Standard Sedan to De Luxe Limousine with custom-coach work, carries the Packard crest and equally upholds the Packard reputation.

PACKARD

ASK
THE MAN
WHO OWNS
ONE

PACKARD

On richly caparisoned horses the most luxurious transportation of their day, Ferdinand and Isabella rode out to receive the surrender of Granada from Boabdil the Moor

PACKARD owners today enjoy personal transportation far more luxurious than even royalty could command a quarter century ago.

It is only natural that Packard should build the finest and most luxurious of vehicles. For the Packard company was founded with that purpose—has had no other object or desire. During 30 years the talents, the facilities and the resources of the vast Packard organization have been exclusively devoted to a single, quality ideal.

Today the Packard name stands for supremely luxurious transportation wherever fine cars are known and appreciated. Today's Straight Eight is acknowledged throughout the world as Packard's greatest achievement—the ideal combination of all that is fine in motor cars.

Luxurious transportation

ASK   THE   MAN   WHO   OWNS   ONE

Luxurious
Transportation

The valiant Norsemen sailed to new continents in the most luxurious craft known to their civilization

FROM its first pioneering efforts Packard has built its motor cars for conquest—conquest of the fine car field! And as the fine car market grows with the natural increase of taste and discrimination among motorists, Packard leadership becomes more marked.

The slender grace of Packard lines has always attracted the favor of the discerning—contributed to the winning of a distinguished clientele. And in the Packard Eight Phaeton—so popular in the open-air, open-road seasons — Packard beauty reaches its most graceful expression. It is only natural that the characteristic Packard design should appeal so strongly. For behind Packard beauty itself lies the satisfying assurance that Packard does not depreciate cars in the hands of owners by frequent and radical changes in appearance. Every Packard—whether new or old—is always unmistakably a Packard!

Supreme safety, the luxury of superb performance and *beauty that is always modern* will be yours in a Packard for many long years of truly distinctive transportation.

ASK THE
MAN WHO
OWNS ONE

PACKARD

PACKARD

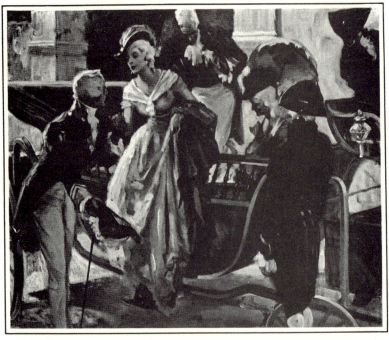

LUXURIOUS TRANSPORTATION

Each year Packard has made truly luxurious transportation available to more thousands of those who want the best. Today Packard transportation is within the financial reach of all those who have been accustomed to paying fifteen hundred dollars or more for their cars.

For him whose means permit the utmost in motor car elegance there is, of course, the Packard Eight De Luxe—and the Custom Eight. But Packard's ever-

In the England of Lady Hamilton's day the light open carriage, ingeniously fashioned and richly upholstered, was the favorite vehicle of gentlefolk

♪ ♪ ♪

growing sales rest chiefly upon the Standard Eight, the car that has made possible the widest enjoyment of Packard beauty and distinction.

Though smaller than the costlier Custom and De Luxe models, the Packard Standard Eight is still a large and roomy

car—complete in every luxurious detail. Fast and powerful, too, with its famous eight-in-line motor. And above all it is a Packard—in quality as well as in distinguished appearance.

It really costs no more to own a Packard Standard Eight than many a lower-priced vehicle. Operating costs are no greater. And the higher first cost is offset by the longer period the owner gladly keeps his Packard.

ASK THE MAN WHO OWNS ONE

186

L U X U R I O U S   T R A N S P O R T A T I O N

Stalwart and majestic elephants, their howdahs and trappings resplendent with rare fabrics and precious jewels, brought the Princes of India to the Durbar ceremonies

PACKARD luxury is mental no less than physical. It is as definitely a thing of the mind as of the body. The Packard owner gains as much satisfaction from Packard reputation as from the quality and appointments of the car itself.

The feeling of complete security born of easy control, safe steering and effortless braking, is a luxury. So is the assurance of brilliant and trustworthy performance—and the pride in a universally acclaimed, unchanging beauty of design and color.

Nothing the world can offer is fundamentally finer than the Packard Eight. That knowledge, perhaps, is the greatest Packard luxury of all.

For more than thirty years Packard has specialized exclusively in luxurious transportation. And today's Straight Eights, refined and improved, excel every famous Packard of the past.

PACKARD

L U X U R I O U S   T R A N S P O R T A T I O N

*Queen Victoria visited the City of London
with all the luxurious pomp and splendor
historically demanded of England's sovereign*

PACKARD luxury goes deeper than richness of upholstery and the comfort of cushions and springs. It is more than grace of body design and beauty of finish—more than abundant power and speed.

Packard luxury is born of a thirty year intent to build nothing but the finest of all fine motor cars. It is the ideal of Packard engineering and the directing force behind Packard manufacturing methods. It governs every detail of the car from the balance of the famous nine-bearing crankshaft to the centralized lubrication of shock absorber arms. Every part of the Packard Eight—great or small—contributes to the fineness of the whole.

New owners sense the luxury of Packard transportation in the very feel of the wheel, the responsiveness of the throttle, the ease of the brakes. And as their years of ownership grow their pride and satisfaction increase.

PACKARD

ASK   THE   MAN
WHO   OWNS
ONE

PACKARD luxury has never been more apparent than in the new series Packard Straight-Eights recently introduced. The three complete lines— Standard, Custom and De Luxe—have all been still further refined and improved, in motor, in chassis and in body.

The characteristic grace of Packard lines is retained, for Packard does not depreciate cars in the hands of owners by radical and unnecessary changes. But the new cars are outstandingly more comfortable, more convenient, more luxurious than ever before.

And as a further advance in truly luxurious transportation, Packard has added to all three lines a practical and beautiful new model—the Five-Passenger Coupe.

This car, pictured below, makes available for five the luxury of seats arranged well forward on the chassis—and at no sacrifice of roominess or comfort. Ample luggage space is provided at the rear.

In the Custom and De Luxe lines, as well as in the Standard line, a Five-Passenger Sedan has now been provided—to meet a growing demand for this model on the longer wheelbase chassis. Packard dealers everywhere are displaying the latest Packard Straight-Eights.

PACKARD

ASK   THE   MAN   WHO
OWNS   ONE

The smoothly gliding gondola, rich with silken hangings and gold embroidery, has long typified in song and story the height of Venetian luxury in transportation

THE PACKARD EIGHT—826

The Packard Eight—826 and 833

MANY NEW and important improvements appeared on this car. The vacuum tank gave way to a mechanically operated fuel pump. New and greatly improved shock absorbers appeared. The chassis lubricating system was made fully automatic. One of the most important improvements was in the system for oiling pistons. It has added greatly to the life of motors.

FOR A DISCRIMINATING CLIENTELE

Through all the ages fine things have been produced because there were those who could appreciate their ownership. The celebrated Goya tapestries executed in Spain in the late 18th century, were woven under royal patronage. Today Packard builds fine cars for those who appreciate and are satisfied only with the truly beautiful and luxurious in transportation

Most popular of all Packard cars is the distinguished and luxurious Standard Eight Five-Passenger Sedan. The Sedan pictured below is of the new 826 series—characteristically Packard in lines and general appearance but embodying added power and beauty, new improvements and refinements in many of its important details.

It costs no more to own this beautiful and distinctive new Packard than to drive any other car of similar size and power, whatever its price. Operating expenses are little if any less for a car of similar size but lesser excellence and lower price. And depreciation, the major cost of motoring, totals no more for the Packard—if the owner keeps it a little longer than he has been accustomed to drive other cars. There is nothing at all unusual in this, for most Packard owners *do* keep their Packards far longer, both in months and miles, than the cars they have previously owned. Not for economy's sake—but because they really want to keep them!

Why not buy a Packard Standard Eight Sedan and provide your family with the beauty, the comfort and the distinction of luxurious transportation? Any Packard man will chart Packard ownership costs for you side by side with those of your present Packard-size car. You will find, undoubtedly, that you are *paying* for a Packard. Why not *have* one?

PACKARD
ASK THE MAN WHO OWNS ONE

For a Discriminating Clientele

The brilliant young Mozart received great inspiration and encouragement from his royal patroness, Maria Theresa. Much of the world's fine music has been stimulated through the interest of those with wealth and appreciation. And so it is with all fine things. The appreciation of those who know and want the best things in life has, over thirty years, built Packard leadership in the realm of truly luxurious transportation

The luxury of Packard transportation—now available at no greater cost than the lesser advantages of many lower-priced cars—has lately brought new thousands to the enjoyment of Packard ownership.

Motorists who thought the Packard Eight beyond their means have discovered that operating costs are no greater for a Standard Eight than for any other car of similar size and power. And also that depreciation, the most important cost of car ownership, is no greater, either, if the Packard is driven proportionately longer, which it nearly always is.

If your present car is of Packard size, undoubtedly you, too, are paying Packard costs. Why not, then, *have* one of the new series Standard Eights—refined and improved in appointments and details, and with added power and speed?

Any Packard man will gladly come and give you the actual figures on Packard ownership costs, so that you can compare them with your current motoring expenses. And you will be satisfied, unless your case is most unusual, that the luxury of a distinguished Packard Eight can be yours at no financial sacrifice at all.

PACKARD

ASK THE MAN WHO OWNS ONE

PACKARD leadership and prestige have been built slowly and permanently. The first Packard car was completed in 1899. And since then the Packard clientele has grown as taste and appreciation have grown.

Once solely a "rich man's car," the Packard, in its Standard Eight Models, is now appreciated by thousands in moderate circumstances who have learned that excellence in transportation means ultimate economy.

For the Packard costs no more to own than any other car of its size and power—even though many are lower priced. It is built to give—and does give—an exceptionally long and trouble-free life. Those who buy a Packard for the first time are always gratified at the long extra service the extra dollars buy. Generally they keep their Packards nearly twice as long as they were in the habit of keeping lesser cars which cost just as much to operate.

The Packard five-passenger Sedan pictured below will provide you with luxurious transportation at the cost of ordinary travel. Packard men everywhere are prepared to prove this. Why not ask them to do so?

PACKARD

ASK THE MAN WHO OWNS ONE

THE PACKARD EIGHT—845

The Packard Eight—840 and 845

SELF-ADJUSTING spring and shackle bolts and a new type vibration damper were other mechanical improvements introduced in the Eighth Series cars. Special attention was given to the details and appointments of body interiors and a new style of smooth "tailored" trim drew widespread favorable comment. The combination of all these and many other refinements made the 840 and 845 the outstanding, fine big cars among the world's finest automobiles.

The Packard DeLuxe may be had in eleven body styles on 140 and 145-inch wheelbases. The two-passenger Coupe, shown here on the longer chassis, provides distinguished transportation for the business or professional man as well as for the woman who likes to drive.

The DeLuxe Coupe is especially appreciated by those families who find need for two cars. Like every Packard, it has all the qualities required by those who know what a truly fine car should be. It is

beautiful, mechanically and to the eye, luxurious in performance as in comfort.

And in the new series cars Packard has gone a step further to provide and maintain luxurious transportation. A fine car must be silent as well as safe, long-lived as well as fast and easy to control. Packard has now made lubrication *automatic.* Chassis parts, once oiled occasionally, then daily, now *cannot* be neglected. They are oiled *continuously,* while the car is in motion.

This new feature maintains factory precision, lessens wear of parts, constantly protects the Packard owner's investment by assuring longer life.

The buyer of a Packard, whether DeLuxe or Standard Eight, makes an investment which the whole world approves. And as the years pass his pocketbook proves that his choice was not extravagant.

P A C K A R D

A S K   T H E   M A N   W H O   O W N S   O N E

195

For a discriminating clientele ~ ~

For the Gonzagas, Medici, Strozzi and other great families of medieval Italy the best artists were constantly employed to decorate both written and printed volumes. Like the 16th century illuminators, Packard today produces its best for families of taste and discernment — builds motor cars for those in a position to know and enjoy truly luxurious transportation

Packard families, in the great majority, keep their cars. Whether they own the costliest of individual custom creations or models of the more moderately priced Standard Eight, they continue to *drive* their Packards with the same good judgment that prompted the original *purchases*.

This is but natural. Those of ample means are seldom extravagant. And when a Packard — of any model or any price — is driven for a period approaching its full, useful life the reward is luxurious transportation at truly economical costs.

Packard, of course, makes it desirable for owners to keep their cars. The fundamental and unchanging beauty of Packard lines protects the owner's investment. A Packard in its fourth or fifth year of operation is as much a Packard in beauty, comfort and distinction as on the day it was delivered.

The new series Packard cars — Standard, De Luxe and Individual Custom Eights—are not exceptions. More powerful, refined and improved throughout, they are the finest cars Packard has ever offered. But as usual they embody no radical changes in appearance — and they will be unmistakably and luxuriously *Packards* throughout their long and distinguished years of pleasurable service.

ASK THE MAN WHO OWNS ONE

PACKARD

LUXURIOUS
TRANSPORTATION

𝒻OR   A   DISCRIMINATING   CLIENTELE

When Josiah Wedgwood in 1763 was appointed Potter to the English Queen Charlotte certain of his creations became known as Queen's Ware. Commissions from nobility and royalty—including the famous Russian Dinner Service of 952 pieces ordered by the great Empress Catherine—from then on inspired the exquisite Wedgwood masterpieces famed today throughout the world

The world of discrimination has always turned to those with reputation established upon a long record of supreme excellence. Packard for 30 years has enjoyed that reputation in the field of fine motor cars.

Yet motorists have found that they can enjoy the luxury and distinction of Packard Eight transportation at no increase in expense.

Depreciation is the one really important item of ownership cost. And depreciation on a Packard costs no more than on a lesser car

—even if bought at two-thirds of the Packard price—if the Packard is kept and driven proportionately longer! And most Packard owners *do* keep their cars far longer.

As to operating and maintenance costs everyone knows they are no greater for a Packard Standard

Eight than for any other car of like size and power, whatever its price.

That is the real secret of enjoying *luxurious transportation.* Buy a Packard Standard Eight and keep it a little longer than has been your custom with lower-priced cars. You gain the advantages of unchanging Packard beauty, Packard comfort, performance and prestige—and the ownership costs are no greater.

ASK THE MAN WHO OWNS ONE

PACKARD

The patronage of Beau Brummell, that famed exquisite of the 18th century, led his crony, the Prince of Wales, and the nobility of all England to the salon of the great Schweitzer, to whom the cut of a coat was a fine art

for A DISCRIMINATING CLIENTELE

The designing and building of a Packard calls for a finely balanced measure of many arts, crafts and sciences. Packard's mastery in each has resulted in a world-wide reputation for beauty, performance and long life.

Wherever Americans travel they are reminded of home and of their home land's preëminence in motor car design and manufacture by the frequent sight of the familiar Packard lines. For literally it may be said that the sun never sets on the Packard. More Packards are exported every year than any other make in its price

class. In 1930 nearly *twice* as many Packards were sold in foreign lands as any other car costing over $2,000. Abroad as at home, Packard dominates the fine car market.

For the world has learned that Packard excellence, while higher in price, really costs no more when

luxurious service throughout an unusually long life is considered. So Packard domestic and export sales alike continue to mount as more and more people advance themselves into Packard ownership—at ownership charges no greater than they have been used to paying.

PACKARD

ASK THE MAN WHO OWNS ONE

PACKARD

ARISTOCRAT OF THE METROPOLIS

PACKARD

WHEN you get a touch of spring fever—coupled with an irresistible yearning to "get away from it all"—there is no surer solace than to go vagabonding in a Packard. At the wheel, you immediately feel in tune with the season—the miles slip by gently, quietly, joyously. Never could motoring be more perfect!

Like flying or speedboating, you must actually experience Packard motoring before you can fully appreciate the thrills it offers you. For a Packard is more than an automobile—it represents the last word in swift, personalized, luxurious transportation.

Fitting to the time of year, Packard offers a galaxy of open and convertible models—every one a true aristocrat. We cordially invite you to come in some sunshiny day and find your affinity in motor cars.

Of unique design is the Derham 4-passenger Sport Sedan on the Packard 845 chassis. The body is low, sporty in appearance, with no division-glass between driver's seat and rear compartment. The floor is recessed, providing greater leg room.

Delivered, $7230

ASK THE MAN WHO OWNS ONE

PACKARD MOTOR CAR COMPANY OF NEW YORK

Eleventh Avenue at 54th Street	Broadway at 61st Street	Broadway at Sherman Avenue
BRONX: 696 East Fordham Road		BROOKLYN: Atlantic at Classon Avenue

PARK AVENUE PACKARD, Inc., 6 East 57th Street   WEST END PACKARD CO., Inc., Broadway at 106th Street

PACKARD
FOR 1932

*I*N announcing its program for 1932, Packard has been conscious of the desirability for stabilization. In presenting now its plans for the year, it hopes to dispel uncertainty —at least insofar as Packard is concerned—as to later developments.

Toward that end it is announcing now two new lines of cars for delivery shortly — the Twin Six and the Light Eight. These new lines will be in addition to Packard's present, very popular Standard Eight and Eight DeLuxe models, and with them will completely cover the fine car field in all price ranges from $1750 upward.

Prices have been established on its entire four lines of cars so low that only an anticipated increase in volume can justify them. Packard expects to supply no other models of these cars before the close of the year and any price changes are more likely to be upward than down.

President—PACKARD MOTOR CAR COMPANY

FOUR LUXURIOUS LINES OF PACKARD CARS AT FOUR DISTINCT RANGES OF PRICE

The Twin Six
The supremely luxurious new Packard Twin Six is a sensational achievement embodying sixteen years of continuous experience with twelve-cylinder designs. It is offered in two wheelbase lengths—142 and 147 inches—with a wide range of standard and individual custom bodies. Chassis include Packard's new Synchro-mesh Transmission, *quiet in all three speeds*; Finger Control Free-Wheeling; Ride Control; the exclusive Angleset Rear Axle and new double drop frame. When you consider the performance possibilities of the conservatively rated and economically developed 150 horsepower of the new Twin Six, you will be truly surprised at the factory price range of this great car—$3650 to $4395.

The Standard Eight
The famous new Packard Standard Eight, the most popular and widely acclaimed Packard car in history, is available as in the past in thirteen beautiful models on 130 and 137 inch chassis. Now, with Synchromesh Transmission, *quiet in all three speeds*, and Finger Control Free-Wheeling, both optional at no extra cost, it becomes an even more outstanding value in the fine car field than ever before. Automatic chassis lubrication and Ride Control add to its riding ease. Complete body insulation excludes noise and temperature, prevents the development of squeaks and rattles. A distinguished car for those with high motoring standards. Factory prices, $2250 to $3250.

The Eight DeLuxe
The new Packard Eight DeLuxe is the companion car to the superb new Twin Six. It is the supreme development of Packard's ten years of straight-eight engineering, and will continue to rank as the world's finest eight-cylinder car. Like the Twin Six it is available on chassis of 142 and 147 inch wheelbase and with a wide choice of standard and individual custom bodies. With its new features—Synchro-mesh Transmission, *quiet in all three speeds* and Finger Control Free-Wheeling, both now available as optional equipment at no extra cost—it brings luxurious transportation in a greatly enhanced degree to the discriminating Packard clientele. Factory prices, $3150 to $3895.

The Light Eight
The new Light Eight— Packard in design, Packard in quality and, therefore, Packard in name—is offered in four large, beautiful and completely modern models, all on a chassis of 128 inch wheelbase, with eight-in-line motor of 110 horsepower, Angleset Rear Axle and double drop frame. Like all current model Packard cars, the new Light Eight provides Synchro-mesh Transmission, *quiet in all three speeds*, and Finger Control Free-Wheeling. Thousands who have long desired the luxury of Packard transportation can now enjoy it, for the Packard Light Eight costs no more to buy or to operate than cars providing far less in size, performance and prestige. Prices at the factory, $1750 to $1795.

A S K   T H E   M A N   W H O   O W N S   O N E

The Packard Eight—901 and 902

THESE CARS, hailed as the finest motor cars Packard had ever built in the shorter wheel-base and lighter type of its famous automobiles, made their first appearance in 1931. They were continued with improvements through 1932. They were provided with a popular four-speed transmission. Later Packard succeeded in building a trouble-proof three-speed transmission in which all forward speeds were quiet, an outstanding accomplishment. Ride Control first appeared on these cars. The Packard-Diesel aircraft engine won the world's non-refueling aircraft duration record with 84 hours, 33 minutes in 1931.

World Supremacy

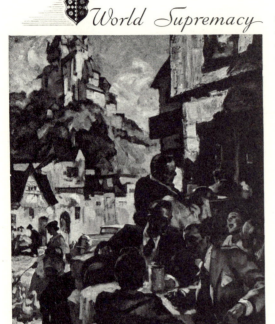

Germany No country in the world surpasses Germany in genuine appreciation of modern design, advanced engineering and precision workmanship. So it is only natural that more Packards are owned by German families of means than any other American car of similar price. On the Continent, in the Orient and in the Americas alike, Packard is supreme among fine cars

NO CAR in Packard's thirty-two year history of fine car manufacture has been more popular, more widely acclaimed, than the big and distinguished Packard Standard Eight. Beautiful, powerful and luxurious in appearance and in riding comfort, this great car has literally brought to its many owners in every part of the world a new enthusiasm for motoring. ¶ The Packard Standard Eight Series includes thirteen handsome and distinctive models built on chassis of 130 and 137 inch wheelbase. All are powered with the refined and improved straight-eight engine, "floated" on rubber mountings. The bodies, Packard designed and built, are completely insulated against both sound and temperature. Shatter-proof glass is standard in windshield and all windows. Interiors are richly upholstered and appointed. ¶ Advanced mechanical features include Ride Control, the original system of dash-adjustable hydraulic shock absorbers and, as optional equipment at no extra cost, Silent Synchro-mesh Transmission, *quiet in all three speeds,* and the new *Finger Control* Free-Wheeling. Prices at the factory range from $2250 to $3250. ¶ If you require a large, substantial and roomy fine car at moderate price, by all means permit your Packard dealer to demonstrate the famous Packard Standard Eight.

PACKARD

Ask the man who owns one

202

— of a

Distinguished family —

THE *Club Sedan, as Packard builds it, is greatly favored for touring. It seats five comfortably, with ample room for baggage, and many owners say it is the easiest riding of all models. The illustration shows the Club Sedan on the superb new Standard Eight chassis. The same body design is available also on the Eight De Luxe and Twin Six chassis.*

Packard now offers a fully complete line of distinguished fine cars, both Eights and Twelves, which today dominates the quality field, from the lowest price at which, in our opinion, any truly fine car is sold to as much as you may want to pay. ¶ Flanked above and below in price by the majestic Twin Six and the new Packard Eight are the thirteen beautiful models of the Standard Eight line and the twelve luxurious body styles offered on the Packard Eight De Luxe chassis—all in the fine car medium price range. ¶ Particularly worthy of your inspection at this time of year are the long wheelbase models of the Packard Standard Eight, especially the Club Sedan pictured above, the various Coupes and the three beautiful open cars. The Standard Eights include every feature, every refinement, found on the finest cars that Packard builds. Before you buy be sure to see *all* that Packard has to offer.

PACKARD

ASK   THE   MAN   WHO   OWNS   ONE

203

THE PACKARD EIGHT—904

The Packard Eight—903 and 904

THE LARGER Packard Eight appeared in 1931 with a device important to all cars of this longer and heavier type—the front end stabilizer. This device, which consists of two harmonic balancers located at each end of the front bumper, effectually dampens out all front end disturbances caused by road shocks. It gave results heretofore unknown in road adhesiveness, riding comfort and balance and accuracy of steering direction. The 903 and 904 cars were equipped with the most powerful eight in line motor Packard ever built.

In Paris, the style center of the world, where taste and the means to gratify it may find the height of beauty and luxury in all things, more Packards are registered than any other American fine car. There as everywhere the Packard is supreme

W O R L D   S U P R E M A C Y

For more than a generation the Packard has been acclaimed as the most beautiful and distinguished of motor cars, both abroad and at home. The new Packard cars are more beautiful and more luxurious than ever. And with their many improvements and refinements they offer exceptional values. · · · The famous Packard straight-eight engine has been given more power—and, because it is now "floated" on rubber, it is smoother and quieter. The Packard-built, synchro-mesh transmission adds to the ease of driving. While *Ride Control*—shock absorbers instantly adjustable from the dash—provides a degree of riding comfort that has never before existed. · · · If you need a new motor car, buy it today. If you desire supreme luxury buy a Packard. Dollars spent for automobiles, which draw on every state in the Union for materials and parts, will do more to revive prosperity than dollars hoarded against better times.

Packard

A S K   T H E   M A N   W H O   O W N S   O N E

Packard

DISCRIMINATING owners of the new Packard Eight DeLuxe Sedan-Limousine say it is the most luxurious car in the world. It gratifies their every desire for the finest and most distinguished in transportation. ¶ Greatly increased power permits the famous eight-in-line engine to meet every demand with silent ease. Now "floated" on rubber, its operation is even more smooth and effortless than ever before. ¶ The body of the new Sedan-Limousine is lower and roomier, newly insulated against sound and weather, more luxuriously upholstered and appointed. The wheelbase is longer and the tread wider. Four-speed, synchro-mesh transmission contributes new driving ease, while *Ride Control*, an exclusive Packard feature, provides traveling comfort never before available in any car. ¶ *Ride Control* permits the instant adjustment of the shock absorbers *from the dash*—to meet changing conditions of road, load, speed or temperature. With *Ride Control* passengers and driver may travel long and far on rough roads or smooth in relaxed and restful comfort. ¶ *Supremely* luxurious transportation is yours in any of the thirteen beautiful and dignified new Packard Continental models.

ASK THE MAN WHO OWNS ONE

Ask the man who owns one

IN THE new Convertible Victoria for five Packard has antici- pated the desires of a discriminating clientele. Preference in body styles in the past has swung from open cars to closed— but now open car smartness combined with closed car comfort is meeting with wide appreciation. And so Packard offers the Victoria, which, with the Coupe-Roadster for two or four and the Sedan for five, provides an exceptional choice of convert- ible models to buyers of either the Packard Eight or the Packard Eight De Luxe. ¶ In all, the new Continental Packard

Eights are available in a complete range of twelve body types. All have longer wheelbases, wider tread, lower and roomier bodies. Power is greater, smoother, quieter. Four-speed, synchro-mesh transmission provides greater driving ease. While the exclusive Packard *Ride Control*—dash-adjustable shock absorbers—insures supreme riding comfort whatever the road, load or temperature. The new Packard cars are more beautiful, more distinguished, more luxurious than ever before—and their riding ease is unmatched throughout the world of fine cars.

PACKARD

207

THIS is the new Coupe-Roadster for two or four passengers—one of two new convertible body styles offered on both the new Packard Eight and the Packard Eight DeLuxe chassis. The other is a convertible Victoria for five. These two new types complete a range of twelve body styles now available for both of the new Continental Packard Eights. With the Convertible Five-Passenger Sedan they provide an exceptional choice of convertible models, all combining open car smartness with closed car comfort. ¶ The new Packard cars offer a luxury of motor travel that in actual truth has never before existed. Bodies are lower—wheelbases longer—tread wider. The motor is far more powerful, smoother, quieter. The transmission is Packard-built, four-speed, synchro-mesh. And the new and exclusive Ride Control—which permits the hydraulic shock absorbers to be adjusted from the dash to compensate for road conditions, temperatures and varying numbers of passengers—provides a degree of riding comfort previously unknown. For *supreme luxury,* you must drive a Packard.

PACKARD

ASK THE MAN WHO OWNS ONE

Packard

The new Packard Sport Phaeton is a smartly beautiful car—trim and yacht-like in its lines, modish and modern in its entire conception. Folding windshields front and rear, with a counterbalanced cowl to protect the tonneau, make it virtually a double roadster. All four passengers enjoy the thrill of open air motoring in *complete* comfort. ¶ The Sport Phaeton is one of the three handsome open models that are available on either the Packard Eight or the Packard Eight De Luxe chassis. The others are the Phaeton and the Touring Car. All embody the many new features and refinements which have established the new Continental Series Packards as supreme in the field of luxurious transportation. ¶ The new Packard cars are longer in wheelbase, wider in tread. The Straight-Eight engine, now "floated" on rubber, is quieter, smoother, more powerful. The transmission is four-speed synchro-mesh—easy and silent. While the new and exclusive Packard Ride Control—which permits instant adjustment of shock absorbers from the dash—provides a degree of riding comfort that has never before existed in motor cars. ¶ The new Packards are truly the cars of tomorrow. Why not have one today?

ASK
THE MAN
WHO OWNS
ONE

209

WORLD SUPREMACY

Royalty everywhere still demands and can afford the finest the world offers. There are few royal garages which do not house more than one Packard marked with an ancient coat-of-arms. The Japanese Imperial Household owns ten

Packard

Packard is the world's favored fine car—a fact proved by registration figures in every country where such records are kept. And now the new Continental Series Packards are still further impressing this world supremacy. Never in history have Packard dealers, both abroad and at home, made so many convincing demonstrations to those who know and appreciate the best the world affords. ⋅ ⋅ ⋅ If you have not driven a new Packard Eight or a Packard Eight De Luxe—if you have not ridden in one as a passenger—you, too, should ask your Packard dealer for a trial trip. You will find that the Packard is literally the last word in luxurious transportation. ⋅ ⋅ ⋅ The speed of the new Packard cars

will deceive you. You will frequently find yourself traveling the open road at from ten to fifteen miles an hour faster than you think. This is due to many things—the quieter, more powerful straight-eight engine now "floated" on rubber, the new insulation of the body against squeaks, rattles and outside noise, and, among the most important causes, Packard's new and exclusive feature—*Ride Control*. ⋅ ⋅ ⋅ Packard *Ride Control* permits you to adjust the hydraulic shock absorbers from the dash to meet changing conditions of road, speed and load—to compensate for the slower flow of oil in cold weather. It assures you a ride of restful comfort at whatever speed you travel.

A S K   T H E   M A N   W H O   O W N S   O N E

The Packard Eight—900

THE 900, first called the "Light Eight", was the sensation of the 1932 New York automobile show. It was first offered at a list price of $1750 and it was completely a Packard. It was the first truly fine car ever produced to sell below $2,000. It had a performance that was new among all motor cars. Although called the "Light Eight" it was not a small car in any way. It had a wheelbase of 127½ inches and a motor of 110 horse power. The Angleset rear axle first appeared in these cars. The 900 had an unusually attractive Vee type radiator, which was completely new in appearance and yet which retained the characteristic Packard lines.

The New
PACKARD

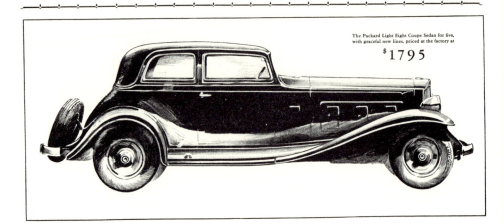

The Packard Light Eight Coupe Sedan for five, with graceful new lines, priced at the factory at

$1795

THE new Packard Light Eight for the first time introduces Packard quality in a current model at a price less than $2250 at the factory. This could never have been done before without a reduction of quality—a thing Packard's thirty-two-year-old policy would never permit.

These sensational prices are possible now only through Packard's taking full advantage of the most unusual circumstances since before the war. Prices on fine materials are at or near pre-war levels. This, combined with advanced engineering and production methods and the assurance of a very substantial volume, makes motor car history by greatly broadening the fine car field.

The new Light Eight Packard line comprises the four beautiful, completely modern models illustrated on these pages, all with 110 horsepower and on a new chassis of 128 inch wheelbase. New cars throughout, designed to fit today's economic conditions—to reflect the new purchasing power of the dollar—these Packards offer many improvements never before available to Packard buyers.

Most important of all are the new Packard Synchro-mesh Transmission, *quiet in all three speeds,* and the new Finger

The Coupe Roadster for two or four, $1795 at the factory

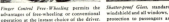

Finger Control Free-Wheeling permits the advantages of free-wheeling or conventional operation at the instant choice of the driver.

Shatter-proof Glass, standard equipment in windshield and all windows, affords complete protection to passengers as well as driver.

OF   A   DISTINGUISHED   FAMILY

212

LIGHT EIGHT

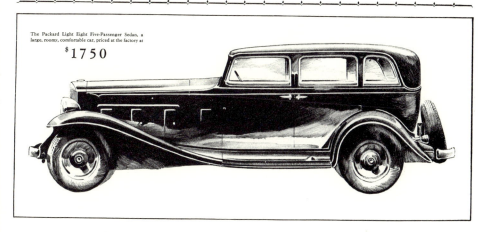

The Packard Light Eight Five-Passenger Sedan, a
large, roomy, comfortable car, priced at the factory at

$1750

Control Free-Wheeling. These two features together revolutionize all conceptions of driving ease, effortless control and *safe* free-wheeling results. The new Angleset Rear Axle and double-drop frame permit a lower center of gravity, and the low, modern design of the body.

Other improvements, just as found on the larger, heavier and more costly Packard models, include Ride Control,

The Coupe for two or four, $1795 at the factory

dash-adjustable hydraulic shock absorbers; complete equipment of shatter-proof glass, and body insulation which excludes outside heat and cold and adds silence to the other interior luxuries. Six-ply tires and bumpers, front and rear, are standard on all models.

Packard is proud to give the Packard name to these aristocratic new Light Eights. They uphold the Packard tradition of engineering leadership and supremacy in beauty of line and luxury of transportation. You will be proud to own one of these new Packard cars. A demonstration will make you dissatisfied with all you have previously experienced in acceleration, ease of control, power and comfort. You will be unfair to yourself if you do not see and drive the Packard Light Eight before buying *any* car at or near its price this spring. You *can* own a Packard.

ASK THE MAN WHO OWNS ONE

Synchro-mesh Transmission, quiet in all three speeds, brings a new ease and convenience in gear shifting, a new quietness in operation.

Ride Control, dash-adjustable hydraulic shock absorbers, provides restful riding comfort whatever the road, load, speed or temperature.

...of a Distinguished family

THESE are days of unusual motor car values. If you are in need of a new automobile *now* is the time to buy it. And if you are considering a car in the $1500 to $2000 class, now by all means is the time to *see* and *drive* the new Packard Light Eight —to *compare* it with the best motor car value that you have ever known. ¶ The new Packard Light Eight is the scion of a distinguished family—truly "Packard" in appearance, personality and prestige and, in addition, youthfully smart and graceful in its own right. With its 128-inch wheelbase you will find it big and roomy—with its eight-in-line, 110 horsepower motor, brilliantly responsive in acceleration and speed. And you will find, too, that it embodies Packard's latest engineering advances—Silent Synchromesh Transmission, *quiet in all three speeds;* simple, *safe* Finger Control Free-Wheeling; and the pioneer system of Ride Control —just as do the larger, heavier and more costly Packard cars. ¶ Here is a car that offers for the first time the luxury and distinction of Packard transportation at factory prices lower than $2000—and with shatter-proof glass throughout, six-ply tires and front and rear bumpers included. Your Packard dealer will gladly accept your present car at its full worth—and the remaining payments will be surprisingly small. Why *not* enjoy *luxurious* transportation?

PACKARD

ASK THE MAN WHO OWNS ONE

214

World Supremacy

A new regime in Madrid has not lessened Spanish appreciation of the luxury and distinction of Packard transportation. Packard cars in Spain outnumber those of every other fine American make. Among families of rank and prominence there, as throughout the entire world, Packard is the supreme fine car

The new Packard Light Eight is a strikingly handsome car. In appearance it belongs unmistakably to the distinguished Packard family. Yet it is smartly new and original in its youthful grace of line and proportion—as is well illustrated by the popular Convertible Coupe below. ¶ When you first inspect the Packard Light Eight, you will be surprised at its size and roominess. It is a big and substantial car, with wheelbase of 128 inches. It is "light" only in com-parison with other cars of the Packard line—the Standard Eight, the Eight DeLuxe and the new Twin Six. ¶ Richly appointed and upholstered, truly advanced in all mechanical features, the Packard Light Eight now offers the luxury of *fine car* transportation to those motorists who have been accustomed to paying from $1500 to $2000 for their cars. For here is an eight—"Packard" in personality, prestige and performance—factory-priced at the astonishing range of $1750 to $1795. ¶ Before buying *any* car be sure to *see* and *drive* the Packard Light Eight. You will thrill to its velvety, 110 horsepower motor, its Silent Synchro-mesh Transmission, *quiet in all three speeds,* its simple, *safe* Finger-Control Free-Wheeling. Why not take your old car to your Packard dealer today? He will allow you all that it is worth—and, if you wish to buy out of income, you will find the payments surprisingly small.

PACKARD   *Ask the man who owns one*

WORLD · SUPREMACY

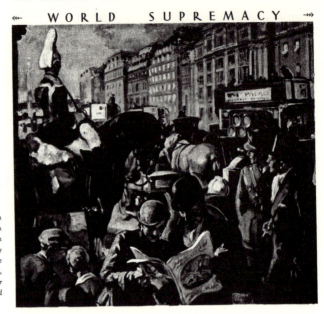

England

In the maze of London's traffic and on the hedge-bordered lanes of the English country-side more Packards are driven by people of wealth and rank than any other fine American make of car. The distinguished Packard has consistently, and by a wide margin, outsold all other American cars of its class in England

The Packard Light Eight—the new car that introduces truly luxurious transportation to additional thousands—is pictured below in its full grace of line and beauty of color. But you must *see* the car itself to appreciate its fineness—you must *drive* it to gain a complete conception of its many performance advantages. ¶ Here is a car that is Packard in design, Packard in quality and, therefore, Packard in name—a car of which Packard is again proud to say "Ask the Man Who Owns One." Yet, because Packard has taken advantage of present economic conditions, lowered prices on fine materials, advanced engineering and new manufacturing processes, it can be offered at a price remarkably low—$1750 at the factory for the Five-Passenger Sedan. ¶ The Packard Light Eight is available in four distinctive and completely modern models—all on a chassis of 128 inches with 110 horsepower motor. It embodies Packard's latest engineering advances—Silent Synchro-mesh Transmission, *quiet in all three speeds,* Finger Control Free-Wheeling, and the new Angleset Rear Axle. Shatter-proof glass throughout, bumpers front and rear and six-ply tires—items charged for as extras on many cars—are included as standard equipment. ¶ Truly, thousands of motorists who for years have admired and wanted the beauty, luxury and distinction of Packard transportation can *now* enjoy it.

PACKARD

A S K   T H E   M A N   W H O   O W N S   O N E

216

The Packard Twin Six

PACKARD ANNOUNCED early in 1932 that it was reinstating the Twin Six at the head of its line. This car offered the first big advancement in automobile motors that had been made in years. It brought many important improvements in both body and chassis to the industry. Because of its balanced design and construction it gave a completely new experience in luxurious highway transportation to the motoring world. Packard engines in Miss America X, the most powerful motor boat ever built with its 6400 horse power, again won the Harmsworth race for Gar Wood and established a world's record of 124.91 miles an hour in 1932, another important engineering triumph for Packard. President Hoover, acting for the Aeronautical Association of America, early in 1932 presented President Alvan Macauley with the famous Collier Trophy, as recognition of Packard's outstanding achievement in building and demonstrating the practicability of the Diesel aircraft engine.

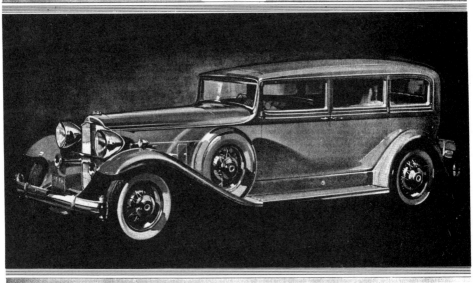

...of a Distinguished family

THE Packard Twin Six is a familiar name wherever men drive motor cars—a name that has taken its place in our very language. ¶ The Packard Twin Six of before the war made motor car history. The world-renowned war-time Liberty motor added to the fame of Packard Twin Six engines—a fame since enhanced by the development of Twin Six marine engines for the world's fastest racing craft and the Packard Twin Six "2500," the most powerful airplane engine built in America today. ¶ And now a superb Packard Twin Six motor car takes to the highway again—a car of beauty, a car of supreme luxury, a car of power, a car that revives the famous title of the first Twin Six—"Boss of the Road." ¶ Today's Twin Six Packard is the climax of sixteen years of continuous experience with twelve-cylinder engine designs—an experience of twice that period in the building of fine and distinguished cars. There is literally nothing by which to judge it, for it is so advanced, so modern that it defies comparison with multi-cylinder cars of conventional type. See and drive this great, new Super-Packard.

PACKARD

ASK THE MAN WHO OWNS ONE

218

World Supremacy

In sunny Italy, where love of grace and beauty and appreciation of fine work are centuries old, Packard is the favored American fine car. To the nobility and to families of eminence throughout the kingdom more Packards have been delivered than any other imported automobile of similar price

Packard, the builder of this country's *first* twelve-cylinder motor car, now offers America's *most advanced* twelve-cylinder car —the new and sensational Packard Twin Six. ¶ Packard has built and sold more twelve-cylinder automobiles than all other American manufacturers combined — nearly ten times as many twelves as all other makes in use today. Packard's experience with twelve-cylinder engine design has been continuous for sixteen years. Famous Packard twin-six airplane and marine motors have been in constant production throughout this period. The *new* and *advanced* Twin Six motor car engine of today is an outgrowth of this long and thorough experience — a natural achievement of the world's master motor builders. ¶ To those who admire advanced and original engineering, to those who appreciate supreme beauty and richness of appointment, Packard extends a cordial invitation to inspect, drive and ride in today's distinguished Twin Six. With its Silent Synchro-mesh Transmission, *quiet in all three forward speeds,* its new Finger Control Free-Wheeling and the original Packard Ride Control, you will find it the highest development of Packard's world-renowned luxury— in performance, comfort and ease of control. ¶ It is priced at the factory from $3650.

PACKARD

Ask the man who owns one

219

PACKARD

THE new Packard Twin Six develops more than 160 horsepower. Seldom, if ever, is it necessary to draw fully on such vast potential power — but the extra power is *there* and its advantages are constantly reflected in the matchless, smooth performance of this great, brand new Super-Packard. ¶ Speed greater than you will ever need is at your quick command — speed that is never labored, speed that always leaves something in reserve. Acceleration — in low, second or high— is as velvety and noiseless as a summer breeze. There has never been a car, we believe, so swift, so smooth, so silent. ¶ And

how easily the Twin Six handles! Steering is almost effortless. Gears shift without a click. Automatic clutch control, available at the flick of a finger, does away with constant

clutch pedal operation and provides free-wheeling results. Brakes, with vacuum assist, operate with the gentlest of foot pressure. ¶ Those who have driven the new Packard Twin Six have freely pronounced it *America's finest motor car.* They base their judgment not only on its brilliant performance but on its majestic beauty, its distinguished luxury, its complete and restful riding ease. Discriminating opinion, wherever the car is known, agrees that today's Twin Six literally obsoletes all Vee-type cars of earlier engineering development. ¶ You are cordially invited to inspect and drive Packard's newest and greatest car.

— of a Distinguished family —

PACKARD   TWIN-SIX

It may never again be so easy
to become "the man who owns one"

PROBABLY you've often wished for a Packard. Perhaps on several occasions you've almost bought one. But somehow you've felt it would be best to wait for better times.

A better time to buy a Packard will probably never come.

Why? For the same reason that a better time may never come to buy sound real estate or seasoned securities.

Today's motor cars are priced to give you more for your money than ever before. But there is still another factor in your favor. When buying turns, allowances on used cars will drop materially. Past experience bears this out. It will take a much greater cash outlay to buy a new car than it does today.

This year two and a half million cars will wear out. Only a million and a quarter new cars will take the road. This means that before long more than a million people must buy new cars—or walk.

Buying must turn. Before it turns is the time to buy your car. And it is a particularly good time to buy a Packard, for today's Packards are the finest of a long line of fine cars.

Take your present car to a Packard dealer. Find out how much you can get for it on, say, a Packard Standard Eight. Learn how easy it is to pay the balance.

Then study the car itself. The Standard Eight has made more friends for Packard than any other model. It combines big car comfort with big car safety. It combines simplicity of design with low service costs. It has Packard's traditional ageless lines—lines that make the car young in appearance when it is old in miles.

And remember this: Your Packard Standard Eight will last for years to come—years that make your Packard a wiser investment than ever.

THE PACKARD YOU NEVER SEE

These gates are about to close on a new Packard that the world will never see. For these are the gates of the Packard Proving Grounds. And the car that is passing through them is going to be deliberately destroyed.

Packard engineers will take this car and give it every punishment they can devise. With scientific thoroughness, they will torture it—strain every part, break it if they can. And they will do so with just one thought in mind—to learn how Packard quality can be still further advanced.

For each new series of Packards must not only do better what other fine cars do well—it must also surpass previous Packard records.

Today's Packard must be able to stand thousands of miles of wide-open speed. Here at the Proving Grounds the world's fastest concrete speedway shows that it will. Today's Packard must provide arm-chair comfort under all conditions. Here mile after mile of the cruelest roads ever contrived say it will. Power plant and chassis must be the strongest that can be built. Packard's man-made "desert" of trackless sand proves they are. The motor—the quietest Packard ever designed—must remain quiet throughout its life. 50,000 miles of 24-hour-a-day driving show that it will.

You will never subject the Packard you buy to such merciless usage. But Packard insists that

each of its cars must have a reserve of stamina, must be capable of heights of performance, far beyond any ordinary needs. And so, upon these Proving Grounds, Packard does its own doubting—that there may be no doubt about the Packard you buy.

Do these statements challenge belief? Good. For you can prove them easily, and get the motoring thrill of your life in doing so. Visit your Packard showroom. Visit it whether you are in the market for a new car or not. You'll get as warm a welcome as if you came to buy immediately. But by all means see today's Packards—ride in them—drive them. Then try to be satisfied with any other car!

PACKARD ❧ ASK THE MAN WHO OWNS ONE

THE STEP THAT ONLY PACKARD TAKES

No PACKARD TWIN-SIX buyer ever has to "break in" his car. He can drive it as fast and as far as he cares to from the very first minute he gets it.

For Packard takes each individual Twin-Six to its Proving Grounds and there, on the world's fastest concrete speedway, scientifically breaks it in.

This means that during its first 250 miles—the most important miles in the life of any automobile—your Twin-Six is in the hands of experts—men who understand every whisper of a motor car. In their hands, 250 miles is a thorough breaking-in for any car.

This test is made, not with a bare chassis, but with a complete car, fully equipped. If any adjustments are necessary, Packard engineers see that they are made. Packard engineers give the motor its final thorough tuning. When these men sign the Certificate of Approval and seal it to the key of a Packard Twin-Six, that car has the best possible start for a long, trouble-free life. It is ready for the sternest usage you may give it.

No other American manufacturer goes so far in preparing a motor car for its owner. This test is Packard's alone. It is the final endorsement that the Twin-Six you receive is the finest automobile that men can build and money buy.

Packard honestly believes that the Twin-Six will give you a motoring sen-sation such as you never had before. Packard would like to have you drive and ride in this car. Whether you have any immediate intention of buying or not, visit your Packard show-room and drive a Twin-Six. Listen to the quietest motor ever designed. Drive with less effort than you have ever known. Then put this car to every test you can think of—traffic, speed, hills, rough roads—and watch it do better what other fine cars do well.

The Packard Twin-Six is priced from $4150 at Detroit. Packard also offers the DeLuxe Eight from $3350; the Standard Eight from $2350; the new Packard Eight from $1895. Prices subject to change.

PACKARD ASK THE MAN WHO OWNS ONE

Where Packard and Nature fight it out

Here, in this desert at the Packard Proving Grounds, Packard engineers lay to rest any doubts that Packard is America's sturdiest automobile.

For here Packards are pitted against the cruelest enemy Nature ever created to torture a motor car. Here Packards plough for days, hub-deep in sand.

Every new mechanical development must survive this "third degree" before it is finally embodied in the Packard. For Packard knows that if there is any weakling part, this ordeal will bring it to light. Once revealed, Packard engineers can study the cause—and learn how to make the Packard still stronger.

In this desert, too, the strength of competitive cars is tested. And Packard must surpass their record every time.

Nor is this the only Packard test of strength. Before the present Packard transmission was incorporated in the car, it was run on a dynamometer under peak load for 350 hours—comparable to driving the car up a hill 2500 miles high and 10,000 miles long. Automotive engineers had said that if a transmission could stand 150 hours of such torture without flying to pieces, it would be a miracle. Yet at the end of 350 hours, the Packard transmission was still operating perfectly.

Such strength is to be found in every part of today's Packards. They stand, we believe, as the greatest cars America has ever seen.

Does that sound like an exaggeration? Accept this offer and prove to yourself that it *isn't!* Go to your Packard showroom, drive one of the new Packards over roads you know by heart. Compare it with every other car you've ever known. Compare it with every other fine car 1933 can offer you. We know then there will be just one car you will really want to own...that car will be a Packard.

PACKARD

ASK THE MAN WHO OWNS ONE

The Packard Eight . . . from $2150 at Detroit
The Packard Super-Eight from $2750 at Detroit
The Packard Twelve . . from $3720 at Detroit

STEICHEN

"I'm not going to wait any longer!"

Perhaps you have wanted a Packard for years, but have felt it was beyond your means.

Then read this letter, written by a man who, like yourself, has felt he couldn't afford a Packard. He says:

"Last Saturday I accepted the invitation of a Packard dealer to slip into the driver's seat and test out a new Packard in my own way. For the best part of the afternoon, my wife and I drove that Packard as we would our own car—over roads we have driven many, many times before.

"That ride was a revelation. I drove faster than I'd ever driven before—yet with a perfect sense of security. The car was so quiet that even at top speeds my wife and I could talk without raising our voices. The steering was so easy it was almost automatic. When we struck a rough road, I set myself for the bumps—but none came. I tried the brake selector and ventilation control and ride control. Why, this car is even adjustable to the mood of the driver!

"That ride made me want a Packard as I had never wanted any other car. But I didn't see how I could afford one.

"Then I got to figuring. I put down all the upkeep costs of a Packard against those of my present car. License, insurance, garage and tires are the same for both cars. With the new economy features of today's Packards, gas and oil run about the same. And repairs? Nothing to worry about there. For last year the Packard factory sold only $15.31 worth of repair parts for each Packard on the road. And while the purchase price of a Packard is a little higher than that of my present car, I know from the experience of my friends that a Packard will last a lot longer.

"That bit of figuring decided me. These new Packards are finer than I thought any car could be—and I'm convinced they will cost less over a period of years. So I'm not going to wait any longer. Tomorrow I'm going to make one of them mine."

We believe the new Packards are the finest cars America has ever seen—and we believe a comparison with other fine cars will prove it. Go to your Packard dealer and take the wheel of a new Packard. Drive it over roads you know by heart. Compare it with every other fine car 1933 can offer. We know then your next car will be a Packard.

PACKARD

ASK THE MAN WHO OWNS ONE

The Packard Eight .... $2150 at Detroit.
The Packard Super-Eight ...... $2750 at Detroit.
The Packard Twelve .... $3720 at Detroit.

Maybe it's time
to talk to your husband about a Packard

PERHAPS, like a great many other women, you have been noticing the new Packards and wishing that you might own one.

Perhaps you have felt that this is a bad time to broach the subject to your husband. You have felt that it is your duty to help economize.

Economy is the very best reason for buying a Packard *right now*.

You know from your shopping experience that "things are down".

Automobiles are no exception. New cars are priced to give more value per dollar than ever before.

Moreover, automobiles are being worn out twice as fast as they are being produced. A million Americans must buy new cars soon. When they start buying, used car allowances will be materially reduced. It will take a much larger financial outlay to buy a car.

Your husband knows the truth of these statements. He also knows that, with the business outlook brightening, the buying tide may turn at any time—and today's opportunity be lost.

Go to your nearest Packard dealer and take a ride in one of the new Packards—learn why today's Packards are the finest of a long line of fine cars.

Upkeep? Millions of miles of owner-driving prove that service costs are the smallest in Packard's history.

Long life? These cars have the famous Packard ability to serve you for years; and the traditional Packard lines that are never out of style.

Their motors were created by the same engineers who designed the Packard motors that drove "Miss America X" 124.91 miles an hour to break the world's speedboat record.

Take all those things into consideration. Then find out how much your Packard dealer will allow on your present car, and how easy it is to pay the balance. Packard cars range in price from $1895 to $4895 at the factory.

ASK THE MAN WHO OWNS ONE

THE FAMILY INVISIBLE

Two families will ride in each new motor car that is bought during the year 1933.

¶ One will be the family of the man who buys the car and the other, the family of the man who built the car—*the family invisible.*

¶ What do I mean?

¶ The motor car stands a tribute to labor. Its raw materials, as the ore in the earth and the tree in the forest, are worth but a few dollars until the hand of labor converts them into beauty and value.

¶ *It would take a man skilled in 80 trades one full year to bring a Packard car from nature's resources to show-room floor—a man with a wife and two or three children.*

¶ There is a double satisfaction in buying *any* new car at this time. The man who buys one gets a value never before approached and he gives a fellow man a job—for one whole year if he buys a Cadillac, a Lincoln or a Packard.

¶ He rides the family invisible as fellow passengers for months if he buys a Plymouth, a Chevrolet or a Ford.

¶ And so with all other cars, large or small.

¶ Think how a man would throw out his chest and pat himself on the back if he could direct a worthy man to a steady job. What's the difference whether he does this directly or indirectly

—as long as the man gets the job?

¶ Remember — a motor car bought means a motor car to be built.

¶ Do I hear someone say "Yes, but who has any money to buy new cars?"

¶ Let's get set on some facts.

¶ Wealth *has* shifted. Income *is* less. But $100 will now buy all that $132 bought in 1929. Why not take advantage of this offset when—

¶ this country has nearly 50% more gold reserve than any other country;

¶ its banks are reported in excellent liquid condition with more than $9,000,000,000 in gold, currency and government securities — the foundation for an enormous super-structure of credit;

¶ it has 44,352,000 savings accounts with $24,281,000,000 on deposit — more than twice the amount of our War Debts and nearly six times enough to buy and scrap every motor car now in use;

¶ it has two savings depositors to occupy the front seat of every one of its 21,045,000 cars and nearly $1,200 in savings to spread out on the rear seat.

¶ Poor America!

¶ All of this savings money is working for 3% or less and neglecting countless opportunities. And though hoarding is a less popular pastime than it was, there is still a billion dollars in hiding without benefit of interest or return.

¶ This billion dollars would more

than pay for all the motor cars sold during the year 1932.

¶ This country is like an enormous cask. One filled with pent up appetite, necessity of replacement and repair, and billions and billions of dollars.

¶ *A cask with staves held by bands of fear.*

¶ Some day, and it may be soon, confidence, *the yeast of business,* is going to start the cask's contents "working" and then we may have a veritable explosion of prosperity.

¶ This country is rich and it is sound. It can be prosperous for years in replacements and repairs alone. It does not need to wait for some big thing to happen or for some new invention. It can do the simple thing. Paint its homes, for example. I believe that every unemployed family head could have work for two months in painting the buildings now going to rack and ruin through nature's ravage.

¶ Let's consider the family invisible. Let's invite it to ride in our new cars and to be the guest in our homes as we buy new furniture and the hundred and one other things we need.

¶ Let's turn some of our lazy billions into work and take advantage of opportunities that may never again come our way.

¶ The reluctance to spend is the greatest single obstacle to the return of better times.

¶ *1933 will be as great as our spending courage.*

President — **PACKARD MOTOR CAR COMPANY**

"Hush!"

There is a deeper significance in the quiet of the Packard Twelve motor than mere solace to your ears.

Such quiet is a reflection of standards so precise as to be almost incredible.

Would you believe that any manufacturer would carry the war against noise into the realm of inaudible sounds? Packard does so. By amplification—the same way sound is stepped up in your radio—Packard locates and eliminates noises that the human ear unaided could not hear.

Would you believe that any manufacturer could reduce even the noise of the wind as it rushes by? Packard has done so—by minutely studying contours, angles, mouldings, and redesigning them.

Such examples are typical of the lengths to which Packard has gone to produce the quietest motor car ever built.

What does this quiet mean in comfort, in motoring pleasure? Take a Packard Twelve out on the road and open the throttle. In a trice you're going faster than you've probably ever dared drive a car before. Yet you drive with a perfect sense of security. For there's no snarl, no roar from the motor to rasp your nerves. So quiet is the whole car that you can converse in a low voice while traveling a mile and a half a minute. You ride relaxed. As mile melts into mile, you realize why Packard Twelve owners have been able to drive a thousand miles in a day without fatigue.

Today's Twelve is not only Packard's masterpiece—it is, we believe, the finest motor car ever produced in America. A car that has withstood tests that have broken other fine cars to pieces. A car that offers years of the finest motoring the world has ever known.

That's saying a great deal. But it's not saying too much, and your Packard dealer would like to prove it to you. He would like to bring a Packard Twelve to your door and have you use it for a few days. Whether you are in the market for a car or not, phone your Packard dealer and accept this invitation. Then drive the Twelve over roads of your own choosing. Compare it with every car you've ever known. Compare it with any other fine car 1933 can offer you. Do this, and we know the only car that will ever completely satisfy you will be the Packard Twelve.

Prices begin at $3,720 at Detroit.

THE TWELVE
BY PACKARD
ASK THE MAN WHO OWNS ONE

STABILITY

WHEN you invest in a fine car, you hope and expect to keep that car for a period of years. This is especially true if the car you invest in is a Packard. The long life of Packard cars—their ability to look beautiful and perform brilliantly for many years — has become traditional in America.

But when you purchase a fine car, you are interested, too, in the stability of the company that makes the car. You want to be certain that service will always be available. You want to be certain that you will never suffer the financial loss that is inevitable to the owner of a "car without a company."

If you are the owner of a Packard, or if you have made up your mind to buy one, you can be justly proud of the position of this company. Packard has come through the critical period just behind us unshaken. Packard faces the upturn with a confidence born of solid strength and preparedness.

The Loyalty of Packard's Clientele

THROUGHOUT these recent lean years, Packard has retained the loyalty of its clientele—the largest fine car clientele in the world. Packard owners have spent more than a billion dollars for Packard cars. They have, in nine cases out of every ten, returned to Packard every time they bought new cars.

Because of the depression, many of these owners have kept their cars far longer than they otherwise would. And in doing so, they have had new proof of the strength, the lasting qualities of Packard cars. With the coming of the upturn, Packard is in better position than ever before to benefit from a huge repeat business.

The Loyalty of Packard Distributers

THROUGHOUT the lean years, Packard has likewise retained the loyalty of its distributing organization. In 1932, changes were made in less than five percent of Packard's distributers —a record probably unparalleled in the industry. And at no distributer point was Packard sales or service interrupted.

As the oldest fine car company in the business, Packard has seen bad times before. And it has come through its entire history without a single reorganization, without a single upheaval in personnel. The present management has been in active charge for more than twenty years. The executive heads of the company average more than seventeen years in Packard service.

A Financial Strength

TODAY Packard stands as a free and independent company. It has no preferred stockholders. It is indebted to no bondholders. It has no bank loans—for it has no need of any. It has one of the finest and most modern plants in the industry and began the new year 1933 with more than twelve and one-half million dollars in cash and United States Government securities—twenty times the amount of its cash reduction during 1932.

The World's Favorite Fine Car

AND results are proving the wisdom of continued and aggressive development—in engineering, in manufacturing efficiency, and in sales and service personnel. In 1932 more new Packard cars were registered in the United States than any other fine car. And Packard exported more cars than any other two fine car manufacturers combined.

Such stability—of clientele, of sales and service, of company organization and finances — offers a most compelling reason for deciding now to choose a Packard as *your* next car.

PACKARD

ASK THE MAN WHO OWNS ONE

To the man who <u>almost</u> owns one

Perhaps you, like the man in the picture, have always wanted a Packard.

And perhaps like him you have felt it was beyond your means.

So you have bought medium-priced cars—cars that have always been a compromise between your desires and your pocketbook.

Now you're about to buy another car. And again you tell yourself, "I can't afford a Packard."

But wait—

Actually you almost own a Packard. Actually you've almost owned one for years.

The gulf that separates you from a Packard is only a few hundred dollars. Spread that sum over the longer life that a Packard will serve you—in the end, a Packard will cost you no more, and probably less, than a "compromise car."

And the extra miles a Packard gives you are miles you enjoy—not miles you merely tolerate. For a Packard is not only built to keep going—it is built to keep its thrill of performance right through the years.

This is truer today than ever before. For these 1933 models are, we believe, the longest-lived cars built in America today. A clutch, for example, was as good as new after 125,000 contacts in traffic. After 50,000 miles of driving, cylinders showed only microscopic wear.

No danger of these cars becoming old-fashioned in appearance either. For they have the traditional Packard lines that never go out of style.

Perhaps you're wondering about upkeep cost.

We can show you that, item for item, a Packard costs no more to run than cars costing hundreds of dollars less. The new Packards use less gas and oil than their predecessors. Because of a new lubricating system, motor parts will last twice as long.

And from this car that really costs you no more, you'll get the greatest motoring thrill of your life. The thrill of driving a car whose motor is so quiet that even when you're travelling up to a mile and a half a minute, you can scarcely hear it. The thrill of riding in a car whose cushions were contoured by an orthopedic expert to let you relax naturally, completely. The thrill, finally, of a car that is even adaptable to your requirements and moods—whose brake-pedal pressure, ventilation and shock absorber resilience can all be adjusted to suit the convenience of whoever is driving or riding in the car.

We would like to prove to you the real economy of owning one of these cars. And we would like to have you drive one over a road of your own choosing.

And bring your old car with you—if it is of average value, it will cover the down payment on a new Packard. The balance can be spread over many months. And the operating economies which your new Packard effects will make the down payments still easier.

PACKARD

ASK THE MAN WHO OWNS ONE

The Packard Eight . . . . from $2150 f.o.b. Detroit.
The Packard Super-Eight . . . from $2750 f.o.b. Detroit.
The Packard Twelve . . . . . from $3720 f.o.b. Detroit.
Prices subject to increase without notice.

Buy your car in '33
the way they did in 1903

PERHAPS you weren't old enough in 1903 to buy a car . . .

. . . but you can imagine what a momentous event such a purchase was in those days. Next thing to getting married or buying a home.

The buyer didn't act on preconceived opinions —no car was old enough to have established much prestige. Instead, he studied every car whose price was near the amount he intended to pay. He compared them in appearance, in features and in value.

Then he did what too many people fail to do nowadays—he rode in each car and compared them all.

Packard believes this year you should go back to the 1903 way of buying a car.

Forget all your opinions about automobiles. This year, ride in every car within your price range—compare them all in every way. Such comparison is especially important if you are considering the purchase of a fine car.

The revolution in the fine car field

In the fine car field, revolutionary changes have been taking place. Spurred on by the terrific competition which the depression years have brought, manufacturers have striven as they never have before to advance their cars mechanically.

And Packard has made the greatest strides of all. You will be amazed—and thrilled—when you take the wheel of one of the 1933 models.

For with these cars Packard has obsoleted all previous standards in the fine car field. Name any quality a fine car should have—brilliant performance, long life, luxurious comfort, perfect quiet— Packard has combined all these qualities in one great series of cars.

An investment that's doubly protected

These cars offer a protected investment without equal in the fine car market.

600,000 miles of testing at the Packard Proving Grounds proved that the new Packards are the most durable cars built in America. A new lubricating system, for example, has doubled the life of motor parts. Even though you pay a little more for a Packard than you might for some other car, you will get your money's worth— with interest—from the added years of service the car will give.

Your investment is protected, too, by the permanent beauty of these cars. For they have the traditional Packard lines that make a Packard, whatever its age, a smart, youthful car—a car you are proud to be seen in.

Cars that are even adaptable to your mood

These Packards introduce a new idea in motor car building—adaptability to the owner's requirements and moods. The pedal pressure of the power brakes, the Packard-Dole ventilation, even the "hardness" or "softness" of the ride, can be adjusted to suit your wishes.

And if you want power, these cars have it. They are the most powerful Packards ever built. If you seek comfort and quiet, you'll find them. The cushions were contoured by an orthopedic expert to let you ride with the greatest relaxation and enjoyment. The motors are so quiet that even at top speeds you can scarcely hear them.

Buy as in 1903—by comparison

Drive your old car to your Packard dealer's— if it is of average value, it will cover the down payment on a new Packard. The balance can be spread over many months. And the operating economies which your new Packard effects will make the monthly payments still easier.

PACKARD

ASK THE MAN WHO OWNS ONE

The Packard Eight . . . . . . from $2150 F.O.B. Detroit.
The Packard Super-Eight . . from $2750 F.O.B. Detroit.
The Packard Twelve . . . . . from $3720 F.O.B. Detroit.

. . . Prices subject to increase without notice . . .

231

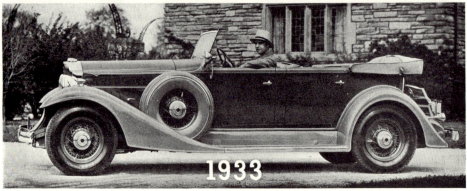

Ask them both --- THE MAN WHO HAS OWNED ONE SIX YEARS
THE MAN WHO HAS OWNED ONE SIX MONTHS

We know of no better way for you to test Packard superiority than to follow our advice and "ask the man who owns one."

First, talk to men whose Packards are rolling into their sixth or seventh year. They can tell you about Packard's long life. And the smart appearance of their cars will prove to you that a Packard, whatever its age, is always beautiful, a car you can be proud to be seen in.

What Packard has done in 1933

Next, ask the man who bought his Packard this year. He can tell you that, with its new 1933 models, Packard has far outstripped the fine car field — has produced cars superior on every basis.

Then ask your Packard dealer to let you drive one of these new Packards. Discover steering so

easy it is almost automatic. Sink into cushions contoured by an orthopedic expert to let you relax naturally, completely. Listen to the motor — a motor that even at top speeds is barely audible.

A Car that's adaptable to you

Discover the thrill of a car that is adaptable to your own requirements. A car whose brake-pedal pressure, ventilation, and shock absorber resilience can all be adjusted to suit your wishes.

Then remember that the new Packards will last longer even than their famous predecessors, and will cost less to operate. 600,000 miles of testing at the Packard Proving Grounds during 1932 have proved that. A clutch, for example, was operating perfectly after 125,000 contacts in traffic. A transmission showed no appreciable wear after 50,000 miles of driving. A new lubri-

cating system has doubled the life of motor parts — and cut repair costs in half.

Why not become a "man who owns one"? Drive your old car to your Packard dealer's today. If you wish to buy out of income, your present car will probably cover the down payment on a new Packard. The balance can be spread over many months. You and your family can be enjoying a new Packard by tomorrow.

PACKARD

ASK THE MAN WHO OWNS ONE

The Packard Eight . . . . from $2150 at Detroit.
The Packard Super-Eight . . . . from $2750 at Detroit.
The Packard Twelve . . . . from $3720 at Detroit.
Prices subject to increase without notice

On Monday, August 21st,
1200 men saw a new world's standard born!

ON MONDAY, August 21st, twelve hundred men saw the new 1934 Packard unveiled.

Packard believes this new car is so significant that it called to Detroit every Packard distributer, dealer and sales executive in the United States and Canada to attend this unveiling.

Packard believes this new car is the yardstick with which all fine cars in the future will be measured—whether those cars are of American or of European manufacture.

Next week the announcement of this epochal car will appear in this magazine.

Twelve hundred men have now driven home their new 1934 Packards. One of these men is your Packard dealer. Ask him about these new Packards—the new Eight, the new Super-Eight, the new Twelve.

For your first glimpse of these new 1934 Packards, look in next week's Saturday Evening Post.

☆   ☆

Packard urges you to borrow this yardstick

IF YOU plan to buy a fine car this year, Packard has a yardstick it wants to lend you.

That yardstick is the new 1934 Packard—a car deliberately designed to be the standard of value with which to judge all fine cars, American or European.

And this year, more than ever, the fine-car buyer needs such a yardstick.

For, within the past three years, there has been a revolution in automotive values. Engineers, taking the depression as a challenge, have accomplished miracles of improvement. The progress of a decade has been compressed into three "hard times" years.

Old prejudices should no longer influence you in your choice of a fine car. Habit and hearsay are not safe guides, if you want to get the most

for your money. Packard believes that this year, of all years, you should *know!*

And the best way to know is to ride in every other fine car America can offer you. *But ride in a Packard first.*

Use the knowledge you get behind the wheel of a new 1934 Packard to judge every other fine car. Measure your dollars in terms of what Packard gives you for them. Then see if you can match Packard value in any other car—on either side of the Atlantic.

And while you marvel at the performance of this new Packard, remember this—if you buy a Packard, you can plan to keep it at least five years. Five years from now your 1934 Packard will still give you peak performance. And five years from now your Packard will still be smart

—for the lines of a Packard never wear out.

Why not telephone your Packard dealer today and ask him to bring a new Packard to your home? Take your choice of the new Eight, the new Super-Eight, or the new Twelve.

Drive it. Dare other fine cars to match it. Do this, and we'll leave it to you which car you'll want to own. We believe it will be a Packard.

PACKARD 1934

THE YARDSTICK WITH WHICH TO MEASURE ALL FINE CAR VALUES

THE PACKARD EIGHT .. THE PACKARD SUPER-EIGHT
THE PACKARD TWELVE

234

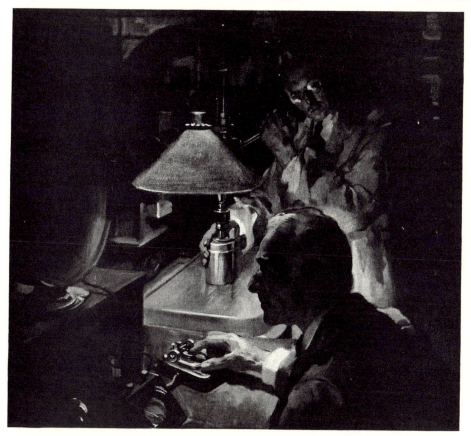

Where silence is not quiet enough for Packard

IN the Packard factory in Detroit is a room unlike any other room, in any other automobile factory, in the world.

It is called the Quiet Room. And it serves as a sentry to guard Packard's reputation as the quietest car made—a sentry which recognizes but one password . . . "Silence"!

Into this Quiet Room goes every ball-bearing that seeks a place in a Packard car. Behind thick walls that shut out all outside noises, each is made to give an account of itself.

Here, silence as the human ear understands it, is not quiet enough for Packard. Packard is on the trail of noises too subtle for any ear to hear . . . noises that are ferreted out by a radio amplifier so powerful that it makes a dropped pin sound like a pistol shot.

Each ball-bearing is rotated in a machine as silent as the bearing itself. Then the amplifier is attached and the degree of noise registered on a dial. If the hand of this dial crosses the line of tolerance by a hair's breadth, that bearing is rejected. It may be silent to the human ear . . . but it's too noisy for a Packard.

Is such minuteness necessary? Aren't other fine cars produced without going to such extremes? Yes, they are.

But without this and similar tests, and the philosophy which inspires them, Packard could not be what Packard is. Without them, Packard would be just another fine car. *With them,* Packard becomes the yardstick with which *all* fine cars can be measured.

Why not call your Packard dealer and ask him to bring one of these new 1934 Packards to your home? The new Eight, the new Super-Eight, or the new Twelve. Drive it. Expect of it more than you have ever expected of a fine car before.

Then decide for yourself whether Packard world-leadership is a claim—or a fact.

PACKARD 1934

THE YARDSTICK WITH WHICH TO MEASURE ALL FINE CAR VALUES

THE PACKARD EIGHT . . THE PACKARD SUPER-EIGHT
THE PACKARD TWELVE

235

Why pay the price of a Packard?

PERHAPS *you* are debating this very question with yourself:

"Why pay the price of a Packard when I can get a good car for several hundred dollars less?"

Then read this story of Fred C. Dierking, a Chicago Packard Salesman, and the 65 Packards he sold in 1928.

The story of 65 Packards

Every one of those cars was sold on the basis of "pay a little more—keep the car much longer."

"Operating costs on a Packard," Mr. Dierking pointed out to those Chicagoans, "are no greater, and frequently smaller, than on a 'compromise car.' The heaviest expense of automobile ownership is the depreciation cost you pay when you trade in your car every two or three years. Pay Packard's slightly higher price and keep the car longer—*keep it at least five years*—and you will be money ahead in the end."

Thus spoke Mr. Dierking in 1928. How true were his words in the light of the intervening five years?

What a census disclosed

Here is a census of those same 65 cars made a

few weeks ago: Two owners have moved away from Chicago. Three have died. Three have disposed of their cars and now own no automobiles at all. Six have traded in their Packards on other makes—a surprisingly small number in an era of shifting fortunes and positions. Eight have replaced their 1928 Packards with new Packards.

But here is the most amazing thing. *42 of the 65 owners, or two out of every three, are still driving their original 1928 Packards!*

If you were to carry such a census throughout the country, you would probably find a similar situation everywhere. You would find owner after owner who *knows*, through years of experience, that Packard is the wisest motor car investment he has ever made!

The finest Packards ever built

You would expect the Packard of today to be finer than the Packard of 1928. And it is—infinitely finer. In fact, the new 1934 Packards are the finest cars ever to bear the Packard name—cars deliberately designed to give America a yardstick with which to measure *all* fine car values, American or European.

Today, see these great cars at your Packard dealer's. Ride in one—the new Packard Eight, the new Packard Super-Eight, or the new Packard Twelve. Compare it on any basis with any other fine car.

And remember that this Packard which so thrills you today will keep on thrilling you for years to come. Mechanically it is built to last, not five years, but far longer than that. And it has the famous Packard lines whose beauty never fades.

Yes, ride in a 1934 Packard—and compare it. We believe your question, "Can I afford to own a Packard?" will become, "Can I afford *not* to own one?"

PACKARD 1934

THE YARDSTICK WITH WHICH TO MEASURE ALL FINE CAR VALUES

THE PACKARD EIGHT...SUPER-EIGHT...TWELVE
ASK THE MAN WHO OWNS ONE

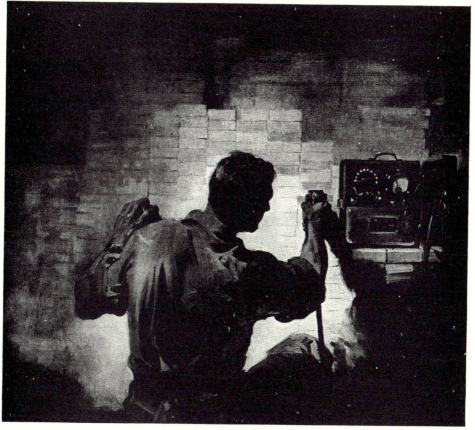

This piece of wood will never get into a Packard body

To the eye and the hand this piece of wood seems sound and dry. Yet it will never go into a Packard body.

For Packard's reputation as the "world's finest body-builders"—a reputation it has held for 34 years—is too precious a possession to be entrusted to the judgment of human sight and human touch. Packard must go much further.

Before a shipment of lumber can be accepted at the Packard plant, it must be combed from end to end by the "moisture detector"—a strange device that ferrets out and registers the slightest trace of dampness in wood. Let the dial of the machine reveal more than the standard of moisture —the wood is refused—unfit for a Packard body.

For damp wood will shrink. Shrinking causes loose joints. And loose joints squeak and rattle. The fact that Packard uses only dry wood is one important reason why Packard bodies are so quiet and last so long.

Nor is the "moisture-detector" the only sentinel that guards the quality of Packard bodies. Everything that goes into them must be tested and counter-tested. Packard's specifications for body steel are so high that steel plants were actually compelled to revolutionize production methods to meet them.

But, you may ask, isn't it possible to make a fine car without such exhaustive tests of quality?

The answer is "yes." You can buy cars—good cars—that are produced without such care. But those cars are not Packards.

For Packard is more than a fine car. Packard, by dint of its insistence on perfection in every part and particle of the car, has become the yard-stick with which to measure all fine car values.

Today, call your Packard dealer and have him bring a new 1934 Packard to your door—the new Eight, the new Super-Eight, or the new Twelve. Drive it. Put it to any test you wish. Compare it, point by point, with other fine cars.

We believe you will then agree that Packard's philosophy of making each part better has produced not merely a great car—but *America's greatest car.*

PACKARD 1934

THE YARDSTICK WITH WHICH TO MEASURE ALL FINE CAR VALUES

THE PACKARD EIGHT...SUPER-EIGHT...TWELVE

ASK THE MAN WHO OWNS ONE

237

ASK THE MAN WHO OWNS ONE

More than thirty years ago, one of the Packard brothers, in answering an inquiry about the new Packard car, said that the best thing to do was to ask the man who owns one.

● Thus, in simple language and out of a great confidence in the Packard car, was born a mighty slogan—a friendly challenge—and a common sense method of buying a car.

● Today, we still say—and we mean it more than ever—Ask the Man Who Owns One.

● When you ask him, you may discover he belongs to one of the thousand distinguished families who have owned Packards continuously for more than twenty years. In any case, you will find him a member of the largest fine car clientele in all the world. And you will find him all over the world. For Packard has sold more fine cars in foreign lands than all other American makers combined.

● Naturally, the man you will want especially to ask is the owner of one of Packard's newest cars. He, too, will not be hard to find. For no car in all of Packard's history has ever won such sweeping approval in so short a space of time.

● If by chance you do not know owners of Packard's newest cars, ask your Packard dealer for their names. Talk to them — find out what they think of Packard's latest and greatest achievement.

● Then ask your Packard dealer to let you drive one of these new Packard cars. Compare it on any basis with any other fine car, regardless of the latter's claims. Make this test — and we believe that you, too, will want to become a "man who owns one."

PACKARD

There are some things that are fundamentally beautiful of line. The Grecian pillar is one. The Packard car is another.

The first step toward having a Packard

THE FIRST STEP toward having a Packard car is one you can take privately and with no investment other than a little of your time.

● Your Packard dealer will be pleased to give you a booklet which will allow you to decide whether you want to drive or ride in one of the new 1934 Packard cars and have your old car appraised.

● The booklet, presenting the most confident offer in the motor car industry, introduces a new method of fine car buying. We say buying because we believe fine cars should be bought rather than sold. You will be delighted to find the Packard salesman working with you toward this end.

● In the booklet you will find a list of those in your own community who have bought Packard cars; a suggested list of questions for you to ask them; and blank pages on which to record the answers you get.

● We suggest that you select a jury of your friends and neighbors, twelve good men and true, who own Packard cars, and then let your purchase of a Packard stand or fall on what they tell you.

● Only a great car could make such an offer. Only a great car makes it. Why not 'phone or call for your copy of the booklet? The sooner you get it, the sooner, we believe, you will have a Packard and then—"Ask The Man Who Owns One" will apply to you.

PACKARD

ASK THE MAN WHO OWNS ONE

240

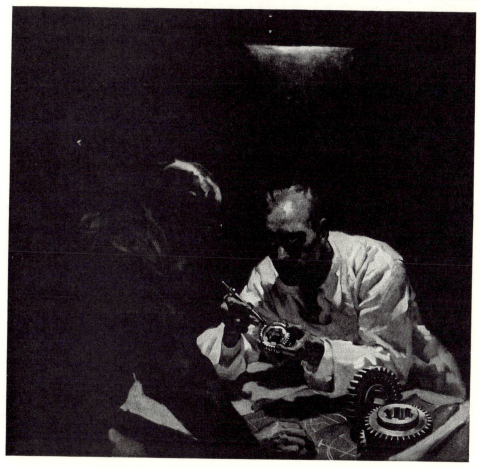

Only in Packard and Rolls-Royce

As a Packard owner, you probably never give a thought to the gears in your car's transmission.

For these gears are so smooth and silent they never call attention to themselves. And one reason is an operation which is performed, to our knowledge, only in the manufacture of Packard and of England's famed Rolls-Royce cars.

This operation is exceedingly difficult—grinding the splines on the inside of the gears. To do it successfully on a large production scale, it was necessary for Packard engineers to design a special machine.

Without this grinding operation, the Packard transmission would still be quiet and velvety-smooth. With it, the Packard transmission sets a new standard in silence.

Turn to the manufacture of any other Packard part and you will find this same adherence to an ideal—an ideal which counts no step too laborious or too costly, if it will make Packard a finer car.

It is the insistence upon this ideal which has made Packard not merely a great car — *but America's greatest car.* It is this practice which has made the new 1934 Packards the yardstick with which to measure *all* fine car values.

Why not call your Packard dealer now? Ask him to bring one of these new cars to your door —a Packard Eight, a Packard Super Eight, or a Packard Twelve. Drive it. Compare it on any basis with any other fine car.

Do this, and we believe there is only one car that will completely satisfy you—a 1934 Packard.

PACKARD 1934

THE YARDSTICK WITH WHICH TO MEASURE ALL FINE CAR VALUES

The Packard Eight · Super Eight · Twelve

Ask the Man Who Owns One

241

THE DAY THAT WAS YEARS IN THE MAKING

● The first car this young couple owned was a small and inexpensive one.

● And even while they were buying it, he told her: "Some day I'm going to buy you a Packard."

● Year followed year. New cars came and went — each but a stepping stone to the car they really wanted.

● And finally the day came. He led her to a window and showed her, there before their home, a gorgeous new Packard. *Their* Packard!

● Yet to them, it was more than a Packard — more than a beautiful, luxurious automobile. To her, it was a vindication of her faith in him. To him, it was a vindication of his belief in his own ability to succeed. To both of them, it was a symbol of everything that is fine in life, of a whole scheme of living.

● Perhaps Packard has meant something like this to you. Perhaps you have wanted one for years, yet have gone on postponing the pleasure it would give you. Why postpone that pleasure any longer? Right

now, give yourself and your family the thrill of owning one of the newest Packards — the one car that, in the eyes of the world, is emblematic of the position in life you have wanted to attain ... Your Packard dealer will gladly show you the newest Packards, or bring one to your door for a trial trip.

PACKARD

ASK THE MAN WHO OWNS ONE

242

ASK !

THIS, we believe, is the most sensible method of selecting a fine car ever proposed. And it's all embodied in the one word, "Ask!" • Ask your Packard dealer for the novel book entitled, "Ask the man who owns one." In this book you'll find the names of people in your community who own Packards. In it, too, you'll find a list of questions covering every phase of motor car performance and upkeep.

• At random, select a jury of your friends. Ask them the questions given, and any others you may think of. • When you've heard their answers, we believe you'll be eager to drive one of the new Packards. Ask your Packard dealer to bring a car to your home. Notice that, in appearance, this car is unmistakably a Packard—with the famous identifying lines that make Packard America's most distinctive car.

• Then drive this Packard—and ask it to do everything you would like a fine car to do. Compare it with other fine cars, American or foreign, on any basis you care to. • When you've done that, decide. • But first—ask!

PACKARD

ASK THE MAN WHO OWNS ONE

243

REST

YOU leave your office at the end of the day, wearied by a hard day's work.

● Ahead of you wait the responsibilities of the evening. If only there could be a little relaxation sandwiched in between!

● There is—for the man who owns a Packard. He steps from his office into his car, and instantly he is cradled in quiet and comfort. The worries of the day are forgotten in the pleasure of driving a car that almost drives itself. He enjoys a bodily peace, a mental solace. He arrives home refreshed.

● For of all the cars man has ever designed, the most restful, we believe, is the new Packard. There's not a sound from its body, barely a whisper from its motor. The cushions, contoured by experts, make you relax. The brakes that stop you so quickly work with such a velvety softness you scarcely know you're stopping. Shock absorbers and spring action are so perfected that ruts and bumps go unnoticed. Instead of riding, you float! You rest!

● We believe that you, as a business man,

deserve the restfulness a new Packard can bring you. We believe you want and need this car. Why not buy it—now? See the new Packards at your Packard dealer's. Or simply phone him —he will arrange for you to ride home from your office in one of these new cars. Very soon after that, we feel confident, you will be making the homeward trip each evening in your own Packard.

PACKARD

ASK THE MAN WHO OWNS ONE

ASK YOUR FRIENDS WHO OWN THEM

PACKARD would like to put into your hands a new way to choose a motor car.

● It is a book—a "Who's Who" of people in your community who have purchased Packards. Many of these people are undoubtedly friends and neighbors of yours.

● Ask your Packard dealer to give you this book. Select a list of those you know. Ask them the questions given in the book, which cover every phase of motor car performance and upkeep. Ask them any other questions you care to.

● We believe the verdict of your friends will make you eager to drive one of the new Packards. Simply phone your Packard dealer and he will be glad to bring a car to your home. Drive it over a road you know by heart — test it in every way. Compare it on any basis you wish with any other fine cars, either American or foreign. And notice, too, that this newest and finest of all Packards has the lines that have made Packard America's most distinctive motor car —lines that make Packard one car the whole world recognizes.

PACKARD

ASK THE MAN WHO OWNS ONE

MAYBE YOU WERE THAT BOY

Sometime—twenty-five, perhaps thirty years ago —you saw a Packard for the first time.

● Measured by the standards of today, it was a crude affair. But there was something about it that spoke the language of fine things. Something that brought a lift to your heart, and a boyish resolution to your lips.

● "When I get to be a man, I'm going to own a Packard!"

● Today, you are a man. Have you kept that youthful promise to yourself?

● We know the excuses that have reared themselves.

"A cheaper car will do me." "I can use the money for other things." But will those other things give you half the pleasure, half the pride of ownership that a new Packard offers?

● Can a compromise between what you want and what will suffice ever thoroughly satisfy you? Doesn't life owe you a few things that are bought for the sheer joy they can bring you?

● And can any other motor car bring you a greater thrill than Packard? Is there any other car whose lines so surely identify it as a car of distinction?

Is there any other car that symbolizes so well your position in life?

● Just take the wheel of one of the new Packards. Compare it on any basis with other fine cars. This Packard is eminently worthy of the promise you made to yourself as a boy. Why not keep that promise by purchasing a new Packard today?

PACKARD

ASK THE MAN WHO OWNS ONE

246

A FAMOUS SLOGAN GOES TO WORK

FOR MORE than 30 years, Packard advertising has carried the slogan—Ask the man who owns one.

● Now this slogan has gone to work. It is helping motorists select their next fine car.

● This is how it can help you. We have prepared an unusual little book which your Packard dealer will gladly send you. This book contains the names of people in your community—many of them friends and neighbors of yours — who have purchased Packards. The book contains, too, a list of questions covering every phase of motor car performance and upkeep.

● From this book, choose any number of those "who own one." Ask them the questions given, and any others you may think of. Then follow their verdict.

● If it's unfavorable, dismiss Packard from your mind. But if it's what we're sure it will be, phone your Packard dealer and have him bring one of the new Packards to your door. Drive it—see how thrillingly it lives up to what its owners say about it. Notice, too, that in appearance, as in performance, this car is unmistakably a Packard ... one American fine car that has maintained its individuality and distinction.

PACKARD

ASK THE MAN WHO OWNS ONE

247

INSURANCE YOU CANNOT BUY

THERE is a fifth kind of fine car insurance that no agent can sell you.

● It covers a hazard more likely than fire or theft, than property damage or collision cost.

● It is insurance against what can be the greatest single expense in fine car ownership—the style depreciation that comes when a car is outmoded by a new model of inherently different appearance.

● No, you cannot buy this insurance. But you get it free when you purchase a Packard motor car. For the makers of Packard have written this insurance for you . . . written it for you in the famous lines that identify this greatest of American fine cars.

● Packard gave these lines to its cars 'way back in 1905. And it has maintained them ever since. They have come to be recognized the world over as the mark of America's most distinctive car.

● This insurance against style depreciation has literally saved Packard owners millions and millions of dollars. For no Packard owner ever has to trade in his car because it has lost its smartness. He can keep it as many years as he wishes and it will still be a Packard. It will still be a car he is proud to be seen in.

● The beautiful new Packards—finest of a long line of fine cars—have these famous distinguishing Packard lines. See these cars at your Packard dealer's. Drive one of them—and compare it. You will know then why these new Packards are increasing Packard's leadership in the fine car field. And you will know, too, why this car is so eminently fitted to be your next fine car.

PACKARD

ASK THE MAN WHO OWNS ONE

248

Let this 20-year-old advertisement tell you
why America prefers PACKARDS

IT is 20 years since this advertisement was published.

Yet, old though it is, it contains a clue as to why nearly half of all the larger fine cars being purchased in America are Packards.

For the idea embodied in this quotation has been Packard's guiding principle for over thirty years. Never, since the first Packard was built, has Packard sacrificed that "excellence of workmanship" so admired by Ruskin for even temporary expediency.

Because more and more fine car buyers have recognized this truth, Packard has won an increasing proportion of the fine car business—

until now that proportion is the largest in Packard's history.

You owe it to yourself, before you buy another car, to discover why such an impressive majority of those who purchase large cars in the Packard price class today prefer Packards. Go to your Packard dealer and take, without obligation, one of Packard's Revelation Rides —either the shorter Ride No. 1 or the all-day Ride No. 2.

Either one of these rides will raise the curtain on a new conception of what motoring can be, no matter what cars you have owned or driven. When you have discovered for yourself the comfort, silence and unmatched performance of the 1935 Packard, you will understand why this car is today an established first in the world of larger fine cars.

PACKARD
Eight · Super Eight · Twelve

ASK   THE   MAN   WHO   OWNS   ONE

249

THIS IS THE NEW

WHAT THE DESIGNERS HAVE DONE — They have produced the most beautiful car in Packard's history — modern, streamlined — yet they have not only retained, they have actually emphasized Packard's famous identifying lines . . . From the inside, they have so designed the body that you find an unbelievable roominess — and the widest, most comfortable seats you ever sat in. They have re-designed the windshield and windows, giving you greater vision than ever before . . . They have designed doors that are easier to get into and out of . . . They have created an entirely new interior treatment for the car, making it more attractive and magnificent than ever.

WHAT THE ENGINEERS HAVE and chassis in the world and have m changes, but by a host of important r the width of the tread and re-distribu easier to ride in and easier to handl parts, they have made last year's sturd have produced a motor so perfect th half-way round the world in a single

250

ACKARD *for* 1935

hey have taken the finest motor
ll finer—not by a few sensational
d improvements . . . By increasing
hey have made the new Packards
g new materials and re-designing
gher, still longer-lasting . . . They
equator a road, you could drive
damaging the motor in any way.

AN INVITATION TO YOU—The great new Packards for 1935 are now on display throughout the country. We cordially invite you to see them, and to ride in them. We confidently believe that such an experience will make you want to be the owner of a Packard. We are sure that no other car will ever again completely satisfy you . . .

PACKARD MOTOR CAR COMPANY
DETROIT, MICHIGAN

ASK   THE   MAN   WHO   OWNS   ONE

251

MR. CHARLES H. MORSE *of Lake Forest*
is one of more than 1000 distinguished owners through whose gateways
Packards have passed for 21 years or more

Packard Twelve Sedan for Seven Passengers

THERE are many things Packard is proud of.

But of its record of uninterrupted ownership by distinguished American families, Packard is proudest of all.

More than one thousand of these families . . . including many of the most prominent names in this country's business, social and public life . . . have owned Packards continuously for twenty-one years or more.

This, we believe, is the greatest testimonial ever given a motor car . . . one that has been twenty-one years in the living, rather than any mere hour in the writing.

No ordinary car could inspire such owner loyalty. And no ordinary car does. Year after year, for more than a third of a century, Packard has offered America its most luxurious transportation.

Nor is that all. Through the years, Packard has come to mean more even than the finest of fine cars. Today, in the minds of millions, it is a symbol of success, a badge of achievement . . . a goal for those who know and desire the finest things of life.

PACKARD EIGHT · SUPER EIGHT · TWELVE

+ *Ask the man who owns one* +

Mr. A. Atwater Kent *of Philadelphia*
is one of more than 1000 distinguished owners through whose gateways
Packards have passed for 21 years or more

The Packard Twelve Coupe Roadster for Two or Four Passengers

IN EVERY well-established family, certain traditions have grown up . . .

Daughters follow mothers to the same finishing schools. Sons follow fathers into the same exclusive clubs.

In many of America's most distinguished families, the Packard motor car has become one of the most firmly grounded traditions. More than 1000 of these families have owned Packards continuously for 21 years or more.

Such a record—the greatest testimonial, we believe, ever accorded a fine motor car—could not have been created by salesmanship alone. It could only have been built up by the car itself—by the service Packard gives, by the luxury Packard affords, by the prestige Packard carries.

From every indication, thousands of fine car owners who have driven their cars years longer than usual are choosing 1935 as the time to replace their old cars with new ones. And from every indication, a majority of these owners are deciding to make their new car the finest of the year's new big fine cars— the 1935 Packard.

PACKARD EIGHT · SUPER EIGHT · TWELVE

+ Ask the man who owns one +

253

MR. EDWIN S. WEBSTER *of Chestnut Hill*
is one of more than 1000 distinguished owners through whose gateways
Packards have passed for 21 years or more

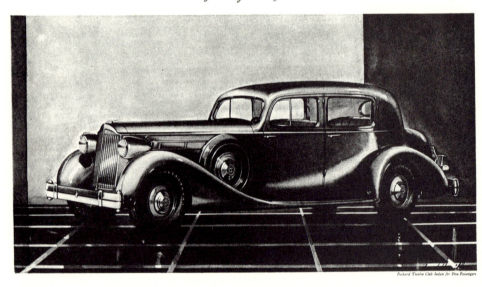

Packard Twelve Club Sedan for Five Passengers

PACKARD is proud of the foreign potentates . . . princes and presidents, maharajas and kings . . . who are on its roster of owners. (Packard has long sold twice as many cars abroad as any other American fine car maker.)

But Packard's proudest boast is the list of more than 1,000 of America's own royal families who have owned Packards continuously for 21 years or more . . . families who represent the flower of this country's wealth, culture and aristocracy.

Such a record of owner-loyalty is, we feel confident, without an equal in fine car annals. And the reason, we believe, is that the car itself has no equal.

For Packard is more than the finest of fine cars. It not only offers the most luxurious motoring that money can buy . . . it also carries with it a prestige that is priceless.

ON THE AIR: Packard presents Lawrence Tibbett, John B. Kennedy and a distinguished orchestra every Tuesday evening, 8:30 to 9:00 E. S. T., N. B. C. Network (WJZ and associated stations)

PACKARD EIGHT · SUPER EIGHT · TWELVE

⋆ *Ask the man who owns one* ⋆

Mr. Morton C. Treadway *of Bristol*
is one of more than 1000 distinguished owners through whose gateways
Packards have passed for 21 years or more

The Packard Twelve Convertible Victoria for Five Passengers

IN PACKARD'S files are thousands of unsolicited testimonials from owners.

But the greatest testimonial to Packard has been *lived*, not written. It is to be found, not in any letter, but in the fidelity to Packard of America's most distinguished families.

More than 1,000 of these families, representing the elect of this country's social, business and public life, have owned Packards continuously for 21 years or longer.

Such loyalty . . . the greatest tribute, we believe, ever paid a fine car . . . could be inspired only by the greatest of fine cars . . . by a car that appeals not only to an owner's love of beauty, not only to his sound business judgment, but to his heart as well.

Such a car is Packard. Even after long years of hard service, it still has the identity of appearance, the prestige that makes owners so proud to say, "I drive a Packard!"

ON THE AIR: Packard presents Lawrence Tibbett, John B. Kennedy and a distinguished orchestra every Tuesday evening, 8:30 to 9:00 E. S. T., N. B. C. Network (WJZ and associated stations)

PACKARD EIGHT · SUPER EIGHT · TWELVE

+ *Ask the man who owns one* +

255

The 1935 Packard Super Eight Club Sedan for Five Passengers

The new 1935 PACKARD has four surprises for you

FOUR SURPRISES? Yes, four *big* surprises!

Surprise No. 1 is the sheer beauty of this new Packard. Here is modern streamlining at its finest. Yet the famous identifying Packard lines are still there. They have even been accentuated.

Surprise No. 2 will come when you open the door of this new car. Was any other car ever so easy to enter? And the roominess of the interior! Packard designers have given you the widest, most comfortable seats you ever sat in.

Surprise No. 3 you'll get when you drive this car. For Packard engineers, by increasing the tread and redistributing weight, have made the new Packard easier to handle even than last year's car. They have made it the easiest riding car you ever rode in. And by redesigning windshield and windows, they have given you greater vision than ever before.

Surprise No. 4 is one that will make you gasp. Last year's Packard motor and chassis were hailed as the finest in the world. Yet, by utilizing new materials and redesigning parts, Packard engineers have actually made this 1935 car still more wonderful. They have created a motor so perfect that, were the equator a road, you could drive the car half-way around the world *in a week* without affecting the motor in any way.

But learn about the new Packard first-hand! Visit your Packard dealer's—see this new car and drive it. We sincerely believe that, after that, you will never again be contented with any other car.

ON THE AIR: *Packard presents Lawrence Tibbett, John B. Kennedy and a distinguished orchestra every Tuesday evening, 8:30 to 9:15 E. S. T., W. J. Z. Network, N. B. C.*

PACKARD

ASK THE MAN WHO OWNS ONE

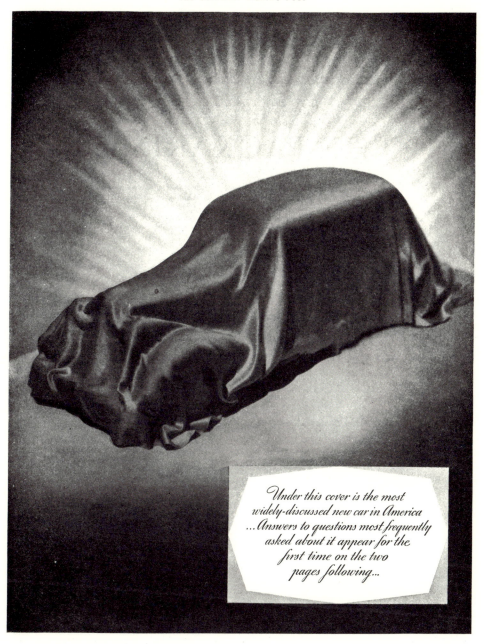

Under this cover is the most
widely-discussed new car in America
...Answers to questions most frequently
asked about it appear for the
first time on the two
pages following...

WITH THIS CAR PACKARD BRINGS FINE-CAR QUALITY

INTO THE LOW-PRICE FIELD

THE PACKARD 120

Few new cars have ever been preceded by such a flood of interest from the motoring public. Letters asking for information about this new Packard have come, not only from all parts of the United States, but from a dozen foreign countries. Because of this intense interest, Packard takes these pages to answer some of the questions most frequently asked.

Q. *Will it look like a Packard?*

A. Yes. It will have the famous Packard identifying lines and traditional Packard beauty.

Q. *Will it have the Packard name?*

A. Yes—it is a car we are proud to call a Packard.

Q. *Is it a real Packard?*

A. Yes, it is a real Packard—every inch of it. From radiator to rear axle Packard has given this new car design characteristics and a mechanical excellence as definitely Packard as its appearance.

Q. *Has it been thoroughly tested?*

A. *First*—the Packard 120 has been given the greatest of all tests—the test of time. Packard motors, clutches, axles, steering assemblies, bodies, have been proved in the millions of miles they have been driven by their owners. And all that Packard has learned through 35 years of research and engineering and manufacturing practice is inherited by this newest, most modern of motor cars.

Second—at the Packard Proving Grounds, in traffic, in country-wide driving under all conditions of roads and climates, this car has been given the most rigorous and exhaustive tests ever given any Packard, and to the best of our knowledge, ever given *any* new car.

Q. *Has it a straight-eight motor?*

A. Yes—a motor designed by Packard and built by Packard; one that includes all Packard has learned in 35 years of motor building. It is, we believe, the most powerful motor ever put in a car of this size.

Q. *What is its horse-power?*

A. 110 horse-power—*active and economical horse-power*, because, contrary to usual practice in cars of this price, the motor has an aluminum head—eliminating the necessity of premium motor fuel.

Q. *Is it economical on gas?*

A. In competitive driving tests, the Packard 120 gave more miles per gallon of gas than any other car its size and weight. Packard engineers got orders to design a motor that would be a miser on gas—and they've done it.

Q. *How much does the car weigh?*

A. The 5-passenger sedan weighs 3685 pounds—heavy enough to provide unusual comfort, safety, and roadability, and light enough to be economical to operate and easy to handle.

Q. *Is it a large car?*

A. Yes. It is a big car with more than ample head room and leg room. Extra wide doors provide unusual ease in getting in and out of the car. It is more than 16 feet in over-all length and 120 inches in wheel base.

Q. *Is it a good performing car?*

A. Yes. While it will easily do 90 miles an hour on the highway Packard is proudest of its ability in traffic and at the stop light. It is, we believe, the most agile of all cars of its size and weight.

q. Has it an all-steel body?

A. It has better than that. Packard has *improved* upon the all-steel body, retaining and plussing the strength of all-steel and eliminating any tendency to develop squeaks, rattles and rumbles. The Packard 120 has a Packard-built Safety-plus body—in Packard's opinion the strongest, safest, most modern body that ever went on a chassis.

q. What is the ventilating system?

A. The standard Packard type—one that lets every passenger have plenty of fresh air without the penalty of drafts, rattling or sticking windows, or other inconvenience.

q. Has it independent wheel suspension?

A. Yes—Packard's own exclusive SAFE-T-FLEX design which introduces for the first time the *safety* of torque-arm construction.

Two steel arms of tremendous strength carry all torque and horizontal load applied to the front wheels, including all braking forces. The springs themselves are relieved of these stresses and strains.

As a result, live rubber cushions can be used throughout the mechanism. These rubber cushions keep road shocks from reaching the frame and passengers—shocks that would otherwise be transmitted if only metal bearings were used.

Advantages:—a far softer ride, greater safety, no "gallop" or sidesway, positive wheel alignment, tires that wear longer, fewer points to lubricate, greater freedom from service adjustment, and a car that is more easily controllable at all speeds on all kinds of roads.

q. Has it hydraulic brakes?

A. Yes—with far greater "stopping power" than you will ever need, even in mountain country. In addition, these brakes have a feature never before found on a car of this price, the Packard-type dirt and water seal.

q. Is it a car my wife can handle easily?

A. The answer to that question is just two words long—drive it! Steering is almost effortless. The improved Packard clutch works with velvet smoothness. The car stops with little more than a tap of the toe. You can park it in little

more than its own length. A ninety-pound woman can drive the Packard 120 all day without fatigue.

q. Is it quiet at high speeds?

A. It is quiet at *all* speeds. Without question Packard has contributed more to the silencing of a motor car than any other manufacturer. Everything that Packard has learned about building quiet into an automobile has been applied to the Packard 120.

q. Will service costs be low?

A. Yes, for three reasons:

First—by examining the car, you will find that Packard engineers have greatly reduced service requirements. For example, there are fewer places to lubricate because the engineers have used more anti-friction bearings than you will find in any other car of this price. And because this is the most completely new car in America, because it was possible to take advantage of the newest engineering developments, the frequency of lubrication has been cut at least in half. *Outside of the crankcase, no point on this new Packard needs attention oftener than six times a year.*

Second—the necessity for frequent adjustments and for the replacement of parts is practically eliminated by Packard precision manufacturing methods which have long been the standard of the industry.

Third—Packard has established the definite policy that charges for service and parts shall not be higher for the Packard 120 than for other cars in its price class.

q. How many body styles will it have?

A. Seven. 5 Passenger Sedan; 5 Passenger Club Sedan; 5 Passenger Touring Sedan; 5 Passenger Touring Coupe; 2-4 Passenger Sport Coupe; 2-4 Passenger Convertible Coupe; 2 Passenger Business Coupe.

q. When can I get delivery?

A. Early in March. By placing your order now at any Packard showroom you can make sure that you will be one of the first to drive one of these great new Packards. *And so great is Packard's confidence in this new car that you may place your order now and take delivery or not as you please when you actually see your own new car.*

q. What will be its price?

A. All America has been waiting for the answer to this question. All America will cheer when it hears the price of the PACKARD 120. So tune in your N. B. C. Network station (WJZ and associated stations) *tonight*—Tuesday, January 8th—8:30 Eastern Standard Time. In a brief interlude between the beautiful melodies of Lawrence Tibbett, Alvan Macauley, President of Packard Motor Car Company, will tell you the amazing price of this amazing new car.

THIS IS THE NEW LOW

IN PACKARD'S opinion, the car shown on this page is the most significant automobile in the motor world today.

It is the first lower-priced car to be built in the fine car tradition. It brings to new thousands the immediate opportunity of fine car ownership.

For all that Packard has learned in its 35 years of motor car manufacturing has been applied to the Packard 120. Figuratively, the car was 35 years old before it was born. Packard design in motors, clutches, axles, steering assemblies, bodies, has already been proved in the millions of miles Packards have been driven by Packard owners.

And with these time-tested features in the Packard 120 have been combined the best, the newest, the most modern advancements.

Witness, for example, the Servo-Sealed hydraulic brakes, with the Packard-type dirt and water seal. Witness Packard's exclusive SAFE-T-FLEX independent front wheel suspension. This design provides a safer and smoother ride; eliminates sideway and "gallop"; holds front wheels in positive alignment and requires a new minimum of lubrication attention. Witness Packard's Safety-plus body, which *plusses* the strength of all-steel and eliminates any tendency to develop

squeaks, rattles and rumbles. Wit[h] straight-eight motor with an alum[inum] rarely found on cars of this price, a[nd] use of premium motor fuel unnece[ssary.]

But perhaps one of the most p[leasing] Packard 120 is its operating econo[my.] ful motor has phenomenal agility [and] will easily drive this big 3685-pou[nd car] hour, it is a frugal user of gasoline[. In] tests, the Packard 120 gave more [than] other cars its size and weight. The f[uel] too, has been cut at least in half.

The Packard 120 Sedan for Five Passengers, One of Seven Attractive Body Styles

RICED *PACKARD !*

rsepower
a feature
nakes the

es in the
ts power-
hough it
miles an
e driving
lon than
rication,
Packard

policy assures you that the charges for service and parts on the Packard 120 will be no more, and often *less,* than for other cars in its price class.

You can get delivery of your Packard 120, in any of seven body styles, early in March. By placing your order now at any Packard showroom, you can be one of the first to drive this newest of Packards. Any Packard dealer will gladly explain to you how easily the Packard 120 may be purchased on a convenient monthly payment plan. *And so certain is Packard that this car will delight you that you may place your order now and take delivery or not when you actually see your own new car.*

PACKARD 120
$980 *to* $1095

List prices at factory—standard accessory group extra

261

The Packard 120 Sedan for Five Passengers, One of Seven Attractive Body Styles

MR. HOUSTON, HERE ARE YOUR ANSWERS

Does the new Packard 120 have traditional Packard long life? Emphatically, yes!

It is a car you will want to drive, and *can* drive, far longer than other low priced cars you have owned.

For all that Packard has learned in its 35 years of building long life into motor cars has been applied to this newest of Packards.

Consider, for example, the Packard 120 power plant, with its 110 horsepower motor equipped with an aluminum head. Consider the Packard transmission; the Packard Angleset rear axle, with gears that actually *improve* with use—all Packard designs whose longevity has been proved by millions of miles of driving.

And to the long *mechanical* life of this newest Packard, add a long *style* life. The famous Packard lines never wear out. Packard style cycles have lasted on an average of eight years—and its newest style cycle is just beginning. Hence, your new Packard 120 runs no risk of being a style "orphan" a year —or three years—from now.

Will the Packard 120 cost much to operate? Emphatically, no! The Packard 120 is unusually frugal of gasoline. It has fewer points to lubricate and service. Outside of the crankcase, no point needs attention oftener than six times a year.

And because of Packard's quality methods of manufacturing, the *need* for servicing and parts replacement is naturally reduced. Too, *it is a definite Packard policy that such service as you do need will cost you no more, and often less, than for other cars in this price class.*

Do you have other questions about the Packard 120? If so, go to any Packard showroom and ask for a free copy of a little book called "The 90 and 9". Read the answers to the questions it contains and we believe you will agree that here is indeed the first lower-priced car of truly fine car quality. Compare it part for part and ride for ride, and we are sure you will be convinced that no other car at or near its price can offer you so much as the Packard 120.

PACKARD 120
$980 *to* $1095
Prices at factory—standard accessory group extra

QUESTION: Will service costs be low on the new $980 Packard?

ANSWER: Yes, and you can prove it <u>before</u> you buy the car.

PACKARD 120

For every $1.00 you would spend for service on the PACKARD 120, you would have to spend for:

CAR "A" . . . $1.24
CAR "B" . . . 1.09
CAR "C" . . . 1.06

PACKARD 120

For every $1.00 worth of new parts in the PACKARD 120, the same parts for three leading cars in this price class would cost:

CAR "A" . . . $1.10
CAR "B" . . . 1.09
CAR "C" . . . 1.02

BEFORE you drive a single mile in the new Packard 120, you can establish this important fact:

Its service costs will not be higher than service costs on other cars in its price field. This is a definite Packard policy. And you can verify it by making a direct comparison of costs on other cars in the Packard 120 price range.

Actually, such a comparison shows that Packard's service costs are frequently *lower* than those of other cars.

The charts at the left show such a comparison for three of the leading cars at or near the price of the Packard 120. These figures are an average of all common repair operations, and an average of all most commonly used parts. No comparison of figures, however, will give you the chief reasons why the Packard 120 is an economical car to operate.

The way Packard builds this car, the long experience in fine-car manufacture that is back of it, the better materials that are in it, and the newest, most precise manufacturing methods in the industry, have combined to reduce service needs far below anything you have ever experienced.

Packard has spent millions of dollars to make the new Packard 120 a car you can afford to purchase—*and a car you can afford to operate.*

ASK THE MAN WHO OWNS ONE

PACKARD 120
$980 *to* $1095
List prices at factory—standard accessory group extra.

263

264

QUESTION:

"HOW DO YOU LIKE YOUR NEW PACKARD 120?"

ANSWERS FROM SOME OF THE FIRST OWNERS

"Our Packard 120 performs beautifully. It's a great 'high speed' car and a wonderfully easy-riding car. But the thing I like best about it is that you know it will stay in style many years, because of those ageless Packard lines."

Mrs. D. S. Cerner
San Francisco, Calif.

"The remarkably sturdy frame construction is what sold me the Packard 120. The car is mechanically perfect. It has amazing snap and getaway."

J. Dodds
Aspinwall, Pa.

"I still cannot understand how it is possible for Packard to make such a fine car for such a low price."

Phillip T. Price
Cleveland, Ohio

"No other car I've ever owned has the all-around ability of the Packard 120. I have never driven any car so responsive to the throttle. The motor is perfect."

W. Fred Hornsby
Windsor, Conn.

"I'm more than pleased with my 120. I've driven it over some terrible roads and it rides better than any other car I've owned. Another remarkable thing—the 120 is more economical to operate than a former car of mine which was both lighter and smaller."

R. S. Ardary
Pittsburgh, Pa.

"I've never had a car that is so easy to park, turn and drive. It has all the fine points of construction that seemed lacking in other cars in this price range. It's very economical, too."

Mrs. J. Hampton Hoge
San Francisco, Calif.

"I recently took a 3600 mile trip in my 120. On one stretch I drove 90 miles in 89 minutes. Went over mountain roads without shifting gears. It's the best handling car I ever had, with the greatest speed, power and pickup."

Dr. E. P. P. Ryan
Scarsdale, N. Y.

PACKARD 120
$980 to $1095
List prices at factory
standard accessories group extra

ASK THE MAN WHO OWNS ONE

WHAT THINGS APPEAL MOST TO PEOPLE
IN YOUR NEW $980 PACKARD ?

The Packard 120 Touring Coupe for Five Passengers, One of Seven Attractive Body Styles

THESE TO MEN

- Its Packard identity, even to its hub caps
- Its fine materials and longer life
- The greater precision of its parts
- Its agility in traffic, its roadability, its performance
- Its thriftiness with gas and oil
- The power of its 110 h. p. straight-eight motor
- Its Packard Angleset rear axle
- Its Safe-T-fleX front wheel suspension
- Its Servo-sealed hydraulic brakes
- Its greater freedom from lubrication and service needs
- Its low service costs
- The convenient finance plan through which it may be purchased

THESE TO WOMEN

- Its Packard identity, even to its hub caps
- Its beauty and simplicity of line
- The ease with which you can get in and out
- Its remarkable riding comfort
- Its handling ease
- Its unusual roominess and interior luxury
- Its effortless operation of clutch and gearshift
- Its level back seat floor, free from the usual "ridge"
- Its spacious luggage compartment
- Its individually-controlled ventilation system
- The safety of its Safety-plus body
- Its easy-operating parking brake
- Its economy of operation

THIS TO EVERYBODY

Its "fourth dimension"—the pleasure and pride of possession a Packard brings to the family who drives one.

A S K   T H E   M A N   W H O   O W N S   O N E

PACKARD 120
$980 to $1095
List prices at factory—standard accessory group extra

Packard presents
for 1936
a new and finer version
of the cars that were chosen by nearly half
of America's fine car buyers in 1935

The

PACKARD

EIGHT
SUPER EIGHT
TWELVE

Ask the man who owns one

The Packard Twelve Town Car with Body by Le Baron

Symbol of a Nation's Preference

THE magnificent Packard Twelve Town Car pictured above is the greatest of a family of great cars.

As the reigning monarch of a noble line, it is the symbol of a national preference that has been increasing for more than a third of a century.

Today, more large Packards are in use in the United States than any three other fine cars combined.

In every state of the Union, there are more Packards registered than any other fine car.

For seven consecutive years, Packard has exported more fine cars than any other three fine car makers combined.

Nor is the preference for Packard a matter of geography alone. It is a matter of family tradition as well. More than one thousand of this country's most distinguished families have owned Packards continuously for 21 years or longer.

During the year just past, this preference for Packard reached the greatest height in history.

During this time, nearly half of all the people in America who purchased cars costing more than $2300 selected Packard over all other fine cars.

And during this same time, the public gave to the new lower-priced Packard 120 a reception so enthusiastic that it forced us to more than double production.

But reputation is a responsibility as well as a reward. Packard owes it to its owners—and to the millions who hope some day to be owners—to build finer and ever finer motor cars.

Probably the best proof of Packard's ability to do this is to be found in the brilliant new Packards for 1936 now on display.

We believe these cars offer the finest motor car values to be found in America. We would like to have you judge if we are right.

Hear LAWRENCE TIBBETT, America's favorite baritone, every Tuesday night, 8:30 P. M. Eastern Standard Time—Columbia coast-to-coast network.

PACKARD

Eight · Super Eight · Twelve

Packard 120

ASK THE MAN WHO OWNS ONE

The 1936 Packard 12 Limousine for Seven Passengers

SACRIFICE

THIS PACKARD has just been checked in at the Packard Proving Grounds. A magnificent new car you'd thrill to call your own. Yet—this is *one* Packard you cannot buy.

Why? . . . Because this is one of those Packards which from time to time are snatched from the delivery line and hustled out to the Packard Proving Grounds, there to be mercilessly abused, racked, tortured—deliberately destroyed if possible.

No one at the factory knows when one of these sacrificial Packards is going to be thus "kidnapped" —no one knows which Packard is the next to be so doomed. But doomed it is—to thousands of flying miles on the world's fastest concrete speedway at wide-open throttle . . . to thousands of grinding, wrenching miles through the most fiendish "bad lands" ingenuity has been able to devise.

Why? . . . Because Packard is constantly searching for any way in which we can build into Packard cars still greater surpluses of strength, safety, endurance, quiet power.

Such unremitting self-examination was of incalculable value in producing the superb Packards of 1935. We believe it is one reason why during that year America purchased almost as many large Packards as it did *all other fine cars combined* . . . why America received the new, lower-priced Packard 120 so enthusiastically that Packard has been forced to *more than double its production*.

But—more important to you today are the contributions of the Packard Proving Grounds which have gone into the beautiful new Packards for 1936—contributions that have helped make these cars beyond shadow of doubt the finest and most luxurious in Packard history.

They await your inspection at your Packard dealer's. We simply ask that you measure them against any other cars that 1936 can offer you.

269

The 1936 Packard Twelve Sedan for Seven Passengers

FIRST

AS THE oldest and largest fine car manufacturer Packard has been awarded many notable *firsts* by motor car owners both at home and abroad.

It is *first* in the size of its clientele. (There are more large Packards in use in America today than any three other large fine cars combined.)

It is *first* in fine car registrations in every state.

It is *first* in the number of cars exported. (Packard annually sends abroad more large fine cars than any three other makers combined.)

It is *first*, we believe, in owner loyalty. (More than 1000 distinguished American families have owned Packards continuously for 21 years or longer.)

It was *first* and has remained the *only* fine car

maker to give to its cars lines of enduring identity — a Packard policy that has saved its owners millions of dollars in depreciation costs.

And during the past twelve months buyers of cars costing $2300 or more purchased almost as many Packard Eights, Super Eights and Twelves as all other fine cars combined!

Nor was this preference limited to Packard's larger cars. America, eager for a smaller, less expensive car that still possessed Packard quality and Packard prestige, gave to the new, lower-priced Packard 120 (in the $1000 price field) a reception so enthusiastic that we were forced to more than double production.

But Packard realizes that success is a challenge to greater accomplishment — that leadership carries

with it the duty to produce finer and ever finer motor cars. So Packard offers, in its new 1936 models, cars which eclipse even their brilliant predecessors. By all means, see and drive these new Packards.

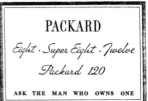

PACKARD

Eight · Super Eight · Twelve

Packard 120

ASK THE MAN WHO OWNS ONE

The 1936 Packard 12 Convertible Victoria for 5 passengers

BIRTHRIGHT

EVERY PACKARD you see carries with it a priceless birthright.

It is the birthright of that quality which is traditionally Packard's—that superiority in engineering design and precision manufacturing that has grown steadily greater through the years—until it has culminated today in the magnificent new Packards for 1936.

Nor is quality the only birthright of a Packard car. To it belongs the name that for thirty-seven years has been synonymous in motordom for beauty, luxury and long life. And to it belongs the most distinguished *and* distinguishing identity among motor cars.

In this birthright of quality, prestige and identity you can find substantial reason why there are more large Packards in use in America today than *any three other fine cars combined*. Why Packard annually exports more large fine cars than any *three* other makers put together . . . why more than 1000 of America's most distinguished families have owned Packards continuously for 21 years or longer . . . why, during the past twelve months, nearly half of America's fine car buyers chose the Packard Eight, Super Eight, or Twelve over all other fine cars.

And the birthright that belongs to every Packard also explains why the new, lower-priced Packard 120 (in the $1000 price field) was greeted so enthusiastically that Packard has been forced to more than double its production.

In the new Packards for 1936, the Packard birthright of superiority is more in evidence than ever. You will notice it when you see these cars, when you drive them—and most of all, when you own them.

PACKARD
Eight · Super Eight · Twelve
Packard 120

ASK THE MAN WHO OWNS ONE

271

The Packard Twelve Town Car with Body by Le Baron

SOLITAIRE

ONLY A FEW jewels achieve the rare distinction of being "solitaires." For only a few can appear magnificent without a flattering setting.

The Packard, we feel, is one of these jewels. Even if you take away its proud name, even if you strip it of its enduring identity—it will still be a monarch among motor cars. It will still be without a peer in mechanical excellence. It will still be without an equal in the luxury men and women love.

But you can no more divorce a Packard from its name, from its prestige and identity, than you can separate it from its comfort, or the swift-flowing ease with which it rides the roads. For more than a third of a century, the Packard name has stood for the utmost in fine motor cars. For a third of a century, Packard ownership has been a symbol of success.

Partly because of this prestige, but more because of the quality that has built it, Packard today has the largest fine car clientele in the world. More large Packards are in use in America than any three other fine cars combined.

During the last twelve months, nearly half of all America's fine car buyers chose the Packard Eight, Super Eight or Twelve over all other large fine cars. And during the same period, America gave to the new, lower-priced Packard 120 (in the $1000 price field) a reception so enthusiastic that we were forced to more than double production.

The new Packards for 1936 are the finest cars Packard has ever produced. We believe they are the finest cars America has ever seen. We would like to have you see them, drive them—and judge.

PACKARD

Eight · Super Eight · Twelve
Packard 120

ASK THE MAN WHO OWNS ONE

The 1936 Packard Twelve Sport Phaeton

A testimonial that has been lived, not written

IN the course of its thirty-six years of life, Packard has received many thousands of testimonials from delighted owners.

Yet Packard's most impressive testimonial is one that has been written, not in ink, but in the *lives* of owners. It is the record of a constantly growing roster of distinguished American families who have owned Packards continuously for 21 years or longer.

Such a record of owner-loyalty — a record, we believe, unmatched in the industry — speaks for itself of Packard's ability to produce cars that are always ahead of the field. It tells of a margin of superiority that is wider than ever today in the greatest Packards of all — the new Packards for 1936.

But the loyalty of Packard owners is only one of the living testimonials to this great car. Today, among the larger fine cars, Packard leads in registrations in every one of the 48 states. During the past year, America purchased almost as many large Packards as it did *all other fine cars combined*. And during this same time, Packard exported *more* large fine cars than any *three* other makes combined.

Equally impressive is the testimonial given to the new, lower-priced Packard 120. In its first year of existence, this newest member of the Packard family was awarded first place in registrations among cars in its price class.

The beautiful new Packards for 1936 — the finest and most luxurious cars in Packard's history — are awaiting your inspection at your Packard dealer's.

When you see them, when you drive them, when you measure them against any other cars 1936 can offer you, we are confident you will vote them the greatest motor cars the world has ever seen.

PACKARD
Eight · Super Eight · Twelve
Packard 120

ASK THE MAN WHO OWNS ONE

273

The 1936 Packard Twelve Club Sedan for five passengers, pictured before the Grosse Pointe Club

Grosse Pointe prefers Packards

IT goes without saying that Grosse Pointe knows its motor cars. As one of the smartest suburbs of Detroit, it has literally grown up with the automobile.

So it is especially significant that, in this motor-wise community, 65.7 per cent of all the large, fine cars are Packards. And among these owners

are many who have driven Packards continuously for more than twenty-one years.

This preference for Packard in Grosse Pointe is in keeping with the trend throughout America. During the twelve months just past, nearly half of all the large, fine cars purchased in this country have been Packards.

The charming Grosse Pointe home of Mrs. Frederick M. Alger, who has used Packards for her personal transportation for more than twenty-five years. Mrs. Alger includes the active leadership of Youth, Inc., among her many important activities.

This driveway leads to the lovely home of Mr. and Mrs. E. S. Bennett of Country Club Lane. The Bennetts have been Packard owners for more than twenty years. Mrs. Bennett's present personal car is a Packard Super Eight limousine.

For more than thirty years Mr. Emory L. Ford, owner of this magnificent Elizabethan residence on Lake Shore Road, Grosse Pointe, has driven Packards. Mr. Ford has long been one of Michigan's most ardent sportsmen.

PACKARD

EIGHT

SUPER-EIGHT

TWELVE

Ask the man who owns one

The 1936 Packard 12 Convertible Victoria pictured before the Sleepy Hollow Country Club

New York's Westchester prefers Packards

A SURVEY of fine car registrations in New York's smart suburban area of Westchester reveals Packard as predominant. Nearly 50 per cent of the fine cars owned in Westchester today are Packards—a significant tribute to the distinguished and distinctive Packard lines.

And this is simply a reflection of the nationwide trend. During the past twelve months, nearly half of all the fine cars purchased in America have been Packards.

Many of the purchasers are among the more than a thousand distinguished American families who have driven Packards continuously for twenty-one years or more.

For twenty years Mrs. R. Clifford Black, the owner of this magnificent home on the Boston Post Road, Pelham Manor, has also owned Packards. Socially prominent, she today enjoys the services of two Packard Twelves and two Packard Eights.

bove is the charming Colonial home of orman Rockwell, on Lord Kitchener oad, New Rochelle. He is, of course, e nationally known artist and a Packard ner for many years.

he home of John Motley Morehead, former S. Minister to Sweden, on Forest Avenue, Rye. r. Morehead now has three Packard Super Eights has been a Packard owner for thirty-one years.

PACKARD

EIGHT
SUPER-EIGHT
TWELVE

Ask the man who owns one

275

If you are-

—A PACKARD OWNER

You will most certainly want to inspect the **1936 VERSIONS OF THE SPLENDID PACKARD TWELVE, SUPER-EIGHT, EIGHT and the PACKARD 120.**

And when you see them, remember that *nearly half* of America's buyers of fine cars chose "your" car in 1935.

—A MOVIE STAR

You will meet your fellow luminaries, during the next few days, inspecting the **NEW 1936 PACKARDS.**

For *two out of three* of Hollywood's most famous names drive luxurious big Packards, and are keenly interested in the newest cars Packard has to offer.

—A MAN OF MODEST INCOME

What a thrill you'll get out of discovering that you can buy one of the **NEW 1936 PACKARD 120's** *almost as easily as any of the lowest-priced cars*—and drive it at no greater cost.

—A WIFE

We believe that, of all the new cars, **THE 1936 PACKARDS** are going to win the greatest praise from you.

They handle so easily, park so easily, are so easy to get in and out of, and are *so safe*, that they have already been hailed as the "ideal cars for women to drive."

—AN EXPORTER

You, as a student of foreign preferences, will be keenly interested in the **NEW 1936 PACKARDS.** For Packard has, for years, sold more cars abroad than any *three* other American fine cars combined.

—A PHYSICIAN

The **NEW 1936 PACKARDS** might well have been made to your own prescription.

What other car, Doctor, can offer you the speed in emergencies, the riding comfort over all types of roads, the dependability, the low maintenance costs—yet be so definitely in keeping with your position in the world?

—AN ENGINEER

You—far more than any layman—will appreciate the ingenuity, the skill and the soundness with which the **NEW 1936 PACKARDS** are engineered.

You will see and applaud the lengths to which Packard goes to build into its motor cars a mechanical life *longer than any owner will ever use.*

—A SPORTSMAN

You have probably noticed the dominant number of Packards at . . .

The Polo Finals at Meadowbrook . . . The National Championships at Forest Hills . . . In fact, wherever leading sportsmen gather.

An inspection of the **NEW 1936 PACKARDS** will convince you that these distinguished new cars will receive an even greater reception in 1936, because of even more brilliant style and performance.

—A BUSINESS MAN

Knowing, as you do, the value of first impressions, you will want to see the **NEW 1936 MODELS** of the car that is recognized the world over not only as a symbol of success, but also as the mark of sound business judgment.

Yet Packard, which stands apart from every other car in appearance and quality, asks no premium for the added value it gives, for the added distinction it confers.

—A SALESMAN

Spending, as you do, a fair share of your life in a car, you'll want to investigate *the most comfortable ride* ever engineered into a lower-priced motor car.

Over good roads or bad, the **NEW 1936 PACKARD 120** brings you to your destination with your salesmanship unmixed with fatigue. And operating costs year in and year out will rival those of the lowest-priced cars.

—A DEBUTANTE

Make a date with Dad right now to see these exciting **NEW 1936 PACKARDS.**

You'll take a keen delight in their smartness, the brilliance of their new color combinations, the easy way they drive.

And *he'll* find it hard to say "no"—when he learns how easily he can buy one for you.

—A "NUT" ON MOTOR CARS

You'll find evidences of mechanical processes in the **NEW 1936 PACKARDS** that will open even your experienced eyes. You will find mechanical designs unique in the motor car industry.

Take one of the cars out on the road, and give it the tests an expert delights in—*then see if any other car 1936 offers can possibly satisfy you.*

—A HOME STYLIST

You, whose home so clearly mirrors your own good taste, will welcome the opportunity to see, in the **NEW 1936 PACKARDS**, the most beautiful motor car interiors in America.

You will delight in their luxurious upholstery, their sculptured hardware, their harmonious color schemes. In every important detail of the car you will see evidence of Packard's ability to blend the ingredients of beauty, luxury and good taste.

—AN ACCOUNTANT

You'll find the **NEW 1936 PACKARDS** ideal cars to keep books on.

Year after year, they will show a favorable operating balance over cars of similar weight and size.

Because of their longer life, these Packards will, in the final analysis, return a saving in depreciation over cars whose original cost is much less.

—AN UNDERGRADUATE

A **NEW 1936 PACKARD 120** will not only see you through your college career, *but will still be smart and youthful after you are launched in business.*

Incidentally, operating costs will tax your allowance no more than many lesser cars.

—AN ARTIST

You'll be curious to see how Packard has taken the car that has won more beauty prizes than any other car in the world, and *made it still more beautiful.*

—A LAWYER

In choosing a new motor car, you will want to use your ability to exercise judgment and form conclusions *based on fact.* When you have briefed the case for every fine car in America, when you have weighed them all, feature for feature and ride for ride, your choice will, we believe, be a **NEW 1936 PACKARD.**

—A SMALL-CAR OWNER

Go to your nearest Packard dealer and ask to see detailed comparative figures covering the costs of owning and operating one of the **NEW 1936 PACKARD 120's.**

A study of these figures will prove to your satisfaction that *the joy of Packard ownership is now within your reach*—that "You are paying for a Packard—why not own one?"

—A SOCIAL LEADER

You will have wise precedent for choosing one of the luxurious **NEW PACKARDS FOR 1936.** *Over 1,000 distinguished American families have owned Packards for twenty-one years or more* —a testimonial given to no other fine car.

—AN AVIATOR

You won't be bored on land if you do your driving behind the wheel of a **NEW 1936 PACKARD.** The world's finest automobile motors provide the kind of flashing performance that will give even you a sensational thrill.

—OR IF YOU FOLLOW
Any One of a Hundred Other Vocations or Professions . . .

And are thinking of buying *any* new car— even one in the lowest-price class—*you can afford the pride and distinction of driving a* **NEW 1936 PACKARD.**

Packard's liberal time payment plan makes this possible. And the long life and enduring beauty of a Packard make such payments sensible—for long after the final payment has been forgotten, your car will still be a delight to own and drive.

—you'll want to see
THE NEW PACKARDS *for* 1936
now on display everywhere

PRICES: *Packard 120, $990 to $1115 at Detroit. Standard accessory group extra. Packard Eight, Super-Eight, Twelve, $2385 to $6435 at Detroit.*

TONIGHT, *and every Tuesday night, hear America's favorite baritone,* LAWRENCE TIBBETT, *8:30 P. M. Eastern Standard Time—Columbia coast-to-coast network.*

HO OWNS ONE

AN OPEN LETTER TO

BEFORE YOU BUY FROM HABIT OR HEARSAY . . .

— match Packard 120 against the field!

THE EDITORS OF "TIME"

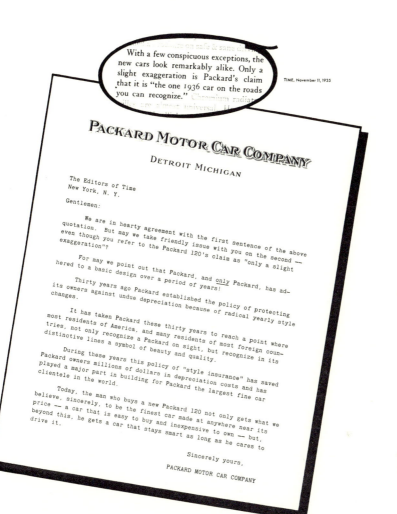

With a few conspicuous exceptions, the new cars look remarkably alike. Only a slight exaggeration is Packard's claim that it is "the one 1936 car on the roads you can recognize."

TIME, November 11, 1935

PACKARD MOTOR CAR COMPANY

DETROIT MICHIGAN

The Editors of Time
New York, N. Y.

Gentlemen:

We are in hearty agreement with the first sentence of the above quotation. But may we take friendly issue with you on the second — even though you refer to the Packard 120's claim as "only a slight exaggeration"?

For may we point out that Packard, and only Packard, has adhered to a basic design over a period of years!

Thirty years ago Packard established the policy of protecting its owners against undue depreciation because of radical yearly style changes.

It has taken Packard these thirty years to reach a point where most residents of America, and many residents of most foreign countries, not only recognize a Packard on sight, but recognize in its distinctive lines a symbol of beauty and quality.

During these years this policy of "style insurance" has saved Packard owners millions of dollars in depreciation costs and has played a major part in building for Packard the largest fine car clientele in the world.

Today, the man who buys a new Packard 120 not only gets what we believe, sincerely, to be the finest car made at anywhere near its price — a car that is easy to buy and inexpensive to own — but, beyond this, he gets a car that stays smart as long as he cares to drive it.

Sincerely yours,

PACKARD MOTOR CAR COMPANY

PACKARD 120—$990 TO $1115

AT FACTORY, STANDARD ACCESSORY GROUP EXTRA

ASK THE MAN WHO OWNS ONE

279

The 1936 Packard 120 Touring Coupe for Five Passengers, One of Seven Attractive Body Styles

1936 will reward lookers!

IF you are planning to buy a new car this year, you are indeed to be envied.

For the new 1936 cars will be a revelation to you, particularly if the car you are driving is three years old or older. You are in for a great thrill, no matter which car you select.

But in every race, there must be a first. Some motor car makers have gone farther than others. This year, neither the make of your present car nor friendly advice should influence your buying.

Find out which 1936 car offers you the greatest value. And Packard believes the surest way to do this is to *match Packard 120 against the field.*

Match Packard 120 against the field in performance. You will discover that never before has such fleetness and agility been built into a motor car of this weight.

Match Packard 120 against the field in roadability. You will find that the car is as easy to steer, turn and park as the smallest car made. Yet it rides as luxuriously as cars costing hundreds of dollars more.

Match Packard 120 against the field in fine-car quality. An inspection of the Packard 120 will prove to you the difference between a car built in the fine-car tradition and a car built to a price.

Match Packard 120 against the field in ease of ownership and economy of operation. Packard's 6% Payment-out-of-Income Plan is both attractive and economical. And Packard's charges for service are as low *or lower* than those of any other car in its price class.

Match Packard 120 against the field on any point you care to name, and make up your mind strictly on the merits of the cars themselves. Then, and only then, consider that the distinguished and ageless lines of the new Packard 120 are your greatest guarantee against owning a style orphan before even a single year has passed.

ASK THE MAN WHO OWNS ONE

BEFORE YOU BUY FROM HABIT OR HEARSAY . . .

— match Packard 120 against the field! $990 to $1115

AT FACTORY - STANDARD ACCESSORY GROUP EXTRA

Like father, like son

THE SIMILARITY of the Packard 120 to the larger, more expensive cars which bear the Packard name does not end with the most famous, longest-lived lines in motoring.

It continues through every point that distinguishes a fine car from a car that is merely good.

You can prove this to your own satisfaction if you will *match Packard 120 against the field*.

For example, Packard's 35 years of experience in building motors for America's finest cars has made possible the remarkable 120-horsepower straight-eight motor which powers the Packard 120—a motor which gives it an effortless, instantaneous response to the throttle that seems incredible in a car of this size and weight.

You will find that the new Packard 120 gives you a ride whose freedom from jar, jolt and noise is literally a revelation. Yet this is understandable when you consider that these have always been Packard's objectives in building luxury cars.

Both in the things you see and the "invisibles" —the evidences of extra qualities that are hidden, the Packard 120 is the product of fine-car experience, fine-car precision and fine-car ideals.

And these things give a tangible, dollar-and-cents return to every Packard 120 owner. They give him a car which, if he buys out of income, is still young in performance and appearance long after the last payment is forgotten. They give him a car in which the *need* for service is reduced below anything he has ever experienced.

Match Packard 120 against the field. You will find the car as easy to buy as it is to own. Packard's 6% Payment-out-of-Income Plan is unsurpassed for liberality. And, if your old car is of average value, you may be able to drive away in a Packard 120 without paying even a cent of cash.

ASK THE MAN WHO OWNS ONE

— match Packard 120 against the field! **$990 to $1115**

AT FACTORY-STANDARD ACCESSORY GROUP EXTRA

One-two-three- and you'll own a Packard 120

1

Learn what a big part of the cost your old car will cover

It may be a surprise to you to learn how far the allowance for your present car will go toward the purchase of a Packard 120.

Of course, it is impossible to quote figures that will suit every situation. But in a surprising number of cases, *the used car allowance equals or exceeds the down payment*. Without obligation, have a Packard dealer appraise your car.

2

Discover the flexibility of the payment plan

The monthly payments on a Packard 120 can be arranged to suit your income. Actually, these payments are never over a few dollars more than those you would make on some lower priced car. And remember, your Packard 120 will still be smart years after the last payment has been forgotten—thanks to Packard's policy of avoiding radical yearly style changes.

3

Learn how low the upkeep and service charges are

A Packard 120 is, we believe, the most service-free car in America.

And such routine service as you do require costs but little. The Packard dealer in your community will be glad to prove this to you *before* you buy the car. He can show you that typical charges for labor and parts actually average a little *less* than on the other prominent cars in the price class of the Packard 120.

These are some of the "money" reasons for choosing a Packard 120. But the most eloquent reasons for Packard 120 ownership will be given you by the car itself. Arrange today to borrow a new Packard 120 from your Packard dealer. Drive the car in traffic and on the open road. Compare it point for point with any car you may be thinking of buying. Do this—and we are confident that you will want a Packard 120 as you have never wanted *any* new car.

ASK THE MAN WHO OWNS ONE

PACKARD 120
$990
to $1115 at factory
Standard accessory group extra

What happens after the honeymoon?

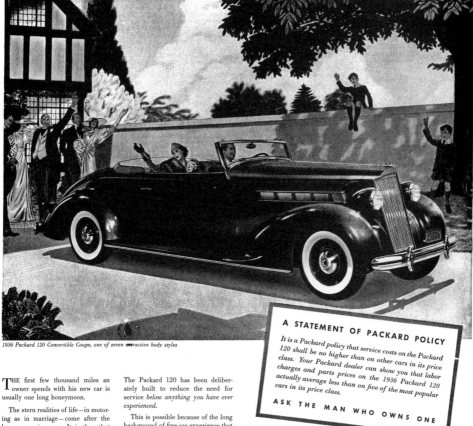

1936 Packard 120 Convertible Coupe, one of seven attractive body styles

THE first few thousand miles an owner spends with his new car is usually one long honeymoon.

The stern realities of life—in motoring as in marriage—come after the honeymoon is over. It is then that an owner faces the question: "How much is it going to cost to support my car?"

And it is then that the owner of a Packard 120 experiences a pleasant surprise. For he discovers that he is driving what is perhaps the most service-free car in America.

The Packard 120 has been deliberately built to reduce the need for service *below anything you have ever experienced.*

This is possible because of the long background of fine-car experience that lies behind the car, the finer materials that are in it . . . and the precision methods by which it is made.

If you will *match Packard 120 against the field,* we believe the comparison will be to the advantage of Packard in actual operating cost.

Match Packard 120 against the field

—in performance, in riding comfort, in prestige, or in any other point you care to name—and we believe you will decide that this is the car you will be happiest with through the years you drive it. It is a fine car that *stays* a fine car, whether you

keep it 2 years or 5. Visit a Packard showroom. Get the facts on how easy the Packard 120 is to buy and own. Your old car, if it is of average value, should cover the down payment. And Packard's 6% Payment-out-of-Income Plan is both attractive and economical.

BEFORE YOU BUY FROM HABIT OR HEARSAY

— match Packard 120 against the field! $990 to $1115

AT FACTORY-STANDARD ACCESSORY GROUP EXTRA

IF YOU WANT TO STAY PROUD OF THE CAR YOU BUY

—match Packard 120 against the field!

ALL the new cars for 1936 offer performance and value that far exceed anything the motorist has ever before known. On the basis of these things alone, *match Packard 120 against the field*. Then, and only then, remember that Packard offers an identity and prestige that no other car can match.

IF YOU ARE THINKING OF A LOW-PRICED CAR

If you question the wisdom of paying a little more for the Packard 120, spend just 30 minutes behind the wheel of one. We'll leave it to you if its agility, its additional riding comfort, its fine-car quality and its long style life don't banish your doubts for good.

IF YOU ARE THINKING OF A MEDIUM-PRICED CAR

Do you think all cars at about the same price offer about the same value? Then match Packard 120 against every car in its price class—and judge whether *any other car* can duplicate Packard performance, Packard comfort, Packard quality, Packard style permanence and the prestige of the Packard name.

IF YOU ARE INTERESTED IN A HIGHER-PRICED CAR

Packard, who has built fine cars exclusively for 35 years, believes that no car costing up to several hundred dollars more than the Packard 120 gives you greater safety, luxury and comfort. Spend an hour in a Packard 120, ask your wife to drive it—and then check these statements.

THESE THINGS MONEY CANNOT BUY

Packard gives you a distinguished motor car. Packard gives you lines that stand out from the crowd—an identity whose smartness does not fade. *And Packard gives you the most respected name in motoring.*

Go to a Packard showroom. Drive the Packard 120 to your heart's content. Get the facts on how easy it is to own. The value of your old car may very possibly cover the down payment. And Packard's 6% Payment-out-of-Income Plan is unsurpassed for liberality.

Hear America's favorite baritone, Lawrence Tibbett, Tuesdays 8:30 P.M., E.S.T. over CBS network.

$990 to $1115

at the factory. Standard accessory group extra.

ASK THE MAN WHO OWNS ONE

BEFORE YOU REPEAT ON THE CAR YOU OWN...
— match Packard 120 against the field!

THERE never was a year in which the automobile buyer was offered so much for his money. Yet Packard—a company that for 35 years has been known for conservative statement, this year issues this sincere invitation ... *Match Packard 120 against the field.*

AGAINST THE LOW-PRICE FIELD

If you doubt the wisdom of spending a little more for the Packard 120's more agile performance, immeasurably better ride, greater comfort and longer life —both style and mechanical—let the car itself dispel those doubts forever.

AGAINST THE MEDIUM-PRICE FIELD

If you think that all cars in the Packard 120's own price class are about equal, inspect the new Packard 120 and see what a difference 35 years of fine-car manufacturing experience makes.

AGAINST THE HIGHER-PRICE FIELD

If you think you need pay several hundred dollars more than the price of a Packard 120 to get truly-fine car safety and luxury, spend half an hour in the new Packard 120.

THIS—ONLY IN PACKARD

In Packard, and Packard alone, you get the distinguished lines that stay smart for years. Because Packard expects its owners to keep their cars at least 5 years, Packard makes no obsoleting yearly style changes. That is why Packard is the *one* 1936 car you can recognize.

See the new Packard 120 and learn how easy it is to buy. If your old car is of average value, it should cover the down payment. And Packard's Payment-out-of-Income Plan is one of the most liberal in the industry.

$990 to $1115

At the factory. Standard accessory group extra

ASK THE MAN WHO OWNS ONE

285

The 1936 Packard 120 Touring Sedan for five passengers

We invite you to forget everything Packard is famous for

WHEN you come in for your first ride in a Packard 120, we invite you to forget everything that Packard is famous for.

You can close your eyes to the car's good looks, you can shut your mind to the prestige of the Packard name, you can ignore the longer style and mechanical life that lie under those unmistakable Packard lines—*and still get the greatest motoring thrill you ever had in your life.*

When you shift into high and step on the throttle, a surge of power sinks you back shoulder-deep into those tailored cushions. The 120 horses of the greatest straight-eight motor ever put in a car of this weight shoot you forward with almost effortless acceleration.

You ride with none of the swinging bounce, none of the half-checked jars you have had to tolerate.

Even chuck-hole shocks are caught and smothered before they reach your body. You *see* road irregularities—but feel nothing. You turn corners without side-sway.

Before a mile has rolled under your wheels, you have a satisfying sense of relaxation. Every control you touch seems to almost anticipate your wish. Steering is finger-light. The Packard clutch and Packard hydraulic brakes, work with little more than tip-toe pressure.

Until you've had a 1936 Packard 120 ride, you don't know—you *can't* know—what modern motoring has to offer you. Only when you've driven and inspected the new Packard 120 can you realize the vast difference between a car built in the fine-car tradition—down to the last bolt and hub cap—and cars built to a price.

And only when you get out pad and pencil will you discover how easy the Packard 120 is to own, especially if you use the attractive and economical 6% Payment-out-of-Income Plan. And long, long after your last payment is forgotten you will be driving a car that is still smart, still a car you are proud of.

You are paying for a Packard, why not own one?

ASK THE MAN WHO OWNS ONE

—match Packard 120 against the field!

PACKARD 120
$990 to $1115
at the factory
Standard accessory group extra

FOR 1937

–get the plus of a Packard "

★ ★ ★ ★

FOUR GREAT NEW CARS !

FOUR NEW LOW PRICES !

On the following pages Packard introduces four
great new motor cars... each the top-quality car
in its price class... *each offering you a* **plus** *for
your money that only a Packard can give.*

THE PACKARD TWELVE
THE PACKARD SUPER-EIGHT
THE PACKARD 120
THE PACKARD SIX

...the ...D SIX

...s price class

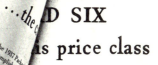

— get the plus

THE ADVANCED PACKARD TWELVE
...the *finest* car that money can buy

THE new Packard Twelve for 1937 is not just an improved version of last year's model. It is a new car—*greatly reduced in price*—and so revolutionary in its performance that it makes all previous standards of fine-car motoring obsolete.

This achievement is the result of *Packard's Completely Re-balanced Design*—a sweeping engineering advance which affects all phases of performance.

This *Re-balanced Design* takes the finest individual wheel suspension ever created—*Packard's own Safe-T-Flex*—and makes it function as no other suspension has ever done before. Riding comfort and handling ease reach heights never before attained in any automobile.

This *Re-balanced Design* assists the Packard-

improved hydraulic brakes to perform in a way that is new and wonderful. A mere touch of the toe, and this great Twelve comes to a stop that seems cushioned in velvet.

This *Re-balanced Design* makes the new Packard Double-Trussed Frame—*a frame some 400% more rigid*—contribute a stability and roadability never before enjoyed in a motor car.

Anticipating the tremendous interest this new car will arouse, Packard has given it a most attractive price—a price hundreds of dollars less than last year's Twelve. Your Packard dealer is eager to show you the new Twelve. See it—drive it—and you will know why we say: For 1937—*"Get the plus of a Packard!"*

PACKARD TWELVE
$3420
and up, at the factory

ASK THE MAN WHO OWNS ONE

288

of a Packard

THE NEW PACKARD SUPER-EIGHT
...a car that will *revolutionize* fine-car motoring

THE Packard Super-Eight for 1937 is a magnificent *new* motor car—a car that succeeds both last year's Eight and Super-Eight.

This great new car is also *new* in price. It sells for a great deal less than the former Super-Eight—*and for even less than the former Eight.*

It is *new* in the combination of qualities it brings to motoring. For it, too, has Packard's epochal development—*Completely Re-balanced Design.*

This significant engineering feat includes four times greater rigidity in the new Packard Double-Trussed frame; it permits full utilization of the finest front-wheel suspension ever created, *Packard's own*

Safe-T-Flex suspension—and it helps bring new efficiency to the Packard-improved hydraulic brakes, the most effective brakes ever built into any car.

In the new 1937 Super-Eight, gasoline mileage has been substantially increased. Oil mileage has been *more than doubled.*

But you have to drive this car to discover the most revolutionary change of all. The new Super-Eight reaches heights of performance, comfort, and handling ease that must be experienced to be believed.

Give the new Packard Super-Eight a thorough trial—and we think you will decide that for 1937, you're going to *"get the plus of a Packard!"*

289

—*get the plus*

THE GREATER PACKARD 120

...the car that surprised America *will now surprise it again*

IN THE 1937 PACKARD 120, the *"impossible"* has been accomplished: a great car has been made conspicuously greater, *and its price has been substantially reduced.*

Your first glance at the car will tell you that it is more beautiful than ever. Yet those famous Packard lines remain—the lines which identify your car as a Packard and protect you against style depreciation.

But what you do *not* see is that the very features of the car which drew the greatest praise are those which have been made still more outstanding!

For example, the comfort of the Packard 120's ride has been the talk of the motoring world. Yet the new 1937 Packard 120 actually *betters* this ride.

The Packard 120 has always been the easiest-

handling car of its weight. Yet, for 1937, it is still *more* responsive to the touch.

But perhaps the most remarkable thing of all is the *extra* economy of this car. Not only does the 120 horsepower motor use less gasoline than ever before, but its oil economy has been *more than doubled.*

During millions of miles of travel the Packard 120 has been called "the most service-free car in America." It will clinch this title even more firmly in 1937. With its new economy features, it will challenge *any* car for low operating costs.

Borrow a new 1937 Packard 120 from your dealer. Let the car reveal itself. Learn how easily it can be purchased out of income. Then we believe you will decide to . . . *"get the plus of a Packard."*

PACKARD 120
$945
and up, at factory. Standard accessory group extra.

ASK THE MAN WHO OWNS ONE

of a Packard

AND — A <u>BRAND NEW</u> PACKARD SIX

...upsetting all former standards in this price class

SHOWN ABOVE is the new Packard Six—a car destined to completely reshape America's lower-price car picture.

It is, Packard believes, the most astonishing value ever offered the public.

It is a tremendously high-powered car, yet it is a marvel of operating economy. It is the safest car of its weight ever built. Heir to Packard's 37 years of experience, brother of the sensational Packard 120, the Packard Six brings to its price class for the first time the important combination of qualities— *long* mechanical life coupled with *long* style life.

Built deliberately into your Packard Six is all the long mechanical life for which Packards are famous.

And guarding this long mechanical life are the lines that assure long style life—the lines that keep Packards looking like Packards, year after year.

Here are quick facts about this astonishing car . . .

Overall length: 192 inches. *Weight:* 3450 lbs. *Motor:* Packard-designed, Packard-built, to Packard precision standards, with a compression ratio of 6.4 to 1. *Horsepower:* 100. *Brakes:* hydraulic. *Front suspension:* Packard Safe-T-Flex individual wheel suspension. *Body:* Packard designed and built.

We urge you to go to your Packard showroom and drive this car yourself. Find out how easily it can be bought out of income. We believe you'll soon be saying, "I'm driving a Packard."

THE MAN OF THE YEAR

To PEOPLE contemplating the purchase of a motor car, we present the man of the year.

He possesses information that will be eagerly sought. And those who seek it will find him eager, in turn, to be of help. They will find him courteous, sincere, friendly...the type of man most people like.

Among others of his kind, he is in a preferred position. For this year, he can offer you definite *plusses* in the purchase of a motor car that no other man can match. He can offer you the top-quality car in each of four great price classes. Each of these cars bears the finest name in motoring. Each of them sells at a new low price.

This man can offer you fine-car mechanical excellence that means long life and freedom from service troubles.

He can offer you the enduring identity of the most beautiful motor car lines in America—lines which protect you against radical yearly style changes.

This man is the Packard salesman. And this year he has *four great new Packards at four new low prices* to show you: The magnificent Packard Twelve, $3420 and up, list at factory; the distinguished Packard Super Eight, $2335 and up, list at factory; the sensational Packard 120, beginning at $945, list at factory*; and the brand-new Packard Six, priced at $795 and up, list at factory*. (*Standard accessory group extra.)

No matter which of these cars you choose, this Packard man will gladly arrange a payment plan to suit *you*. Drop into your Packard showroom and have a chat with him. He is a man well worth knowing.

ASK THE MAN WHO OWNS ONE

"From now on, Son you ride in a Packard"

This <u>New</u> <u>Packard</u> <u>Six</u> lets your dreams come true

A GLANCE to the right will show you that there is now a Packard at an unbelievably low price.

This is big news. But it is far from the biggest news about the Packard Six. What makes it the outstanding car of 1937 is the fact that it combines two qualities that have been missing from its price class —*long life and enduring identity.*

For the first time in history, there is a low-priced car that is not outstyled a year or less after you buy it. For the first time in history, a low-priced car has the long life for which Packard is famous.

But to get the full picture of the new Packard you must add the following facts . . .

The Packard Six is powered by a Packard-built high-compression 100 horsepower motor. Handling ease, riding comfort, agility, are phenomenal. The car is niggardly with gasoline. It has unheard-of economy with oil. And—its body is Packard designed and built.

Give yourself the fun of driving this great car— the brother of the sensational Packard 120. Your Packard dealer will gladly loan you a Packard Six. Try it out to your heart's content. Then find out how easily you can buy one out of income.

Do this—and we believe that nothing in the world will stop your owning one.

Every Tuesday Night—THE PACKARD HOUR, starring Fred Astaire—NBC Red Network, Coast to Coast, 9:30 Eastern Standard Time

ASK THE MAN WHO OWNS ONE

PACKARD SIX

$795

and up, at factory. Standard accessory group extra.

—get the plus of a Packard

293

WHY YOU SHOULD READ THIS BOOK BEFORE BUYING <u>ANY</u> MOTOR CAR

LET'S say that you're one of the millions who will buy a new motor car in 1937.

If you're like a majority of these people, Packard is one car you have always wanted to own. Yet you have gone on, year after year, buying some other make of car—never seriously considering Packard—because you thought you couldn't afford one.

We have a feeling that the thing that is really keeping you from the pleasure of Packard ownership is not a lack of money—but a lack of information.

Far Lower In Price

For, while Packard ownership may have been beyond your reach a few years ago, the advent of the new Packard 120 and the still newer Packard Six has changed all that. Today, nearly everyone who can afford any new car can afford a Packard.

To prove that to you—to give you information that can save you both dollars and disappointments—we have printed a booklet called "The Business of Buying and Owning a Motor Car."

It is an unpretentious little book that you can read in a few minutes. Yet it contains facts that will undoubtedly surprise you—facts that have already changed the car-buying habits of thousands of people.

Easy To Buy

For this book shows you that, because of the flexibility of the Packard payment plan, and because of Packard's method of handling used cars, a Packard Six or 120 is extremely easy to buy. And it shows you how Packard's *double life*—long mechanical life *plus* long style life—not only can bring you motoring joy such as you have never known before, but at the same time can save you money, even over cars whose first cost is actually lower than Packard's.

HOW TO GET THIS BOOKLET

The quickest way to get it is to stop in at your near-by Packard showroom and ask the friendly dealer there for a copy. (It's free, of course!) Or, just send us your name and address, and we'll mail the book to you. Either way, we urge you to get *your* copy of this book *at once!* The Packard Motor Car Company, Detroit, Michigan.

ASK THE MAN WHO OWNS ONE

BUT <u>IS</u> THIS JUST "ANOTHER SPRING ?"

And we believe that many a man to whom a motor car is more than simply steel and rubber and transportation is going to make this the year when he gets the car he has always wanted—a Packard.

The urge to own a Packard goes back to boyhood —not simply to last year's Auto Show. The things that Packard stands for—the things that only Packard can give you—are part of the heritage of America's proudest motor car.

And now it is easy—easier than ever before—to own a Packard. For Packard has entered the low-price field with two genuine and thrilling *Packard* cars—the Packard 120 and the Packard Six. Both are *real* Packards mechanically. Both have the traditional Packard lines, which make a Packard the smartest car on the roads today, which keep it smart year after year.

See these new Packards! Drive them. And learn, to your pleasant surprise, how easily either a Packard 120 or a Packard Six can be purchased out of income, and how economical it is to own.

• • •

Every Tuesday night—THE PACKARD HOUR, starring Fred Astaire—NBC Blue Network, Coast-to-Coast, 9:30 Eastern Standard Time.

NOT many mornings from now the jonquils will begin to come up in that sheltered bed that gets all the sun.

Not so many noons from now you are going to find it a lot more comfortable to go to lunch without a topcoat.

Not so many dusks from now you are going to hear the winter stillness broken by the shrill-voiced advance guard of the army of spring peepers.

Then you'll know it is spring again. But we don't believe that this is just "another spring."

This year, as the ice goes out of the lakes, we believe a lot of the ice is going out of living.

The past twelve months have seen an easing of the tension under which most of us have lived. This year we can think more of having fun...of getting some of the things we've longed for and done without during the leaner years.

This year we believe that many a golfer is going to start the season with the fine set of matched golf clubs he has been eyeing with envy.

We believe that the fly fisherman is going out to

buy the rod which has just the action he has wanted. We believe that many a skeet shooter is going to lay aside his old gun for a new one with the fit and pattern he has long felt would spell the elusive 25 x 25.

PACKARD
PACKARD 120 ★ PACKARD SIX

Let your Packard dealer give you complete price information and tell you the easy terms by which you can own a Packard. Ask for booklet "The Business of Buying and Owning A Motor Car," an invaluable guide in the selection of any car.

ASK THE MAN WHO OWNS ONE

"I'm keeping a promise I made to this boy"

"Years ago, a little freckle-faced boy watched with envy as a magnificent new motor car went by.

"To that boy, it was *more* than a motor car. It was a symbol of a way of living that reached above the mere necessities of life. It was an emblem of success.

"And as his longing eyes followed the disappearing car, I promised him that some day, he, too, would own a Packard.

"Yes, *I* was that boy. And today I'm keeping the promise I made to myself some twenty-five years ago.

"*I'm going to get my Packard.*"

· · ·

If you, too, have long wanted a Packard, *you need wait no longer to realize your ambition.*

For Packard now offers you *two* great motor cars priced within the means of almost every one who will buy a new car.

These cars are the 1937 Packard 120 and the sensational new Packard Six.

Either can be bought for little or no cash, if your old car is of anything like average value. And the monthly payments are only a few dollars more than those of even the *lowest*-priced cars.

Furthermore, both the Packard 120 and the Packard Six are astonishingly thrifty to operate and service, and this can be proved to your satisfaction in any Packard showroom.

Don't fail to see these new Packards. You'll find them thoroughbreds, through and through. They offer you the smartness, the long mechanical life, the traditionally beautiful lines, the long style life, for which Packards are famous the world over!

The car illustrated is the Packard Six Touring Sedan for Five Passengers

Listen to THE PACKARD HOUR, starring Fred Astaire—NBC Red Network, Coast-to-Coast, Tuesday Night, 9:30 Eastern Standard Time.

PACKARD

PACKARD 120 ★ PACKARD SIX

Let your Packard dealer give you complete price information and tell you the easy terms by which you can own a Packard. Ask for booklet "The Business of Buying and Owning A Motor Car," an invaluable guide in the selection of any car.

ASK THE MAN WHO OWNS ONE

THREE GREAT *FIRSTS* IN A MAN'S LIFE

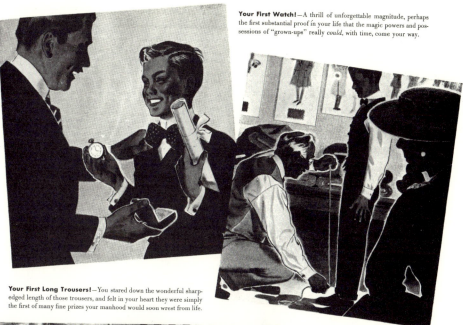

Your First Watch!—A thrill of unforgettable magnitude, perhaps the first substantial proof in your life that the magic powers and possessions of "grown-ups" really *could*, with time, come your way.

Your First Long Trousers!—You stared down the wonderful sharp-edged length of those trousers, and felt in your heart they were simply the first of many fine prizes your manhood would soon wrest from life.

The car illustrated is the Packard 120 Touring Sedan

Your First Packard!—A thrill as you look at it—realizing that your boyhood dream of someday owning a Packard has really come true.

And today, that dream *can* come true—*easily*. For, this year, Packard prices are lower than ever before. The car you now drive will probably cover the down payment. The balance can be paid out of income.

See the new Packards—*drive* one—learn what it feels like to *be* "the man who owns one"!

Listen to THE PACKARD HOUR, starring Fred Astaire —NBC Red Network, Coast-to-Coast, Tuesday Night, 9:30 Eastern Standard Time.

PACKARD

PACKARD 120   ★   PACKARD SIX

Let your Packard dealer give you complete price information and tell you the easy terms by which you can own a Packard. Ask for booklet, "The Business of Buying and Owning a Motor Car," an invaluable guide in the selection of any car.

ASK THE MAN WHO OWNS ONE

297

"We're tired of leading a second-best life"

The whole thing started when we were celebrating our wedding anniversary. Suddenly Jane fell silent. Then she spoke. "By the way, young man, what ever happened to all our dreams, and hopes, and ambitions?

Where are all the fine things we were going to have? Can it be true that we've become content 'with second bests'?"... Shortly, our little party at an end, we went out to the car to drive home.

Looking at our car, we were reminded of what we had said when we were married: "*And some day . . . we'll own a Packard!*" This was a good, serviceable, take-you-there-and-bring-you-back car. But it was no Packard.

Illustrated is the Packard Six, 5-passenger Coupe

Yes, we remembered our wedding-day hopes. We decided it was not good for young couples to become content with the second-best things in life. And we made up our minds right then that, by golly, we *would* have our Packard!

Next day we marched down to the Packard showrooms to see the new Packard Six. We saw that it was a *real* Packard, with the traditionally beautiful Packard lines. We drove it—and found in it all the

verve and spirit only Packard puts into a car. We learned (happy surprise) that the allowance on our old car took care of the first payment, and that the remaining payments were pleasantly easy!

So today—*we own our Packard!* And life is fuller and richer because of that Packard. Imagination? Perhaps. Psychological? Maybe. But our pride in our Packard is deeper than the usual "new-car pride." We like to be seen in it. And because driving is a thrill again, we're out more, enlarging our world and our horizons, having fun again. Yes, we have our Packard—*our* dream has come true!

You'll never know how good a Packard is until you drive one! See your Packard dealer, and borrow the new Packard 120, or the new Packard Six. Watch it behave like a living, thinking thing in traffic. Thrill to its long-lived smartness, its distinguished identity! Learn how easy it is now to *be* the man who owns one!

PACKARD

PACKARD 120 ★ PACKARD SIX

Let your Packard dealer give you complete price information and tell you the easy terms by which you can own a Packard. Ask for booklet "The Business of Buying and Owning a Motor Car," an invaluable guide in the selection of any car.

ASK THE MAN WHO OWNS ONE

298

"REACHING FOR THE MOON" —AND GETTING IT!

LOOK BACK into your memories...

In them, isn't there a picture like this? Didn't you, in the years when you were younger, stop as a sleek Packard purred by in all its magnificence, and say:

"Some day I'll own a Packard. Some day I'll drive by in my Packard and then people will envy me."

The dreams of the very young! The propensity of youth for "reaching for the moon!"

But wait. Today, the moon is within your grasp. Today, for nearly everyone who plans to buy any car, it is literally true...*if you can afford a car at all, you can afford a Packard!*

For Packard has entered, and completely *altered*, the low-price field with two genuine and thrilling Packard cars—the *Packard 120* and the *Packard Six*.

These new Packards are the brain-children of the very same engineers... and are built by the same incomparable workmen... who have made the big Packards the finest cars in the world today, and the name of Packard the most honored in all motordom. And they have the traditional Packard lines, which are lasting in beauty and lasting in identity.

See these new Packards! Drive them. Learn for yourself how amazingly they perform, how superbly they handle, how soothingly they ride, how reassuring is the safety of their sturdy Packard-built bodies and their Packard hydraulic brakes.

And learn, to your pleasant surprise, how easily either a Packard 120 or a Packard Six can be purchased out of income, and how economical it is to own.

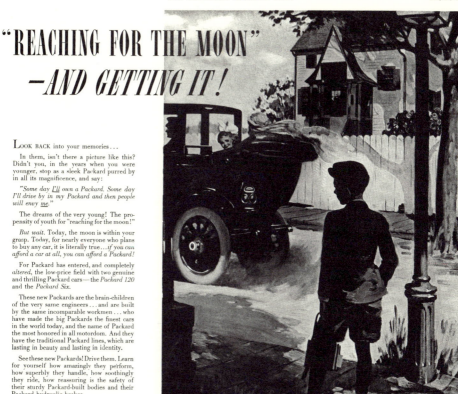

The car illustrated is the 1937 Packard 120 Convertible Coupe

You'll never know how good a Packard is until you drive one! See your Packard dealer, and borrow the new Packard 120, or the new Packard Six. Watch it behave like a living, thinking thing in traffic. Thrill to its long-lived smartness, its distinguished identity! • Learn how easy it is now to *be* the man who owns one!

PACKARD

PACKARD 120 ★ PACKARD SIX

Let your Packard dealer give you complete price information and tell you the easy terms by which you can own a Packard. Ask for booklet "The Business of Buying and Owning a Motor Car," an invaluable guide in the selection of any car.

ASK THE MAN WHO OWNS ONE

....HE WANTED

"I want a car that is long on mechanical ruggedness—and I mean *long!* These days *all* automobiles are first-rate performers the first few thousand miles. But I want to drive *our* car much longer than that. So I want to be sure it's a car that'll serve us nobly throughout a mighty long life!"

SHE WANTED....

"I want our car to be a *beauty*—furthermore, one that *stays* a beauty! Mechanical long life is just dandy, of course. But how much fun is it if each year drastic changes in the style lines make your car look *more* and more like an antique? Please, oh *please*, let's get a car that's smart...and will *stay* smart!"

...SO THEY BOUGHT A PACKARD AND GOT <u>BOTH</u> !

The car illustrated is the Packard Six Touring Sedan

Built into the Packard 120 and Packard Six for 1937 is that extra ruggedness for which all Packards are famous.

And guarding thát long mechanical life are those famous lines that make Packard the smartest car on the road to-day, and that will *keep* it smart no matter how long you drive it.

See the new Packards—ride in them! Let your Packard dealer give you complete price information and tell you the easy terms by which you can own a Packard.

PACKARD

PACKARD 120 ★ PACKARD SIX

Listen to THE PACKARD HOUR, starring Fred Astaire—N B C Red Network, Coast-to-Coast, Tuesday Night, 9:30 Eastern Standard Time.

ASK THE MAN WHO OWNS ONE

—"and we're going to California in our Packard"

IT STARTS EARLY—this recognition of Packard as a shining symbol of all that is smart in motor cars.

This is true today. And it has been just as true throughout Packard's 37 years of life. Probably you, if you look back into your memories, will realize that your admiration for Packard started back in your childhood.

This is perhaps the chief reason why Packard's two lower-priced cars—the Packard 120 and the Packard Six—are the sales sensations of the year. For both of them now make it possible for most Americans to realize the life-long dream of some-day owning a Packard.

Even a brief inspection of these two Packards will prove to you that, inside and out, they have the smartness, verve and distinction that have made

Packard your longed-for car. You will agree that both cars are *real* Packards, embodying not only Packard's famous lasting identity, but also Packard's celebrated long mechanical life.

These two Packard "lives"—long mechanical life and enduring beauty—are two important reasons why the Packard 120 and the Packard Six are shattering precedents and sales records.

The *other* reasons for the cars' sensational triumph you will discover before you nave driven them a mile. You will discover an agility, a fleetness of acceleration, you never suspected could be built into cars of such generous size. You'll find them thrillingly easy to handle, turn and park.

And when you take out your pencil and start to figure, you'll get the pleasantest surprise of all. For you will find that both cars are very easy to buy, and even easier to maintain. You will find

that, without straining in the least, you can be the man who owns one.

For example, your present car will probably fully cover the down payment on a Packard Six. And the usual monthly payment comes to *less* than $35 a month!

Why not drop in on your Packard dealer this week?

PACKARD

PACKARD 120 ★ PACKARD SIX

Let your Packard dealer give you complete price information and tell you the easy terms by which you can own a Packard. Ask for booklet "The Business of Buying and Owning a Motor Car," an invaluable guide in the selection of any car.

ASK THE MAN WHO OWNS ONE

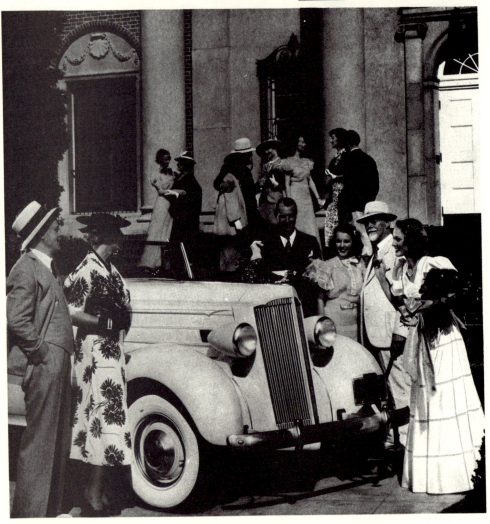

A FAMILIAR SCENE ON MANY AN AMERICAN CAMPUS THIS JUNE

TODAY, more than ever, America's first families prefer Packards.

In fact, this year, the country is buying more large Packards than any other large fine car.

What could be more natural, then, than that the socially-prominent families who have given Packard their loyalty for years, should select for the personal transportation of their sons and daughters, the smart new Packard Six?

For this graceful new Packard, alone among America's low-priced motor cars, carries with it Packard's traditional smartness, distinctive appearance, fine-car quality, and pride of ownership.

PACKARD

ASK THE MAN WHO OWNS ONE

SOCIALLY—AMERICA'S <u>FIRST</u> MOTOR CAR

MEETING "THE CANNON BALL" AT SOUTHAMPTON, LONG ISLAND

AT THOSE vacation and week-end resorts which year after year attract America's most socially prominent families, more large Packards are habitually in evidence than any other fine car.

This is a striking fact, but a most natural one. For in such families Packard ownership has become as traditional as attendance at certain schools, membership in certain clubs.

In fact, more than a thousand of America's most distinguished families have owned Packards continuously for twenty-five years or longer.

PACKARD
THE TWELVE
THE SUPER·EIGHT
ASK THE MAN WHO OWNS ONE

303

The Touring Sedan, one of five beautiful Packard Six models for 1938

...and no other 1938 car

INTO the new 1938 Packard *Six* and *Eight* have been crowded more really sensational improvements than usually come to light in a five-year period.

Below, in all sincerity, Packard makes you a series of promises that cannot be matched by any other 1938 car, regardless of size or price.

We promise you an absolutely new sensation in riding comfort; the *gentlest* ride ever built into a motor car; a ride that actually makes bad roads seem smooth, and smooth roads seem even smoother than they are.

We promise you the surest rear-wheel traction ever found in an automobile. The rear wheels hold the road as if they were grooved there. Your Packard rounds turns as though it were running on rails, like a train. This vastly increased "sure-footedness" is the greatest contribution to safety since the advent of four-wheel brakes.

NOTE: *The foregoing promises, are made possible by, not one, but THREE epochal improvements in the rear suspension. Working together, these developments produce advancements in comfort and safety that go far beyond the fondest drafting board dreams.*

We promise you that you need lubricate the new Packard *Six* and *Eight* chassis *only twice a year.* And there are only 15 points that ever require lubrication.

We promise you the first really quiet all-steel body with an all-steel top. Packard has discovered how to eliminate body noises in steel bodies through long and patient research in cooperation with a great University.

We promise you just about the roomiest cars of their respective prices you have ever stepped into. Bodies are far wider. The wheelbase of both the Packard Six and Packard Eight has been increased *seven full inches.* And the enlarged trunks will hold enough luggage to carry you round the world.

We promise you two lives—long style life and long mechanical life, *and no other car can make this*

304

Announcing the new 1938 PACKARD EIGHT

FORMERLY CALLED THE PACKARD 120

The Touring Sedan, one of the nine beautiful Packard Eight models for 1938

can make all these promises

promise. This year's Packard lines are more smartly streamlined than ever, although they still preserve their Packard identity, still proclaim your car a Packard, still guard it from early style obsolescence. And Packard's famous long mechanical life has been still further lengthened.

We promise you that there is no pride of ownership equal to that of driving the car that bears the most distinguished name in motoring.

We promise you that no other cars can equal these new Packards in all-around excellence — an excellence that could only come from 38 years of experience in making the world's finest motor cars.

We promise that if you can afford any new car you can afford a Packard; because, your present car will probably cover the down payment, and convenient monthly terms can be arranged on the balance. And in economy of operation and maintenance these new Packards challenge the *lowest* priced cars.

So far these are only promises. All we ask is the chance to make good on every one of them. Go to your Packard showroom, and drive one of these 1938 Packards. Test it against every promise we have made. Do it as soon as you can — and we promise you the greatest motoring satisfaction you've ever had in your life.

ASK THE MAN WHO OWNS ONE

AND WHAT ABOUT PRICE
Naturally, you are eager to know how much these new Packards will cost, delivered to your doorstep. May we suggest that you visit your own Packard dealer, who will give you the exact local price on whatever model you are interested in, and show you how easy it is to own one. *This much we can assure you, these new Packards are the greatest dollar value in Packard history.*

Each Tuesday night at 9:30 E.S.T. over the NBC Coast to Coast Red Network, Lanny Ross and Charles Butterworth have as their guest one of the topmost stars of radio, stage or screen. Don't miss Packard's big star-studded full hour show.

305

The Touring Sedan, one of the nine beautiful Packard Eight models for 1938

TEAR OUT THESE CLAIMS..AND MAKE US PROVE THEM!

TEAR
HERE

This year, be a cynic.

Say that no car could be as good as we claim the new Packard Six and the new Packard Eight to be. Tear out the following claims, bring them to a Packard showroom. Say: *"I dare you to make good on these statements"*...

For the new Packard Six and Eight, we claim...

1 That these new Packards give you the *gentlest* ride you ever had in a motor car; that they make bad roads seem smooth, and smooth roads seem even smoother than they are. *Make us prove it.*

2 That Packard has designed an exclusive new rear suspension which, through a combination of ingenious engineering principles, now gives the *rear* wheels the superb riding effect of independent wheel suspension. *Make us prove it.*

3 That increasing the wheelbase of the Six from 115 to 122 inches, and the Eight from

120 to 127 inches; that adding more beautiful interiors... have made these cars the most luxurious ever offered at their respective prices. *Make us prove it.*

4 That Packard, working with a great University, has developed the first really quiet all-steel body with an all-steel top. *Make us prove it.*

5 That these cars have a new feeling of security on curves and wet pavements, that side-sway on turns is minimized, that the danger of skidding is reduced. *Make us prove it.*

6 With normal mileage you need to lubricate these cars only twice a year, and then at only 15 points. *Make us prove it.*

7 That these new Packards are the only cars in their price classes to offer *both* long mechanical life and long style life. *Make us prove it.*

8 That if you ride in a Packard, you'll want one more than you have ever wanted any car. *Make us prove it.*

9 That you—right now—can afford one. *Make us prove it.*

These are our statements—and we mean every word of them. Your nearest Packard dealer is waiting for you to come in and challenge them.

1938 PACKARD
SIX & EIGHT*

*Formerly called the Packard 120

Each Tuesday night at 9:30 E. S. T. over the NBC Coast-to-Coast Red Network, Lanny Ross and Charles Butterworth have as their guest one of the topmost stars of radio, stage or screen. Don't miss Packard's big star-studded full hour show.

ASK THE MAN WHO OWNS ONE

306

When heaven was at the corner of Sycamore and Main

BACK HOME, when I was a boy, there was a place at the corner of Sycamore and Main that was as wonderful to me as anything out of a fairy tale.

For on that corner was the Packard showroom. Just about once a year, father would go there, and he always took me with him.

We never actually bought a Packard, for father's income was never more than modest. But we got a great kick out of feasting our eyes on those magnificent cars and imagining what it would be like to own one.

This year, my wife and I decided we needed a new car. As we passed the Packard showroom I said, "Let's go in, just for the fun of looking," exactly as my dad used to do.

Imagine our surprise when we found a Packard wasn't just something to dream about, but a car we could really afford. We found that—with the recent $100 price reduction on the Packard Six— we could have a Packard without paying a cent of cash. Our old car more than covered the down payment. And the monthly payments were only a few dollars more than we should have had to spend for one of the lowest priced cars.

So we're driving the car we've always wanted. And we're as thrilled as a couple of kids with it. Its lines tell the world we're Packard owners. And those same lines will keep our car smart and recognizable as a Packard over the many long years we expect to drive it.

Best of all, our Packard costs us no more to run—and less to service—than the car we used to own!

Moral: *Get the facts—they'll lead you to a Packard.*

Packard

· ASK THE MAN WHO OWNS ONE

The new 1938 Packard Eight Touring Sedan

ARE THESE "PUFFS" OR UNDER-STATEMENTS?

MAYBE THERE'LL BE a big question mark in your mind about some of the statements we're going to make about the new 1938 Packard Six and Eight. If so, we urge, and ask, you to check up on us—and *then* decide whether we've stepped over, or *under*, the truth.

WE SAY that these new Packards make all roads seem better than they are—that they give you the gentlest ride you ever had in a motor car. Do you doubt it? *You'll get the proof in a Packard.*

WE SAY that these Packards mark an epochal advance in safety—that they have the greatest rear wheel traction ever put in an automobile—that they have the "sure-footedness" of a mountain goat, even on hairpin turns—that sidesway has been practically eliminated. *You'll get the proof in a Packard.*

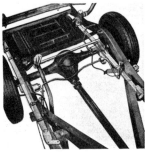

WE SAY that the foregoing contributions to comfort and safety are Packard's and Packard's alone, made possible by three new and vital improvements to the rear end—that the rear end now has the superb effect of independent wheel suspension. *The proof is in a Packard.*

WE SAY that the wheelbase of both the new Packard Six and new Packard Eight has been increased *seven full inches*—that bodies are far wider—that trunks are huge. *The proof is in a Packard.*

WE SAY that you only need to lubricate these cars *twice a year*—at intervals as far apart as Christmas and the 4th of July—and then at only 16 points. *The proof is in a Packard.*

WE SAY that a team consisting of Packard engineers and University scientists have discovered facts which make possible the *first* really quiet all-steel body with an all-steel top. *The proof is in a Packard.*

WE SAY that no other cars in their price classes can match these new Packards for all-around excellence—that you'll be *prouder* of a Packard—and that you'll *stay* proud of it because it's the only American car whose long style life matches its long mechanical life.

And we say that you can afford the car you've always wanted. You'll have to sit down with your Packard dealer to get the proof of this. You'll probably discover that your old car will cover the down payment on a Packard . . . You'll find you can arrange easy monthly payments on the balance. And we believe you'll say to yourself, "Why have we denied ourselves a Packard for so long?"

1938 PACKARD SIX & EIGHT*

*also known as the Packard 120

•

ASK THE MAN WHO OWNS ONE

"Our Packard pays us $39 cash every month"

IN THE last few months, Betty and I have been having a pretty surprising experience.

We've been getting money *out* of a car, instead of putting money into it.

You see, ever since we've been married, we've made monthly payments on some car. We got used to that way of doing it, and arranged our income to provide for it. And just about the time we'd finish paying for one car, it would be so much out of style we'd go and get a new one.

About two years ago we decided to get a Packard. We found that our old car covered the down payment, and our monthly payments came to only a few dollars more than we'd been used to paying. The car has been such a delight to own and drive that we've never regretted the little extra it cost.

Then a few months ago, Betty said, "Jack, do you realize we've finished paying for the Packard? I've already set the money aside just as usual, so what do you say we bank it?" Well, it came to me then that a Packard is almost like an insurance annuity. You pay in for awhile, and then begin to collect.

So here we are with a car that's all paid for. But *this* time it's a car that's still smart, still in style, and running like a fine watch. Moreover, it's still a car we are proud of.

So we're going to drive our Packard another year—and tuck an extra $39 in our bank account every month!

MORAL: *Get the facts— they'll lead you to a Packard!*

With the recent $100 price reduction on all body types of the new 1938 Packard Six, the 4-Door Touring Sedan as shown is only $1070—delivered at the factory in Detroit with standard equipment; State taxes extra. Convenient terms can be arranged through your Packard dealer—and if your car is of average value, it will probably cover the down payment on a Packard Six. The minimum down payment on the above factory delivered price would be $357.

Packard

ASK THE MAN WHO OWNS ONE

DRIVE THE NEW 1938 PACKARD SIX....

...AND CHECK (✓) THESE STATEMENTS AS YOU GO

When you read this ad you'll probably say, "It's too good to be true". So we're making it as simple as possible for you to check on whether these statements are facts or just puffs.

#1 ☐ The new Packard Six gives you a ride that is incredibly *gentler* than any you ever had before. Roads of every type seem *better than they are.* Check?

#2 ☐ You round curves so fixedly you'd think the car were grooved to the road. Side-sway has been greatly minimized. You can *feel* that the danger of skidding is reduced. Check?

#3 ☐ An utterly new type of rear suspension, involving three new Packard developments, gives the Packard Six a degree of comfort and safety you never before experienced. Check?

#4 ☐ The car has one of the roomiest bodies of any car in its price class. Wheelbase is now 122 inches—seven full inches longer than last year. Check?

#5 ☐ You are surprised at the low noise-level in the body. Packard, working with a great University, has created a really *quiet* all-steel body with all-steel top. Check?

#6 ☐ If you did not know the motor was a Six, you might guess any number of cylinders up to twelve. A combination of chassis and engine improvements results in a smoothness unknown before in a six. Check?

#7 ☐ The car has Packard's famous identifying lines in a new and more beautifully streamlined form. Only Packard offers you both long mechanical life and long style life. Check?

#8 ☐ Look where you will, you will find only 15 points that require chassis lubrication. And none of these points need lubrication, in normal usage, oftener than *twice a year.* Check?

#9 ☐ You can afford to buy, operate and maintain a Packard Six. You can't prove this in the car, but you *can* prove it in your Packard showroom. Check these points, and you won't want *any* other car.

NEW 1938

PACKARD SIX

Visit your own Packard dealer, who will give you the exact local price on whatever model you are interested in, and show you how easy it is to own one.

ASK THE MAN WHO OWNS ONE

Enjoy Lanny Ross, Charles Butterworth, and guest stars on radio's most thrilling program, THE PACKARD HOUR, every Tuesday night 9:30 E.S.T. NBC Red Network

"An old flame never dies"

"There's a lot of truth in that song," I said to my wife as it came in over the radio the other night.

"You mean you have an old flame?" she said.

"Certainly," I told her. "But it isn't a girl, it's a car—a Packard. I've wanted one for years."

"So have I," sighed Anne, "ever since I wore pigtails. Don't you suppose we could afford one?"

"I don't know," I told her. "But it won't cost a thing to find out."

Well, with that start, we didn't let any grass grow under our feet. The very next day we went down to the Packard showroom and asked the man to let us see the new Packard Six.

At first, we couldn't believe the car he showed us *was* the Six. It's a *big* car—100 horsepower . . . 122 inches in wheelbase . . . *seven inches* longer than last year!

And when we took it out on the road, that car simply took our breath away! The economical Packard Six challenges any competitive eight on smoothness and performance.

Could we afford it? Since the $100 price reduction on the Packard Six—with no change whatever in the car itself—almost anyone who can afford *any* new car can afford a Packard! The car we traded in covered the down payment, and the monthly payments were only a little more than those of our old smaller car. And we found that the Packard Six costs no more to run—and even *less* for typical service operations—than many *small* cars.

PACKARD

With the recent **$100 price reduction** on the new 1938 Packard Six, the 4-Door Touring Sedan is only **$1070**—delivered at the factory in Detroit with standard equipment; State taxes extra. The minimum down payment on the above factory delivered price would be **$357**.

● *ASK THE MAN WHO OWNS ONE* ●

311

IF YOU THINK YOUR WIFE HAS EVERYTHING
YOU MAY BE WRONG

DRESS BY JAY-THORPE . . . JEWELS BY MAUBOUSSIN

PERHAPS, as you cudgel your wits for the best way to play Santa Claus this year, it *does* seem that your wife has everything.

You can't whip up much fine Christmas enthusiasm over contributing another piece of jewelry to her already well-stocked jewel box.

You can't imagine any very exciting way in which you might add to her always admirable wardrobe.

And a check, generous as you would make it, hardly seems what you'd most enjoy giving a lady with her own ably managed bank account.

May we, then, recommend that on Christmas morning you present her with the keys to her own—her very own—new 1938 Packard 12 or Super 8?

Surely no other gift can give her a thrill comparable to that of owning America's most magnificent large, fine motor car—this year finer and more luxurious than ever before. Surely no other present will bring her the lasting joy she'll get from her Packard's smart, ageless beauty and matchless mechanical perfection through all the years she cares to keep it.

And surely nothing else you could give will give *you* such deep satisfaction . . . because you know your wife's new Packard 12 or Super 8 will protect her always with that safety of big-car size and weight for which there is no substitute . . . because you know you have given her *the safest, quietest, most comfortable motor car the world has ever known!*

SOCIALLY—AMERICA'S *FIRST* MOTOR CAR

PACKARD
FOR 1938

THE 12
THE SUPER 8

ASK THE MAN WHO OWNS ONE

The new 1938 Packard 12 Sedan for 7 Passengers

BEFORE YOU START FOR NEWPORT

SOCIALLY — AMERICA'S *FIRST* MOTOR CAR

THE PACKARD 12 CONVERTIBLE SEDAN FOR FIVE PASSENGERS

POSSIBLY the most enjoyable time of the year to acquire a new motor car is that season which takes you to your favorite resort . . . to Newport . . . or, perhaps, Harbor Springs . . . or Santa Barbara.

So now, before you start, we'd like to suggest that you insure a maximum of pleasure for this summer by taking two pleasant preparatory steps.

First: decide to get your new car *now*. And second: accept our invitation to use, without obligation, a new 1938 Packard 12 or Super 8 over one of these nice weekends.

Frankly, we are extending this invitation because we are so utterly confident of the ability of these Senior Packards to convince you that they are the most magnificent Packards ever built —the finest of all large, fine motor cars.

You will delight in recognizing those enduring, *always* recognizable basic Packard lines. You will revel in the new Senior Packard's supreme comfort, its almost uncanny quiet as you ride. And, as you put the car to any test you like, you will realize its mechanical perfection and extreme, inherent safety.

After that, it may surprise you to discover that a 1938 Packard 12 or Super 8 actually costs hundreds of dollars less than any comparable car you can buy, foreign or domestic.

You can enjoy this interesting prelude to your summer by looking under "Packard" in the telephone book for the Packard dealer nearest you, then calling and telling him when he may place one of these cars at your disposal.

PACKARD
The 12 · *The Super 8*
★
The Six · *The Eight*
ASK THE MAN WHO OWNS ONE

SOCIALLY — AMERICA'S *FIRST* MOTOR CAR

PACKARD 12 COUPE-ROADSTER FOR TWO OR FOUR PASSENGERS

WE SUGGEST YOU SHOW THIS PAGE TO YOUR SECRETARY

THE easiest, pleasantest and, ultimately, the most satisfactory way you can approach the purchase of your new motor car, we believe, is by showing this page to your secretary with instructions to accept for you the invitation it extends.

The invitation? Simply this: we ask you to accept for a few days, without obligation, a new 1938 Packard 12 or Super 8—to use as though it were already your own.

We do this because of our complete conviction that these Senior Packards for 1938 are the finest motor cars ever built . . . and that their superiority is so marked as to be immediately apparent to anyone who rides in them.

Certainly you will recognize at first glance those distinguished, *always* recognizable basic Packard lines. You will note during your first ride the extraordinary degree of comfort and quiet with which a Senior Packard serves you. When you put it to whatever tests occur to you, you will promptly sense the car's mechanical perfection and extremely high safety factor.

And you may well be surprised to discover that a 1938 Packard 12 or Super 8 actually costs hundreds of dollars less than any comparable car, foreign or domestic.

So . . . we suggest that you show this page, today, to your secretary and say, "Please accept this invitation for me!"

NOTE FOR SECRETARY: Look under "Packard" in the telephone book for the Packard dealer nearest you. Call him and tell him when your employer would like to accept a 1938 Packard 12 or Super 8 for trial. Thank you.

PACKARD

The 12
The Super 8

*

ASK THE MAN WHO OWNS ONE

PACKARD 12 ALL-WEATHER CABRIOLET — BODY BY BRUNN

R.S.V.P.

HERE is an invitation which, by its very nature, is limited to a small number of people—people of your own station in life—people who as a matter of course own large, fine motor cars.

It is an invitation for you to spend a week-end with a 1938 Packard 12 or Packard Super 8.

We invite you to take one of these new automobiles, without obligation, and use it over the week-end exactly as though it were your own.

We know these Senior Packards for 1938 are the most magnificent we have ever built. We extend this invitation because we are certain that once one of these cars is in your hands, there is but one conclusion you can come to—that a Senior Packard is the finest of all motor cars.

Accept our invitation. You will, of course, note with satisfaction the enduring beauty of the distinguished, always identifiable Packard lines. You will, we think, be enchanted by the greater comfort and well-nigh incredible quiet in which you ride. You will, we are confident, convince *yourself* of the mechanical perfection and extreme, inherent safety of a big Packard.

And it may surprise you to learn that a 1938 Packard 12 or Super 8 actually costs hundreds of dollars less than any comparable car you can buy, foreign or domestic.

You can arrange to have one of these cars placed at your disposal by looking under "Packard" in the telephone book and calling, today, the Packard dealer nearest you.

R. S. V. P.

PACKARD
The 12
The Super 8

★

ASK THE MAN WHO OWNS ONE

315

FOR KEY MEN

SOCIALLY — AMERICA'S *FIRST* MOTOR CAR

PACKARD 12 SEDAN FOR SEVEN PASSENGERS

IF YOU are the sort of man who fills one of the key positions in America's industrial or professional life, there is no question about the sort of new motor car you are going to buy.

Naturally it will be a car appropriate to your station in life—a large, fine car.

So it is to you that Packard extends a rather remarkable invitation . . . an invitation to accept for a few days, quite without obligation, what we honestly believe to be the *finest* large, fine car of 1938—a new Senior Packard.

We want you to take one of these cars (either a Packard 12 or a Packard Super 8) and use it as though it were your own—to test it in whatever ways you wish. And we want you to do this because we are supremely confident that these

1938 Senior Packards are the most magnificent cars ever built . . . and that you cannot, after this brief, intimate acquaintanceship, help but come to the same conclusion.

You will, we know, be pleased to note that these cars retain those distinguished *always* recognizable Packard lines. You will, we are sure, warm to the extraordinary comfort and quiet in which a Senior Packard cradles you. You will, most certainly, sense with approval the car's mechanical perfection and extreme, inherent safety.

And you will, we imagine, be distinctly surprised to learn that a 1938 Packard 12 or Super 8 actually costs hundreds of dollars less than any comparable car you can buy, foreign or domestic.

Under "Packard" in the telephone book, you will find the Packard dealer nearest you. Simply tell him when you would like one of these cars placed at your disposal.

PACKARD

The 12
The Super 8

*

ASK THE MAN WHO OWNS ONE

You Are Cordially Invited to Inspect
America's Newest Motor Car

The Packard Super-8
*Now only $2035**

A Great Companion Car for the
1939 Edition of
The Famous Packard 12

ASK   THE   MAN   WHO   OWNS   ONE

THE NEW PACKARD SUPER-8 offers you something entirely new in motor car performance and value.

This beautiful new automobile was deliberately designed to combine, for the first time, super-luxury and super-power with a delightful nimbleness and an unusual ease of handling.

We urge you to see and drive this new Super-8 at your very earliest convenience. Visit your Packard dealer, or have him bring a car to your door.

*The Four-door touring sedan illustrated ... delivered for $2035 at the factory in Detroit—represents a really remarkable value. The price includes standard equipment. (State taxes are, of course, extra).

S O C I A L L Y — A M E R I C A ' S   *F I R S T*   M O T O R   C A R

For 1939 Packard has created an entirely new motor car—

The New
Packard Super-8
only $2035 *

Combining Super Performance + Super Luxury with Extraordinary Nimbleness

WE **knew that,** in these days of crowded streets, people like easy maneuverability to be a feature of their cars.

But we also knew that many people still want the gratifying size, the thrilling power and the comforting luxury that only a truly *big* fine car can offer.

So we deliberately set about designing a car that would give you *all* these things—super performance and super luxury combined with extraordinary nimbleness.

And now we present it for your inspection . . . a new car we have proudly given one of the most honored names in motoring...the Packard Super-8.

No Packard as luxurious as this one has ever sold at anywhere near this price.

This newest motor car creation, in appearance, in upholstery, in fittings, in roominess, takes second place only to the Packard 12.

It has all the new improvements that make Packards the gentlest-riding, quietest, easiest handling cars on the road . . . Packard Safe-T-fleX Suspension front and rear, the exclusive Packard *Fifth* Shock Absorber, Packard noise-insulated all-steel body with all-steel top, and Packard Handi-shift—the improved steering column gear shift that

puts your gear lever up under the steering wheel, clearing the front floor and making operation infinitely easier.

And a specially-built 130 horsepower straight-8 Packard power plant gives this car an incredible deftness in traffic, a spectacular dash on the open road. In short, the New Packard Super-8 is *one* car you just *must* see and drive . . . *NOW!* There are six attractive models, including a 7-passenger sedan and 7-passenger limousine.

Available at slight additional cost, is the new Packard Econo-Drive which lets your engine run 27.8% slower—thus even quieter and· smoother —at speeds over 30 m.p.h., cutting engine wear, reducing gas and oil consumption.

THE NEW
PACKARD SUPER-8 FOR 1939
THE NEW 12...THE NEW 120...THE NEW SIX
ASK THE MAN WHO OWNS ONE

SOCIALLY — AMERICA'S
FIRST MOTOR CAR

*$2035 for the Four-Door Touring Sedan, as illustrated, delivered at factory in Detroit, with standard equipment; State taxes extra.

What's new about America's Newest Motor Car?

1. **LARGE-CAR LUXURY** and power, extreme ease of handling are triumphantly combined in this beautiful new motor car creation — the Packard Super-8 for 1939. It offers you the sumptuous roominess and smooth-as-silk ride of a truly fine big automobile, with the thrilling super-power of a specially-built 130 horsepower straight-8 Packard engine. And this new car is a positive joy to handle! Just one of many reasons is its Packard Handishift, the improved steering column gear shift that puts your gear lever up under the steering wheel, clearing the front floor.

2. **AND ITS PRICE IS ONLY $2035,** for the 4-door touring sedan, as illustrated, delivered at factory in Detroit with standard equipment; state taxes extra. Remember—such super-performance and super-luxury have been available heretofore only in cars approaching $3000 in price. You should see this Packard Super-8 *now*. Above all, you should *drive* this car—and learn how completely new and different it is!

SOCIALLY—AMERICA'S FIRST MOTOR CAR

THE NEW

PACKARD SUPER-8 FOR **1939**

THE NEW 12 • THE NEW 120
THE NEW SIX

★

A S K T H E M A N W H O O W N S O N E

3. **AND IT GIVES YOU** what only a Packard can give! The new Packard Super-8 is endowed with purely *Packard* improvements that have resulted in the smoothest-riding, easiest-handling, quietest cars on the road . . . Packard Safe-T-fleX Suspension front and rear . . . the exclusive Packard *Fifth* Shock Absorber . . . the Packard noise-insulated all-steel body with all-steel top. And, inside and out, this is the *smartest* Packard you ever have seen! Furthermore, it has those dis-

tinguished Packard lines that have long protected Packard owners from style obsolescence. In six attractive models, including a 7-passenger sedan and a 7-passenger limousine.

Available at additional cost, is the new Packard Econo-Drive, a new and perfected fourth-speed gear which lets your engine run 27.8% slower—thus even quieter and smoother—at speeds over 30 m.p.h., reducing engine wear, and saving on gas and oil.

ONE ANSWER TO <u>TWO</u> QUESTIONS

PROBABLY the first question to arise when you begin considering the purchase of a new car is:"What car will best meet my desire for true large-car luxury, comfort, and power?"

And the answer to that question assuredly is: *"The new Packard Super-8 for 1939".*

But there's another question you may well have in mind at the same time—a question prompted by modern driving conditions. That question is: "What car can give me the extreme *nimbleness*—the easy maneuverability—that is so necessary in facing today's traffic and parking problems?"

And—perhaps surprisingly—your answer to that question *also* is: *"The new Packard Super-8 for 1939!"*

For Packard has deliberately *combined* these motor car virtues in this one car. Drive it just once—and discover how deftly it sifts through traffic and into snug parking spaces. Sit back in it—and begin to realize how luxurious is its comfort, roominess, richness of appointments . . . how fine are *all* the details that make this car a worthy companion to the magnificent Packard Twelve.

Until now such luxury has been available only in cars approaching $3,000 in price!

One ride in the new Packard Super-8, we are certain, will convince you what an extraordinary car it is. Won't you take that all-revealing ride—*now?*

"I wanted to grow up and marry Mr. Washburn"

AT THE TENDER AGE OF EIGHT, I fell madly in love with a gentleman named Mr. Washburn.

He used to drive by in a beautiful Packard, magnificent with its proud lines and gleaming brass. And to the smitten little girl who watched him, it was as though imperial Caesar passed by in his conquering chariot, Roman eagles and all. I used to dream of riding in that gorgeous car beside my hero, to the envy of my playmates.

Looking back across the bridge of years, I'm not sure whether I lost my childish heart to Mr. Washburn, or to Mr. Washburn's Packard. Not to be too unromantic, I suspect it was to the Packard.

At any rate, ever since then a Packard has always been my beau ideal of a car. But because the man I married isn t exactly rolling in wealth, I despaired of ever owning one.

Then, one day last month, Jim and I happened to pass a Packard showroom. And just for the fun of looking at those stunning Packards, we went inside.

Well, just out of curiosity, we asked how much it cost to own a Packard. The figures simply bowled us over! We could get one for only a very few dollars a month more than our payments were on our last car!

In fact, the difference amounted to little more than we spend a month for cigarettes!

Then and there, we snapped up a stunning blue Packard Six—a perfect dream of a car that has our friends' eyes simply popping. Our old car fully covered the down payment, so there wasn't a penny of cash to pay. And it costs no more to run and keep up, than the ordinary cars we've owned.

We're proud as a couple of peacocks! For we have a car that *stays* smart, *stays* looking like a Packard!

• • •

If you, too, have long wanted a Packard, **don't** delay! Go to your nearest Packard showroom **now**. We can promise you a pleasant surprise!

PACKARD

When you drive a Packard,
the whole world knows it's a Packard

•

ASK THE MAN WHO OWNS ONE

321

Announcing two NEW PACKARDS

ABOVE: The new Packard Six for 1939 . . . BELOW: The 1939 Packard One Twenty. (Also known as the Packard Eight)

...*every traffic sign says "see them!"*

T&T ENGINE ... FIFTH SHOCK ABSORBER
CHANGE THE ENTIRE BEHAVIOR OF MOTOR CARS

The most revealing way to find THE car of 1939 is to test a new model Packard Six or Packard 120 against America's traffic signs. Each sign will demonstrate some phase of motoring *now radically bettered* for you!

Packard's improved TRAFFIC & TRAVEL engine now gives you flashier, thriftier performance in *both* traffic and on the open road. You'll get away from a light faster—usually *first*. You'll get *more* engine satisfaction out of a gallon of gas.

Every jolt-reducing mechanism ever used has been designed to absorb *up-and-down* shocks. Yet most road shocks hit *cross-wise* as well. Packard's new, exclusive FIFTH shock absorber smothers cross-shocks *for the first time.* It gives a *new* riding ease.

This FIFTH shock absorber adds to your safety and comfort in three ways. *First,* it checks rear-end side-stepping. You can take S-curves "in a groove." There's no objectionable side-sway nor body-roll.

Second, it increases steering accuracy. If you must, you can miss danger by inches, and know you'll *stay* inches away! You actually *feel* this added steering security.

Third, it stops the lateral shocks which, like the pressure of some giant hand, have encouraged your car to skid. These new Packards are harder to skid than any car Packard has built in 40 years of fine-car manufacturing!

Shift gears, and you'll discover again what Packard quality means. For these Packards have a design borrowed from the Packard Twelve—Packard UNIMESH transmission. Gears are in constant mesh, so shifting becomes quieter, easier than ever before!

Lastly, you'll be *prouder* of one of these new Packards. You'll step out of one knowing that you're driving America's most beautiful car—with the distinctive lines that have been smart year after year.

And here's *more* good news ...

As IF the developments above weren't enough of a sensation in these new cars, here are *more* Packard "headlines" ...

First—an improved steering column shift—the Packard Handishift—is now standard equipment on both the Packard Six and One Twenty. This better shift puts your gearshift lever up under the steering wheel, clears front floor. Nothing new to learn; in fact, it is definitely easier to operate.

Second—available on both of these Packards is an ingenious device called the Packard Econo-Drive, one of the greatest boons to your pleasure and your pocketbook ever put on a car! The Econo-Drive works with a foot-touch at speeds over 30, and *lets your engine run 27.8% more slowly—much more quietly and smoothly!*

Hence, when the Econo-Drive cuts in, you ride with an entirely new sense of effortless motion. And your gas and oil consumption, as well as engine wear, take a nosedive! The cost? Only a few dollars additional.

And, remember that *only* Packard can offer you the distinguished lines that have protected its owners from the depreciation caused by radical yearly style changes. A Packard keeps up its smartness, retains its identity.

So, to discover the car that offers you the greatest thrill for 1939, hurry to your Packard dealer and *take the traffic sign test.* And remember, if your old car is of average value, it will probably cover the down payment on a new Packard Six. Convenient monthly payments can be arranged through your Packard dealer.

your next car should be a 1939 Packard

Illustrated: the new Packard Six Four-Door Touring Sedan for 1939.

round S-curves without side-stepping, steer with greater accuracy—and greatly *reduces a car's tendency to side-skid!*

Shift gears—for two surprises

"*Stop,*" the sign says. You do so, swiftly and surely. Then you shift gears—and are delighted by two things.

First, you no longer reach down and feel for a gear lever. For you're using the handiest gear shift lever that ever blessed a car—the Packard HANDISHIFT. It's an improved lever under your steering wheel, leaving your front floor clear, and it's *standard equipment* on both the Packard Six and Packard One Twenty. *Second,* you've never experienced such velvety shifting! That's because your gears are in constant mesh—thanks to the Packard UNIMESH transmission, a transmission design taken from the magnificent Packard 12!

But—words are a poor substitute for the real thing. Go now to your Packard dealer's. Look your fill at the smartest, most beautiful lines in motoring— the lines that say "Packard" the world over. Get the facts on how easy a Packard is to own. Then borrow either one of these new Packards—*and let the Traffic Sign Test make you a proud and happy owner!*

• • •

New! Another brilliant Packard plus!

Packard's ingenious Econo-Drive—optional at additional cost. This new and perfected fourth-speed gear lets your engine turn 27.8% more slowly at speeds over 30 miles an hour. Think what this saves you in gas and oil, and in decreased engine wear. Yet Econo-Drive is more than worth its extra cost —in smoother, quieter, more pleasurable motoring!

THE NEW 1939

PACKARD

SIX and 120*

*Also known as the Packard Eight

How Much . . . ? You can expect a most agreeable surprise when your Packard dealer shows you how *little* it costs to buy one of these new Packards—*delivered right to your door.* He will tell you the exact local price on whatever model you prefer—the small down payment, which very likely will not require any cash outlay—and the astonishingly low monthly payment figures that prove how easily you can own and drive a 1939 Packard.

ASK THE MAN WHO OWNS ONE

Protected Investment!

No PACKARD owner has ever been left with a style orphan.

No Packard owner has ever awakened one morning full of pride in his still-new car, only to find that radical style changes have branded it an "out-of-date model."

For Packard, ever since 1905, has followed the policy of protecting its old owners in its quest for new ones.

Does this mean that Packard opposes style changes? Of course not—for change is the essence of progress. But Packard believes that style, like ambition, is a good servant but a poor master—that style can, and should be, used in the best interests of the car owner, and not against them.

This is why Packard makes its style changes with restraint rather than sensationalism.

This is why every Packard for the past thirty-four years has been altered and modernized so skillfully that it has still looked like a Packard . . . so artfully that it never shamed the owner of an earlier model.

Ask the man who owns one, and he will tell you that this is one of the things about Packard he prizes most. It is one of the reasons why Packard has such an outstanding record of loyalty among its owners.

Unique—for 1939

So, again for 1939, you will find Packards refined, re-styled, more beautiful than ever. But you will also find them unmistakably Packards—no one has to guess what they are. *Can you say as much for other 1939 cars?*

Before you sign the order for any new car, ask yourself whether you can expect your pride in the car to outlast your first few thousand miles—or your payments.

Then consider that, when you buy a Packard, you are buying a car that is *built* to last longer, styled to *look well* longer, and labelled a Packard —not in words—but in lines.

Why not see your Packard dealer and talk it over now? You'll find a Packard surprisingly easy to own and run.

ASK THE MAN WHO OWNS ONE

PACKARD SIX & 120

When you drive a Packard, the whole world knows it's a Packard!

With its 4 year plan completed

Packard makes this promise to you!

1939 PACKARDS THE FINEST PACKARDS EVER BUILT

These cars, now reduced in price, are the same spirited, mechanically great 1939 Packards that have thrilled and delighted the "man who owns one." Never in 40 years has Packard received such a torrent of enthusiastic letters from new owners.

ASK THE MAN WHO OWNS ONE

A lot more car for your money!

NO OTHER AUTOMOBILE shall offer you as much for your money as a Packard.

This is Packard's promise for the future. And the reason why it can be fulfilled goes back four years, to Packard's entry into the lower price field.

Four years ago Packard formulated an orderly plan which would so reduce costs *as to make lower prices a permanent Packard policy.*

This plan has now been completed. Packard's two great factories have been extensively rearranged and replanned. Many millions of dollars have been invested in a huge expansion and equipment program which effects important manufacturing economies.

Add to this the fact that Packard enjoys an unusual financial position—with no loans, no mortgaged overhead, no interest charges to increase the cost of its cars, and you have the major reasons why Packard can now offer you unheard-of values!

New prices $100 to $300 lower

Make no mistake about this—the beautiful Packard that now sells for $888 instead of $990, the Packard 120 and Super-8 that sell for $100 to $300 less than before, *are cars that have not been cheapened or changed in even the smallest detail!*

So let nothing stop you from seeing your Packard dealer, driving your favorite model of the finest Packards ever built, and deciding for yourself that Packard offers you—not just more car—but *a lot more car for your money!*

PACKARD NOW

AND UP, delivered in Detroit, State taxes extra

327

"Look—the Wards have a new car!"

"Look—those lucky Eatons have a gorgeous new Packard!"

THESE REMARKS POINT OUT <u>THREE</u> FACTS:

Fact No. 1: When you buy a new Packard, your car immediately proclaims you a Packard owner. People recognize your car's smart lines—*at once.*

Fact No. 2: It's more news in your neighborhood when you buy a Packard than when you buy any other car of equal price.

Fact No. 3: Packard is America's most *beautiful* car—and this *isn't* just Packard's opinion.

Recently, an independent research organization conducted a nation-wide poll to determine which American car people considered the best looking. When the results were tabulated, *Packard led every other 1939 car—regardless of size or price!*

And Packard's stunning lines are planned with consideration for Packard owners. Because Packard makes its style changes *gradually*, never in 34 years has any Packard owner been left with a "style orphan."

How to pick a better car

Another thing. We know that the new 1939 Packard Six and One Twenty are better-built cars. And the strange fact is, that *you* can sense this simply by driving one. Even in a short ride, you'll get the feeling that you're handling a piece of finely-built, superbly-engineered machinery.

One more discovery—and an important one. Your Packard dealer will show you that it's really easy for you to get a Packard—right *now.* For instance, your old car, if of average value, will probably cover the down payment on a new 1939 Packard Six. Your monthly payments will be little, if any, more than those you've been used to. And your service costs may run you even less!

P. S. New Econo-Drive transforms touring—this perfected Packard automatic fourth-speed gear lets your engine run 27.8% slower (thus even quieter and smoother) at speeds over 30 m.p.h., reducing engine wear and saving on gas and oil. Available at moderate extra cost.

ASK THE MAN WHO OWNS ONE

PACKARD

The 1939 car that America's motorists voted the most beautiful

THE SIX · THE 120

3 figures *that took* 4 *years to write*

FINEST PACKARDS EVER BUILT NOW AMERICA'S GREATEST VALUES

To see for yourself whether Packard's confidence is justified, go to your nearest Packard dealer and borrow the particular model you fancy.

Drive it. Ask your wife to drive it. Take it over the worst—and best—roads you can find. Test it on hills and in city traffic. Be as thorough, and as critical, as you know how to be. And see if you don't end up more genuinely thrilled and enthusiastic over this Packard than you've ever been over any car since your first one!

A LOT MORE CAR FOR YOUR MONEY!

A FEW YEARS AGO, nobody ever dreamed that a really big, luxurious 122-inch-wheelbase Packard would be priced at the astonishingly low sum of **$888***.

To make these three magic figures a reality has not been easy. It has taken Packard four years to reach a point where *an entirely new and permanent policy of pricing* would be possible.

During these four years, significant changes have taken place. Both of Packard's huge plants have been extensively rearranged. Millions of dollars have been invested in ultramodern machinery for more efficient production. Step by step, an important program of expansion has drawn to completion.

Nothing changed but the price

A few months ago Packard's four-year plan was completed—and before a day had passed the prices of 1939 Packards had been reduced $100 to $300! *And this without the changing or cheapening of so much as a shackle-bolt on the cars themselves!*

Public response has been impressive. Since the establishment of this permanent new pricing policy, Packard business has steadily increased. In these months for which comparable figures are obtainable, nearly a third more people bought Packard cars than last year.

The reason is obvious. Equipped for and schooled in the manufacture of fine cars, Packard believes it can now offer you more quality, and more car, than you have ever been able to buy for a given price before!

ASK THE MAN WHO OWNS ONE

PACKARD NOW

$888*

*AND UP, delivered at Detroit, State taxes extra

329

1940's best business card for outstanding auto salesmen who are looking to the future.

To top-flight automobile salesmen
who have their eyes on bigger things!

THIS is the kind of opportunity that comes to an automobile salesman once in a blue moon.

Here, in brief, is our situation.

Packard, ever since its entry into the lower-price field, has been growing fast. But this year—with the prices of Packards at a new low and the cars at a new high in excellence—the spurt has become almost a landslide.

Packard sales up 72%. People switching to Packard by the thousands. In short, business expansion—*and we need more car salesmen capable of sharing this growth!*

Are you the man?

We want *top* men. Men with a record behind them. Men who can team up with Packard and do us—and themselves—proud.

For such men there's opportunity unlimited.

The door is wide open. Packard is going places and you're invited to come along.

The field is uncrowded. You'll have all the scope you want. And the opportunity isn't confined to any one section—it's as broad as the U. S. A.

Since the first of last September, 577 new dealers have heard opportunity knock and joined the Packard ranks. More are being, and will be, added. And these dealers—as well as many old ones—need top-flight salesmen *now*.

Four cars to sell

When you join Packard, no price hedges surround you. You have four cars to offer—ranging in price from **$867 to $6300** (delivered in Detroit, State taxes extra). Every car owner is a potential Packard owner.

And Packard owners *stay* Packard owners. Packard owner loyalty is almost a legend in the

trade. That means that when you build a clientele, you *keep* it.

So if you're the man for Packard, do one of two things. Contact your nearest Packard dealer. Or mail this coupon *now* to headquarters.

W. M. PACKER, Vice-President of Distribution
Packard Motor Car Company
Detroit, Michigan

DEAR SIR: I'm interested. Last year my sales totaled_____cars, and I'd like to do still better. I know I can top that record with the right product and the right dealer. Please put me in touch with him.

*Name*_____

*Home address*_____

*City*_____*State*_____

Even the porter knows it—

GREAT THINGS HAVE HAPPENED!

YOU CAN NO MORE KEEP news like this quiet than you can hush up a gold strike.

Even the porter at the Packard showroom knows that great things have happened at Packard—things even more far-reaching in their consequences than the unveiling of a sweet and sensational new 1940 car.

For with its 4-year program of plant rearrangement completed, with millions of dollars invested in ingenious new machinery, Packard can now offer you —not just a new Packard, but *a masterpiece at a price!*

It's a speed-streamed sensation!

Gaze on those stunning, speed-streamed lines! They're as new as television—yet as Packard as the red hex hub caps.

Look at those smartly styled interiors. Rub your eyes—for you'll wonder how so much luxury can be price-tagged so astonishingly low.

Touch that responsive accelerator. You shoot ahead, with the speedometer hand climbing like a treed cat. For this lithe and nimble new Packard packs *so much more horsepower per pound of car weight* that it makes run-of-the-mine cars seem pokey.

You'll glory in a ride like nothing you've ever experienced—a ride unbelievably free from jolts, jars, and sway—even on the worst stretch of broken-down macadam.

Credit this uncanny comfort to Packard's improved Safe-T-fleX suspension, front and rear—the finest in the business and the envy of the industry.

In looks and breeding, in comfort and luxury, in sheer delight of ownership, this dazzling new Packard is a dream-on-wheels come true!

It's crowded with news—from its new Sealed-Beam lamps, that bring near-daylight to the roads at night, to its greater trunk space.

You've simply *got* to get your hands on one of these thrilling new 1940 Packards before you're an hour older.

And why not? With a Packard now within handshaking distance of even the lowest-priced cars—*why wait another day?*

•

ASK THE MAN WHO OWNS ONE

PRICES STILL FURTHER REDUCED *as much as* $133 *less than a year ago*

1940 PACKARD

$867

AND UP, delivered in Detroit, State taxes extra

Model illustrated is Packard One-Twenty Touring Sedan $1146* (white sidewall tires extra)

What a car to drive anywhere—
GEOGRAPHICALLY *or* SOCIALLY

new 1940
PACKARDS
LOWEST PRICES IN PACKARD HISTORY

PACKARD 120 · $1038
AND UP,*delivered in Detroit, State taxes extra

PACKARD 110 · $867
AND UP, delivered in Detroit, State taxes extra
Prices subject to change without notice

YOU MAY BE about to take off for Mexico or Montreal . . .

Or you may be stepping out to the swankiest white tie function in years . . .

In either case, you can't climb into any other car that will fit the picture so well, and take you there with so much ease and comfort as this dazzling new 1940 Packard One-Twenty!

For this big, 127-inch wheelbase blue-blood has more sleek good looks than ever. And its straight-eight, 120 horsepower motor makes greased lightning worry about a new rival!

Popular though this famous car has been from the beginning—and much-loved though past One-Twenties have been by their owners—the 1940 One-Twenty is a car that, unless we miss our guess, is going to smash all existing Packard sales records. For it's a one-in-a-million car in every department of modern motoring! And if there's the slightest

doubt in your mind about that statement, drop in at your nearest Packard showroom.

How to spoil yourself for other cars

The moment your eyes fall on that longer, sweeping bonnet, that narrower, rounded radiator, those gleaming side-grilles . . . you'll know that here is beauty you've *got* to have around!

Slip into the driver's seat, and let that straight-eight motor begin to whisper. Because this speed-streamed One-Twenty has so much *more horsepower per pound of automobile weight*, you'll feel as though you were hitched to a comet!

Now for one you'll find hard to swallow—till you try it. Find yourself a bad road you know. This last is important—for unless you *know* how bad the road is you won't believe it in this new One-Twenty! It makes a neglected, back-country road seem as smooth as new-laid concrete! . . . for which miracle you can thank Packard's improved Safe-T-fleX

suspension, the envy of the automotive industry.

Yes, Mr. and Mrs. America, this year's One-Twenty is a millionaire's car at a family-on-a-budget price. It's as easy to buy as it is thrifty to run.

Come and try one out. We bet we never get it away from you!

·

ASK THE MAN WHO OWNS ONE

332

More car for your money!

Doesn't anybody YAWN *any more?*

HAVE THEY DISAPPEARED from the face of the earth? . . . the yawn-smotherers, the shoulder-shruggers, those blasé souls who can't get a thrill any more?

Or does something happen to them when they walk into a Packard showroom?

For we've yet to discover the man or woman who can gaze at this new speed-streamed Packard, and not get as enthusiastic as a press agent!

And Packard's pulse-quickening new beauty is only part of 1940's most exciting motor car story.

What's new? What isn't?

This year, you'll have to scrap your standards of value and get yourself a bright new set.

For with its 4-year expansion program behind it, with factory costs reduced in hundreds of ways—*Packard has made $867* bring you the best-looking, best-performing, biggest-value Packard in all Packard's history!*

Slip into that luxurious driver's seat, set yourself for action—and you'll soon see just what we mean.

Touch the accelerator, *and watch things happen!* For this glamorous new Packard has so much more power per pound of automobile weight that it makes your usual transportation seem pokey!

Now hit for the back country—the home of the forgotten roads. Take even the worst stretch of broken-down macadam in your stride. To your utter amazement, that pitted road will flow under your wheels almost as smoothly as though it were level as a card table!

No other car can match this ride—for no other car has Packard's improved Safe-T-fleX suspension, the envy of the automotive industry!

And if you want still another thrill, wait till dark and switch on those new Packard Sealed Beam lamps—that bring near-daylight to the roads at night.

Yes, if you don't see and drive a new 1940 Packard, you'll miss the greatest motor car sensation that ever brightened a value-conscious world!

ASK THE MAN WHO OWNS ONE

LOWEST PRICES IN PACKARD HISTORY
new 1940
PACKARD
$867

*AND UP, delivered in Detroit, State taxes extra
Prices subject to change without notice

333

"The fourth Packard owner got me"

1. A lot of my friends bought Packards this year, and one of the first was Ed Byrne. So at lunch the other day, I said "Ed, I've got to buy a new car and . . ." "Buy a Packard," he broke in without letting me finish. "I looked them all over and there's nothing that even comes *close* in value." He rattled off a lot of figures to prove it before I had to leave.

2. Dr. Yates came to look at Jimmy's sore throat one day, and I noticed *he* had a new Packard. "Doctor," I said, "you must use your Packard a lot and I'd like to ask you this question—how is it on upkeep?" He laughed. "Mine has gone 10,000 miles and, except for routine lubrication and check-up, it hasn't been in the shop yet." And with that he was gone.

3. I got home one day to find Esther Work there. My wife, giving me a meaning look, asked Esther about their new Packard. Esther's face lit up. "Honestly, I want to tell you that I've never *known* such comfort—it rides like a dream. And it's the easiest car to handle that we have ever owned, by all odds, I'm simply *crazy* about it."

4. Finally, I said to Walt Glenn, a statistician: "I *know* your Packard is a fine car. I *know* it performs like greased lightning. But, does it cost much *to run?*" "No," he said. "It's easy on gas and oil. And take a look at this clipping the dealer gave me. Shows Packard service charges are in line with those of even *small* cars." **P.S.** *MY* new Packard is simply great!

PACKARD $867

AND UP. *Packard 110, $867 and up, Packard 120, $1038 and up. Packard Super-8 160, $1524 and up. Packard Custom Super-8 180, $2228 to $6300. Prices delivered in Detroit, State taxes extra.*

ASK THE MAN WHO OWNS ONE

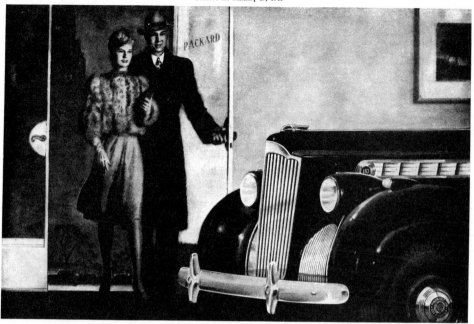

When you cross this threshold,
your Purchasing Power goes up!

AS YOU ENTER A PACKARD SHOWROOM, something new and wonderful happens to your worldly wealth.

In effect, the purchasing power of your money definitely steps up. For the same number of dollars that will buy you a certain amount of car anywhere else, will now buy you considerably *more* car in a Packard showroom!

This simple discovery is leading thousands of *value-seekers* to Packard ownership this year—already promising to be the biggest year in Packard history.

For example, take the question of size. Packard's 122-inch wheelbase is longer than that of practically every car priced at Packard's level, and longer than several cars *higher* in price.

More car for your money

Performance is difficult to reduce to cold figures, but its best yardstick is *horsepower per pound of car weight*. Check the Packard figures against those of any car you may be considering, and you'll appreciate this Packard's rocket-like performance!

But you'll have to look behind the price tag—surprisingly low as it is—to *really* get the picture of Packard value-for-your-dollar.

For here you'll discover Packard quality. Here you'll find breath-taking new beauty of form and line. Here you'll find the prestige of the Packard name. You'll come upon, too, a car whose beauty is *distinctive*—a car that looks unlike every other car, but like a Packard!

So—for a once-in-a-lifetime experience, take this glamourous new Packard out on the highway. And when you come to a pock-marked road—throw caution to the wind that's rushing past! For thanks to Packard's exclusive complete Safe-T-fleX suspension, that bad road becomes a good road—just like *that!*

Right about this time—and this is a promise—you will realize that your purchasing power has indeed gone up! And yours will be the warming discovery that, 4 times out of 5, the car traded in *more* than covers the down payment—and that monthly payments are surprisingly low.

PACKARD
$867

AND UP, delivered in Detroit, State taxes extra. Prices subject to change without notice.

ASK THE MAN WHO OWNS ONE

The New Master of America's Highways

"THE ENGINEER'S ENGINE!"

You are looking at the most amazing engine in America!

This brand-new, Packard-designed, Packard-built husky of 160 horsepower is a masterpiece of mechanics—an engine whose utter perfection wins the admiration of motorists and engineers alike.

It Is The Most Powerful 8-cylinder motor being put into any American passenger car today. It gives the new 1940 Packard One-Sixty so much spirit, fleetness, and getaway, that this Packard is to other cars what a whippet is to a poodle!

Yet this quiet and brawny engine eats less gasoline than many a feebler motor. In fact, the new Packard One-Sixty comes close to equalling the gasoline mileage of cars weighing hundreds of pounds less, and with 40 to 60 less horsepower.

Drive A New Packard One-Sixty and any other car will seem dull by comparison. It has looks, litheness, luxury . . . it has a ride which cradles you in unbelievable comfort—*all at a price hundreds of dollars less than for any previous Packard of comparable size and luxury.* Drive this car—you'll lose your heart to The New Master of America's Highways!

ASK THE MAN WHO OWNS ONE

Model illustrated is Packard Super-8 One-Sixty Touring Sedan $1632* (white sidewall tires extra)

1940 PACKARD ONE-SIXTY

$1524.

*AND UP, *delivered in Detroit. State taxes extra
Prices subject to change without notice*

337

Four-wheeled amazement!

Illustrated: Packard One-Sixty Touring Sedan, $1647* (white sidewall tires extra)

Available in eight body styles and three different wheelbase lengths. Long, lithe, handsomely appointed, this car is a joy to look at as well as a dream to drive.

PACKARD SUPER-8 160

$1524

AND UP. *Packard 110, $867 and up; Packard 120, $1038 and up; Packard Super-8 160, $1524 and up; Packard Custom Super-8 180, $2243 to $6300. *All prices delivered in Detroit, State taxes extra.*

IF your ideas of the best a motor car can do are premised on the best any other car has ever shown you . . . this new Packard One-Sixty will change those ideas. *And quickly!*

Measure its ability by any yardstick you may choose and you'll agree it's the New Master of America's Highways!

LIVELINESS? Beneath its racy hood is the most powerful 8-cylinder motor being put into any 1940 American passenger car—*160 horsepower.* More power per pound of car weight than any other car on the road!

GET-AWAY? Its pick-up is so fast it will take you from 5 to 60 in less than 21 seconds —in high gear!

LOW MAINTENANCE COSTS? Comparable with the best you could get from cars of hundreds of pounds less weight and 20 to 25 less horsepower. In fact, you pay very little more for its premium performance.

HANDLING EASE? Around hairpin turns, through crowded streets or on open roads, this car will stir you to superlatives.

RIDING COMFORT? It's a "good roads movement" on four wheels . . . so smooth it can even smother the "thuds" as tires cross expansion joints!

Drive this great Packard. You will get a new conception of motor car ability. And —*costing less than any previous Packard of comparable size and luxury*—it will also give you a new conception of motor car value!

Dialogue with thousands of dittos!

1. TOM: "George, why do you hang on to that small car of yours—when you could be driving a big new Packard like mine *for the same upkeep*? I tell you I *know*—haven't I compared its costs with smaller cars I've owned?"

GEORGE: "Wait, Tom. I . . . "

2. TOM: "Why, you'd never guess how little my Packard costs to run. It gets *grand* mileage out of gas and oil, and has cost me next to nothing to service. But don't take my word! Figures show Packard's service costs are right in line with those of even small cars like yours!"

GEORGE: "Sure, I know. You can't tell me . . . "

3. TOM: "One more minute, George, till I tell you how I picked it out. I looked into 5 other cars. And in *my* not-too-humble opinion, not *one* of 'em could touch Packard with a ten-foot claim for downright value. So, why..."

GEORGE: "Hey, wait—will you? I've been trying to tell you that I haven't *got* that small car any more! I traded it in on a 1940 Packard."

ENTHUSIASM LIKE THIS becomes a living part of every 1940 Packard owner. It's understandable, too. For the 1940 Packard is the finest we've ever built—on any basis you want to name. It offers more in smart new styling . . . pick-up and performance . . . comfort and roominess. It's easy to buy, thrifty to run. And for *proof* that Packard service charges are comparable to those of even *much smaller* cars—just study the table at right! Why not drop in on your Packard dealer now?

ASK THE MAN WHO OWNS ONE

COMPARISON OF SERVICE CHARGES

Type of Service Operation	Average Charge Packard 110	"Lowest-priced 3"
Service brakes, adjust complete . . .	$2.70	$2.53
Re-line and adjust brakes, 4 wheels . .	13.65	12.81
Clean and adjust carburetor	2.40	2.43
Tune engine	4.75	4.07
Piston rings—renew all, align rods . .	23.65	24.12
Carbon and valve job	13.00	13.98
Front wheel toe-in, check and adjust .	1.25	1.02
Clutch, pedal clearance, adjust . . .	.50	.53
Fan belt, renew	1.90	1.57

SPECIAL NOTE: Prices taken from an impartial flat rate manual used by over 30,000 garages. Being *average* costs, they may be somewhat higher or lower in your city, but they do illustrate the small difference in upkeep between Packard and much smaller cars.

PACKARD $867

AND UP. *Packard 110, $867 and up. Packard 120, $1038 and up. Packard Super-8 160, $1524 and up. Packard Custom-Super-8 180, $2243 to $6300. Prices delivered at Detroit, State taxes extra.*

339

Announcing the "PICTURE PACKARD" *contest*

Photograph America's Most Beautiful Car—and WIN IT!

Limitless possibilities! Just picture any 1940 Packard . . . Any place . . . Any situation

| Beach Scenes | Snow Scenes | Scenic Beauty | "Candid Shots" | Children . . . Pets | Family Groups |

229 Awards—including Five 1940 Packards and $3,600 in cash

CONTEST STARTS JANUARY 15th—COSTS NOTHING TO ENTER!

5 NEW 1940 PACKARDS AS NATIONAL PRIZES!

FIRST PRIZE . . . .
120 Convertible Coupe

SECOND PRIZE . . . .
120 Touring Sedan DeLuxe

THIRD PRIZE . . . .
110 Touring Sedan

FOURTH PRIZE . . . .
110 Club Coupe

FIFTH PRIZE . . . .
110 Business Coupe

START TODAY! If you don't own a camera, borrow one! Remember, it's the *picture* that wins, not the equipment used. Originality . . . beauty . . . drama . . . appeal . . . qualities like these count as much as technical excellence.

But be sure to include a 1940 Packard in the pictures you "shoot"—whatever the situation. Packards at work, Packards at play . . . any color, any body style—just as long as it's a *1940* Packard!

See your Packard dealer or photographic store *today* for official rules and entry blank. Your Packard dealer will gladly give you a copy of "Winning Hints" —packed with picture ideas and professional suggestions. And study the 1940 Packards on display in his showroom for "camera angles".

Don't delay! The "Picture Packard" contest starts Jan. 15—ends March 15. The sooner you start, the better your chance to win a 1940 Packard!

ALSO 74 CASH PRIZES TOTALING $3,600

6th Prize — $500 • 8th Prize—$200
7th Prize — $300 • 9th Prize—$100

10 Prizes of $75 Each
15 Prizes of $50 Each
20 Prizes of $25 Each
25 Prizes of $20 Each

150 AWARDS OF MERIT

50 Silver Medallions
100 Bronze Medallions

Enter today—See your Packard Dealer or Photographic Store

340

It's happening on a thousand Main Streets!

1. THIS YEAR, something has been happening on Main Streets all over America. For increasing thousands of average-income motorists have discovered that they don't have to keep on buying ordinary cars . . . they can own a truly *fine* car. Take the case of the Harry Browns . . . typical Americans. Our close-up shows their first eye-opener—the discovery that their neighbors in the modest house next door have bought a Packard!

2. A FEW DAYS LATER, the Stedmans took them riding. "Such a big, roomy car!" admired Mrs. Brown. "Watch her go," said Bill Stedman. Miles slipped by. Hills bowed down . . . rough spots vanished magically.

3. GHOSTING HOMEWARD, Harry fired questions at his neighbor . . . found that Bill hadn't had to pay a penny down! His old car *more* than covered the down payment, so that his monthly payments were unbelievably low. (This happens 4 times out of 5.)

4. NOW—weekends find this note in the Brown's milk bottle. They have a beautiful, smart new Packard of their own. Its flashing performance and its astonishingly low operating costs delight them. And this same experience can be *yours.*

THE SWING'S TO PACKARD!

This year, thousands of new owners have joined the Packard family.

Ask *any* of them what he thinks of his 1940 Packard. Then *try* to break away from his enthusiasm for the newly-styled Packard lines, for the car's verve and spirit, its all-around fineness. And operating costs? He'll declare his Packard a veritable miser on gasoline—and that he can hardly remember when he last had to "add a quart" of oil!

Add these owner facts to what your Packard dealer will *show* you: that service charges on a big, roomy Packard actually compare favorably with even those of the so-called "economy cars"! But drive a new 1940 Packard *yourself*—and you'll know—*immediately*, why this promises to be Packard's biggest year!

ASK THE MAN WHO OWNS ONE

PACKARD
$867

AND UP. *Packard 110, $867 and up. Packard 120, $1038 and up. Packard Super-8 160 prices begin at $1524. Packard Custom Super-8 180, $2228 to $6300. All prices delivered in Detroit, State taxes and white sidewall tires (as shown) extra.*

FIRST WITH A <u>REALLY</u> REFRIGERATED CAR!

When heat makes you swelter and humidity wilts you down, there's *new* relief in sight—step into a new Packard and banish *both!*

You can step OUT of summer heat—when you step INTO your stunning new Packard! Yes, Packard makes possible this long-awaited motoring comfort for summer's sweltering heat —the first mechanically refrigerated air-cooling system ever offered to motor car owners.

Dehumidifies as well as cools! It may be 90 or 100 in the shade *outside*—but *inside* your smart new Packard it's early Spring, cool and clean and comfortable. What's more, this miraculous Packard Air Cool-ditioning *dehumidifies* as well as *cools*. It is Packard's latest "famous first" in a long distinguished line!

Real refrigerated air—This Packard cooling unit cools by actual *refrigeration*—not merely by fan-driven air. In refrigerator-plant rating its rating is 1½ *tons of ice* at a motor speed of 60 miles an hour.

Supplies clean, filtered air! If you can't get away during the hay fever season, your next best bet is an Air Cool-ditioned Packard. For in its spacious, comfortable interior you'll breathe *clean, fresh, filtered* air.

Quiet, forced circulation! The fresh, clean, refrigerated air is circulated to every part of the car by a fan—concealed and quiet. Here is how it works: air follows along the top of the car, returns to the floor, under the rear seat to the cooling coils—where it is re-cooled and re-circulated. The comfort of an Air Cool-ditioned Packard is a revelation beyond that you have ever known in motoring.

And—don't shout, they can hear you! In this superbly comfortable air-cooled Packard, you ride free from open-window traffic noise and the rush of wind which so often carries away one's words with it! In this greater silence, front and rear seat passengers converse with ease and complete audibility. You enjoy a ride that is infinitely more restful than any you have ever experienced.

• • •

So add this newest achievement in super-comfort to the many reasons why your next car should be a beautiful new Packard. It is available installed at the factory, at extra cost. And your nearest Packard dealer will be glad to show you what a grand thing it is!

PACKARD
$867 to $6300

delivered in Detroit, State taxes extra.
Prices subject to change without notice.

Air Cool-ditioning is available on closed models of the Packard 120, Super-Eight 160, and Custom Super-Eight 180 at extra cost, installed at the factory.

ASK THE MAN WHO OWNS ONE

Illustrated: Packard One-Twenty Business Coupe, $1038* (white sidewall tires extra)

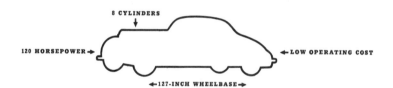

8 CYLINDERS

120 HORSEPOWER →

← LOW OPERATING COST

← 127-INCH WHEELBASE →

Choose a car as you choose a friend!

NO other eight we know of has such winning ways. No other eight has quite the same ability to make warm and loyal friends.

This, because the Packard 120's unique qualities parallel those which men instinctively seek in the lasting friendships they make. Qualities to be admired and esteemed. For your car, like a friend, must win your complete confidence.

And recognition of this crops up in your *first* chat with the *first* member of the One-Twenty's loyal family you meet. He will pull out all the stops in his praises of this great Packard's stunning appearance, flashing pick-up, and the luxurious feel of "riding on air" which its *extra length* provides.

And he will tell you tall but *true* tales of the mileage his car spins from gasoline and oil. If he has had his car long enough for any of the commoner service operations—he will confide happily that One-Twenty service charges are right in line with those of *much smaller and cheaper cars!*

Such enthusiasm is worth looking into, so drive this Packard 120 *yourself!* Note its eager answer to your half-formed wish. Its stirring tempo when you give it the gun . . . its "sixth sense" in its noiseless drift through traffic. And when you've done all this, compare this truly fine car with *any other eight!* Chances are dollars to dimes, on the record of 1940, you'll choose a Packard One-Twenty!

PACKARD 120
$1038

AND UP. *Packard 110, $867 and up. Packard 120, $1038 and up. Packard Super-8 160, $1524 and up. Packard Custom Super-8 180, $2243 to $6300. *All prices delivered in Detroit, State taxes extra.*

ASK THE MAN WHO OWNS ONE

Here is your hope!

IF YOU'VE DREAMED OF A
MIRACLE IN MOTOR CAR LUXURY
—THIS IS YOUR CAR!

Illustrated—The Club Sedan, $2297 (white sidewall tires and Weather-Conditioner extra)*

EVEN FOR THOSE to whom the luxurious is commonplace, this magnificent new Packard One-Eighty holds eye-widening wonders.

You wonder that ingenuity could conceive this car, that craftsmanship could offer so much in beauty and style and luxury—for you may have in this new car the unbelievable comfort of conditioned air—filtered, and heated or cooled—every day of the year!★

Indeed, of generations of fine cars, this is Packard's very finest. Of this car we are proudest.

And we are scarcely less proud of *this* achievement: *this car is priced hundreds of dollars less than were any of its noble ancestors.* No comparable Packard has ever cost so little.

Open a door—no car ever whispered a more

irresistible invitation to "come in." You enter—a veritable salon of spacious roominess is yours. So different from the cramped, the conventional—so like the home of some gracious host.

To ride in it, we promise you, will be a thrill. For whether you creep along in crawling traffic or whisk over miles in a few fleeting minutes—you marvel that this car can do either with equal ease.

You seem to feel that something has miraculously smoothed your road—so smoothly do you glide along—and you are right.

For Packard's Safe-T-fleX suspension keeps jolts from plaguing you—you lounge in the lap of luxury-cushions. You end the longest ride eager for more.

Your Packard dealer will be glad to bring this car

to your door—if you will phone him. And by all means do. By all means—drive this car. If you ever hoped for a car incredibly fine, beautifully appointed, a dream to ride in—this car is your hope!

•

ASK THE MAN WHO OWNS ONE

PACKARD ONE-EIGHTY
$2228

*AND UP, *delivered in Detroit. State taxes extra. Prices subject to change without notice.*

SOCIALLY—AMERICA'S *FIRST* MOTOR CAR

★ *Cooled by Mechanical Refrigeration in Summer*

—and heated by the same unit in winter—1940 Packards set a new standard in motor car comfort. By means of this latest Packard "first," the air inside your car is not only cooled or heated to the degree

you may desire, but it is also filtered—cleaned of pollen and dust—and, in summer, dehumidified. This year-round accessory, the Weather-Conditioner, is available at extra cost, installed at the factory.

As "position" in a class magazine was of prime importance to an advertiser, Packard's claim to the page facing the TABLE OF CONTENTS in several periodicals made an enviable record during the great years . . . On this and the following two pages an imitation gold-colored ink was used for the background blocks in the original ads. Since this ink demonstrated a propensity for absorbing the facing page's imprint, a glance at these backgrounds will confirm the Company's preeminence in *Fortune* magazine.

INTRODUCING THE 1940 PACKARD CUSTOM ONE-EIGHTY

A CAR IN WHICH LUXURY REACHES A NEW HIGH ...AND PRICE A NEW LOW

Illustrated— The Formal Sedan, leather back and top, $2894(white sidewall tires extra)*

IT IS SAFE TO SAY that never in Packard's 40 years, has so much luxury graced a motor car!

It is safe to say that here is a car so outstanding in value that you'll look twice before you believe its price. For the magnificent new Packard Custom Super-8 One-Eighty costs hundreds of dollars less than any previous Packard of comparable size and luxury.

It is safe to say that never has such a stunning Packard taken to the roads. The new speed-streamed body, the narrower radiator, the longer, rounded bonnet, the chromium side-grills, are new and different—yet the car is still unmistakably a Packard.

No matter what other cars you may have known, we predict that this Packard One-Eighty will make them seem sadly outclassed.

In fact, it is no mere turn of phrase to say that

this car reaches new heights of luxury, not alone in the things that meet your eye, but in the things that contribute to your physical and mental enjoyment.

For example, tremendous horsepower has been balanced against weight to such a nicety that this car is a performing wonder. To drive this new Packard Custom Super-8 on crowded streets is an eye-opening experience! And at cruising speeds on the open road, no Packard has ever demonstrated so brilliantly the luxury of power. Thanks to this brand-new engine, the car actually seems to loaf at whatever speed you drive. Cruising becomes a completely new sensation.

Nor have you known the luxury of comfort until

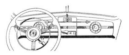

you drive this great Packard. Its ride is literally unbelievable—and no wonder. For it is the combined result of Packard's Safe-T-fleX suspension—and of cushions which use not one, but *three*, luxurious cushioning elements.

Superfine upholstery, superb tailoring, and the graceful new fittings and trim, make the interior of this car a delight. You'll find yourself put to it to

choose from among the ten custom-styled models.

We urge you to get acquainted with the most thrilling creation in Packard history—the 1940 Packard Custom Super-8 One-Eighty. Phone your Packard dealer—and he'll gladly bring one to your door.

•

ASK THE MAN WHO OWNS ONE

PACKARD ONE-EIGHTY

$2228

*AND UP,*delivered in Detroit, State taxes extra*

SOCIALLY—AMERICA'S *FIRST* MOTOR CAR

To people who refuse to be second

THIS NEW CAR JUST CAN'T BE CHALLENGED BY ANYTHING ELSE ON WHEELS!

Illustrated—the seven-passenger, 148" wheelbase Limousine, $2723 (white side wall tires extra)*

THIS YEAR, those who insist that their car be *first* in luxury, *first* in performance, *first* in beauty will find their choice of a motor car simple.

For Packard's newest masterpiece – the new Custom Super-8 One-Eighty – is exactly that *topmost car.*

Gloriously new from bumper to bumper, this car is Packard's proud best—the finest Packard built today. The finest Packard *ever* built. Even its price is something new. For this car costs *less by hundreds of dollars* than any equally large, equally luxurious Packard ever created.

For your eye, this car offers a feast of beauty—of jewel-like appointments. And this luxury is

more than surface-deep. Step into this car, look around you—and you'll see what we mean.

First among the unusual luxuries this car offers is the luxury of ample room. There is leg room for the longest and elbow room for the widest. A veritable living room on wheels!

And there are luxuries about this car your eye can never ferret out.

Its motor, for instance, has tremendous power. But motor power and car weight have been mated so perfectly that you seem to glide at whatever speed you go. You may creep along some crowded

city street, or you may flash along some wide and open road—either ride will thrill you.

Actually, you don't seem to ride, you seem to *drift.* There is a refreshing lack of huff and puff. Never before have you seen a motor do wonders so easily.

And you are literally cradled in comfort — by

Packard's complete Safe-T-fleX suspension. You settle back into cushions so deep, so luxurious, that no ride, however long, seems long enough.

Phone your Packard dealer. He will gladly bring the 1940 Packard One-Eighty to your door. Drive this car—and a completely new motoring joy will be yours!

ASK THE MAN WHO OWNS ONE

PACKARD ONE-EIGHTY

$2228

*AND UP, *delivered in Detroit, State taxes extra. Prices subject to change without notice.*

SOCIALLY — AMERICA'S *FIRST* MOTOR CAR

346

Glamour car of the year!

(OF COURSE, IT'S A PACKARD!)

★ One look at it starts little fires in your eyes. For this superbly styled Custom Packard is easily the most exciting car that ever kindled your urge-to-own.

It is all this era's dash and dare, all its dignity and distinction fashioned into one.

It is the car which motor-show goers throughout America have honored with more citations of praise, seemingly, than any of the other 1940 motor cars.

Such admiring comments as these: "The most beautiful" . . . "The most modern" . . . "The very finest."

Yet this distinguished car, as illustrated above, is priced at only $4570*.

Look inside—ingenuity and good taste have performed a score of miracles. No other car in America is more magnificently appointed.

And drive this car. It boasts no less than 160 horsepower. The most powerful 8-cylinder motor in any American passenger car whispers beneath its bonnet. The ability of this car is as eye-widening as its style. And its 127-inch wheelbase provides a steady, stable ride that spells rest-cure comfort.

Actually, from your first look to the end of your trial trip this will be the most surprising car your searchings have ever discovered.

In fact, there is perhaps only one thing about this car that isn't surprising—one thing you would expect so fine a car to be. And that is—it is a Packard!

The Packard Custom Super-8 One-Eighty is available in numerous body styles and several wheelbase lengths. Packard has prepared a special brochure

giving detailed information on these distinctive custom creations which is yours for the asking.

347

Brimming with Beauty

This stunning new Packard One-Ten Deluxe Sedan is available in many brilliant Multi-Tone combinations—both inside and out. Like all of the new 1941 Packards, it's completely restyled, bumper to bumper, roof to road. Nothing like it on the road!

—the Class of

—Bursting with News!

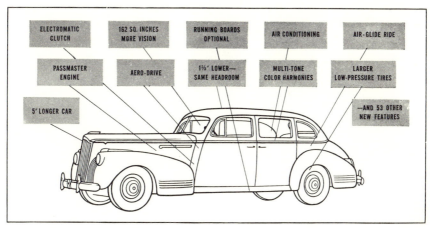

ELECTROMATIC CLUTCH	162 SQ. INCHES MORE VISION	RUNNING BOARDS OPTIONAL	AIR CONDITIONING	AIR-GLIDE RIDE
PASSMASTER ENGINE	AERO-DRIVE	1½" LOWER— SAME HEADROOM	MULTI-TONE COLOR HARMONIES	LARGER LOW-PRESSURE TIRES
5" LONGER CAR				—AND 53 OTHER NEW FEATURES

The NEW 1941 Packard

YOUR FIRST delighted glance will tell you the 1941 Packard is both the *newest* and the *smartest* car on the road! Completely redesigned! Inches longer . . . inches lower . . . and "luxury" the watchword!

Its stunning new Multi-Tone color combinations are available with a variety of equally stunning upholstery options inside.

And the chart above highspots only 11 of the engineering advances which total 64 in this superlative new car.

New! Passmaster Engine Cuts Fuel Costs 10%!

Along with the dash and fire of this spirited power plant comes a new mechanical master stroke!

Without sapping an *ounce* of this great engine's flashing power, Packard engineers have succeeded in cutting its already-low gasoline consumption by *no less than 10%!*

Couple these welcome savings with negligible oil consumption and low upkeep cost, and you have a thrifty trio that's hard to beat.

New! Electromatic Clutch Lets Your Left Foot Loaf!

In the new 1941 Packard, the *car itself* operates the clutch! Your left foot loafs. This Packard-perfected clutch works on a new principle, free from the defects of earlier devices. If desired, the conventional foot-clutch can be employed by touching a button. There's nothing complicated, nothing new to learn, about using Electromatic Clutch —and it's available at *very low* extra cost.

New! Aero-Drive Doubles Fun of Driving!

One ride tells you that Packard's Aero-Drive doubles the fun of open-road driving! For it lets your engine turn lazily over—*27% slower*. And when you want to pass a car, in cuts a mountain-climbing gear — automatically —

and you fairly zoom past! (Aero-Drive, optional at extra cost, is a money-saver, too— cuts gasoline consumption up to 20%!)

New! Air Conditioning— A Packard FIRST!

No mere ventilating device, but real, refrigerated air conditioning. (Costs extra, but you'll bless it every mile you drive!)

Check all 64 features that make Packard the year's smartest buy. And remember Packard's low upkeep! A recent survey shows a Packard needs servicing less often than *any other car!* See your Packard dealer now!

ASK THE MAN WHO OWNS ONE

Your Packard dealer has the good news about 1941 prices!

Packard makes this a great year for left feet!

THE 1941 Packard starts eliminating work right down at the foot—*your* left foot.

Yes, your left foot loafs—doesn't have to do a thing but enjoy the ride! For this blessing, you can thank the engineering genius behind the new Packard Electromatic Clutch*—a *radically different* clutch using a new vacuum and electric principle.

A dozen things recommend it over other devices. There's no "creeping" forward. No danger of oil leaks. No slippage after engagement. No lag. Getaway is lightning fast—and the clutch engages with much more smoothness than anyone but an expert driver could achieve. Furthermore, a dash control permits conventional clutch operation when wanted —for easier sub-zero starting and for second-gear braking while descending steep mountain grades.

Try it! And try the amazing Packard Aero-Drive*. It saves gas, oil and engine wear—and combined with Electromatic Clutch, it saves *shifting*, too!

But these are only *two* of 64 new features in the 1941 Packard. See glamorous new Multi-Tone interiors—with 261 trim combinations, 122 of them at no extra cost! Passmaster Engine, 10% more economical! Real Air Conditioning* (a Packard *first*) . . . Air-Glide ride—and 58 other improvements.

Your dealer extends this cordial invitation, "Come in! Drive this Packard with Electromatic Clutch— and while your left foot loafs—discover *all* the reasons why Packard is the class of '41!"

ASK THE MAN WHO OWNS ONE

PACKARD—*the Class of '41*

$**907** TO $**5550**
FIVE LINES OF NEW CARS—
40 BODY STYLES

★*delivered in Detroit, State taxes extra. Prices subject to change without notice.* *Available at extra cost.*

Illustrated: 1941 Packard One-Ten Special Coupe, $907★ (white sidewall tires extra).

350

Cuts your footwork in half!
Packard Electromatic Clutch

Illustrated: the new Packard One-Ten Deluxe Touring Sedan

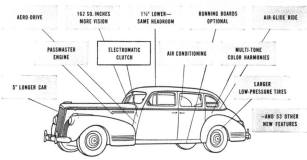

AERO-DRIVE

162 SQ. INCHES MORE VISION

1½" LOWER— SAME HEADROOM

RUNNING BOARDS OPTIONAL

AIR-GLIDE RIDE

PASSMASTER ENGINE

ELECTROMATIC CLUTCH

AIR CONDITIONING

MULTI-TONE COLOR HARMONIES

5" LONGER CAR

LARGER LOW-PRESSURE TIRES

—AND 53 OTHER NEW FEATURES

ONCE YOU TOUCH THE STARTER of the new 1941 Packard, you've opened the door to amazement in motion—new and more effortless than you ever dreamed of!

For in this brilliant new Packard, your left foot loafs. It just goes along for the ride, the *car itself* operates the clutch.

The Packard Electromatic Clutch takes over the clutch operation . . . the letting-out and letting-in that used to keep your left foot so busy. This moderately-priced Packard optional feature has none of the defects that marred earlier self-operating clutches. It engages at *just the right rate,* neither too slow nor too fast. A combination of electrical and vacuum control does a smoother job of operating the clutch than *you* would do for yourself.

It has the further advantage of making the conventional foot-clutch available, if desired, by touching a button. And, in combination with the Aero-Drive, this Packard improvement not only eliminates footwork on the clutch—but reduces gear-shifting as well!

The Electromatic Clutch is only *one* of 64 bright new features that make the 1941 Packards the most exciting cars of the year. There's glamorous new Multi-tone beauty—inside and out—with no less than 261 color harmony combinations.

There's the Passmaster Engine, 10% more economical than preceding thrifty Packards. There's Aero-Drive*, giving you a dividend of *one mile free in five!* There's Air Conditioning* (a Packard *first*) which puts heat and humidity to rout with real refrigeration. There's Feather-light handling ease, Air-Glide ride, —and these are only the starting points!

Make no mistake, the new 1941 Packard is *new* from stem to stern. Longer, lower, lovelier, infinitely more luxurious, it's truly the Class of '41. See it now, and—*Ask the man who owns one!*

**Available at extra cost.*

P. S.

Your Packard dealer has the good news about 1941 prices!

NEW PACKARD—the Class of '41

351

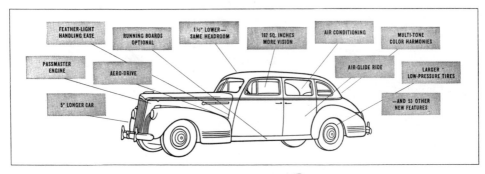

Full of surprises as a Christmas stocking

Illustrated: the new Packard One-Ten Deluxe Family Sedan

NUMBER ONE surprise of the new-car season comes with your first wide-eyed look at this longer . . . lower . . . lovelier . . . infinitely more luxurious Packard! With no less than *64 new features!*

Take the Passmaster Engine—packing all the famous Packard dash and spirit, but now giving you a dividend of *10% greater fuel economy!*

Or take the new Packard 1941 Aero-Drive, which lets your motor loaf even at cruising speeds, slowing your engine down 27% . . . and when you want to pass, automatically cuts in a mountain-climbing gear that *sprints* you by the car ahead. Well worth its extra cost for added driving pleasure alone, yet

Aero-Drive also cuts gas consumption up to 20%!

And for another top-of-the-stocking surprise, there's the Packard Air-Glide Ride—motoring's mellowest. On boulevard or back road, the Packard Safe-T-fleX spring suspension and larger, low-pressure tires combine to iron out the bumps with magic smoothness.

Yes, match the surprising features of this new Packard against the field. Note Air Conditioning—a Packard *first!* Real, mechanically cooled air conditioning, an optional extra cost feature that pays big comfort-dividends the whole year round! Try Tru-course steering . . . test Packard handling ease . . .

feast your eyes on the Multi-tone custom interiors, boasting 261 possible trim combinations (122 of them at no extra cost!)

Don't miss a point! And then, find out for yourself how very, *very* economical this stunning surprise-packed Packard is to own. See your Packard dealer now! Ask him for the facts on Packard low upkeep cost—or better yet, *ask the man who owns one.*

Five lines of new cars—40 body styles

$**907** to $**5550**

Delivered in Detroit, State taxes and white sidewall tires extra! *Prices subject to change without notice.*

NEW PACKARD—the Class of '41

This little foot went to market....

(BUT JUST FOR THE RIDE)

Driving is a lot easier—a lot *surer*—when you get behind the wheel of a 1941 Packard with Electromatic Drive*. Even in reversing, you never touch the clutch pedal. There's *nothing* for your left foot to do—it just goes along for the ride!

Get-away is lightning fast! With Packard Electromatic Drive you *zip* ahead from stop lights—no trace of "lag." The clutch engages, *automatically*, but with all the quick, positive response you are used to, and whisks you smoothly on your way.

Stopping for a red light? You don't have to touch clutch or gear shift—nothing but the brake pedal. Nor do you ever have to use the brake pedal to keep the car from "creeping" forward on the level after coming to a full stop.

And that's not all! Shifting is easier—and you have full control at all times. You shift when *you* want to, not when the car wants to. No wonder Packard owners cheer for *Electromatic* Drive!

And what a blessing in traffic! Electromatic Drive lets you stop-and-go with effortless ease—quickly, smoothly, with what it takes to keep you out in front. Just forget the clutch—the car itself does the work *and does it better!*

But sometimes a clutch pedal is mighty useful—for instance, to avoid "drag" in cold-weather starting, or for engine-braking on a steep grade. So Packard provides a handy dash control to permit conventional clutch operation whenever you wish it.

Simplified driving, at its very best, is just *one* of 64 improvements that we've packed into the stunning 1941 Packards for your amazement and delight. There are many other mechanical marvels, such as real, refrigerated Air-Conditioning*. . . the thrifty Passmaster engine, 10% more economical . . . and the famous Packard Air-Glide Ride. Here, definitely, is a car you *must* see and drive. There's a great big WELCOME on your nearest Packard dealer's doormat, and it's meant for you. Drop in and see this wonder car today—won't you?

ASK THE MAN WHO OWNS ONE

The big, roomy 6-passenger Packard One-Ten Sedan, $990★ (white sidewall tires extra)

PACKARD
the Class of '41
$907 TO $5550

*delivered in Detroit, State taxes extra. Prices subject to change without notice. *Available at extra cost.*

353

"Luxury's Lap" is now on wheels!

STEP UP AND MEET the 1941 version of "Luxury's Lap"—designed by Packard!

What catches your eye first in this roomy, oversize interior? Right! Those Multi-tone custom effects in upholstery and trim! And below you see only *one* of the 261 combinations available—122 of them *at no extra cost!*

Not until you sink back into the lower . . . softer . . . deeper seats, however, do you fully realize that you are—beyond the shadow of a doubt—cradled in luxury's lap! These cushions are *orthopedically* contoured! There's room in abundance—and clear vision wherever you look.

More revelations? No less than 64! Packard Passmaster power has cut gas consumption by 10%. Electromatic Clutch* lets your left foot loaf. Packard's famous Safe-T-fleX suspension joins with larger, low-pressure tires to give you the Air-Glide ride—motoring's smoothest!

Then there's thrifty Aero-Drive* that reduces engine speeds and gives you 1 free mile in 5! You may even have *real* Air Conditioning* with refrigerated, dehumidified air.

Yes, "Luxury's Lap"—with upkeep that challenges the *lowest*—is now on wheels. What's more, it's waiting for you at your nearest Packard dealer's. *Ask the man who owns one.*

Harmonizing tones, even in the new Beaut-ility instrument board, with its handsome new lacquers and plastics. Your Packard dealer's "Color Harmonies" selector will show you all the available combinations—some at a slight extra charge, others at no charge at all.

Smart new styling is in evidence everywhere. This pleasingly soft-toned upholstery, bound in contrasting leather, with the sparkle of chrome for added charm—is typical of the many tasteful trims awaiting your selection.

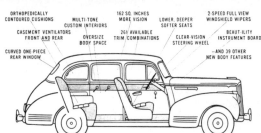

ORTHOPEDICALLY CONTOURED CUSHIONS
MULTI-TONE CUSTOM INTERIORS
162 SQ. INCHES MORE VISION
LOWER, DEEPER SOFTER SEATS
2-SPEED FULL VIEW WINDSHIELD WIPERS
CASEMENT VENTILATORS FRONT AND REAR
OVERSIZE BODY SPACE
261 AVAILABLE TRIM COMBINATIONS
CLEAR-VISION STEERING WHEEL
BEAUT-ILITY INSTRUMENT BOARD
CURVED ONE-PIECE REAR WINDOW
—AND 39 OTHER NEW BODY FEATURES

NEW PACKARD
the Class of '41

Five lines of new cars—40 body styles

$907 to $5550

Prices delivered in Detroit, State taxes extra. Subject to change without notice. *Available at extra cost.*

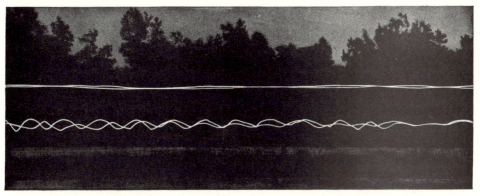

A 4-color picture of comfort

Cameraman taking night photo of the famous "Packard Air-Glide ride." Car was run over railroad ties. Exposed negative traced paths of lights fixed to hubcaps and windows, as shown in large picture above.

(Above): **The Result!** All the words in the dictionary would not give you so graphic a picture of comfort as those tell-tale lines of light.

The lower pair of dancing lines indicates the wheels, bouncing over railroad ties. Those even upper lines, at window sill height, trace the level, superbly mellow Packard Air-Glide ride.

You can give most of the credit to Packard's famed, improved Safe-T-fleX suspension—the finest suspension that ever cradled a motor car. In addition, ample weight, scientifically distributed... larger, low-pressure tires...no less than 25 rubber chassis cushions—all contribute to unsurpassed riding comfort.

Delightful as the Air-Glide is, it's only *one* of 64 all-star *news* in this longer, lower, more luxurious 1941 Packard. Drive it!...with the gas-saving Aero-Drive*, the thrifty Passmaster engine, amazing new Electromatic Clutch*, and *real* Air Conditioning*—a Packard FIRST!

Yes, drive it—and let this superlative new Packard prove it has everything you want in your next car!

ASK THE MAN WHO OWNS ONE

$907 TO $5550
FIVE LINES OF NEW CARS
40 BODY STYLES

*Delivered in Detroit, State taxes and white sidewall tires extra. Prices subject to change without notice. *Available at extra cost.*

PACKARD – *the Class of '41*

Packard Custom Convertible Victoria—$4685* as illustrated

What could it be <u>but</u> a Packard?

WHENEVER YOU see an unusual stir around a curb or driveway this year, it's more than apt to be occasioned by the glamorous car above.

This car is, naturally, a Packard. When you see a car so head-and-shoulders above the field . . . so smart, so sophisticated, so patrician . . . it is hard to imagine it being anything *but* a Packard.

Owners tell us that wherever this distinguished Custom Packard parks or pauses, traffic is well-nigh disrupted by admirers.

And engineering ingenuity has made this Packard just as outstanding *mechanically* as it is in looks. It offers one of the most powerful 8-cylinder motors in any American car, and its ride is no less than cushioned luxury. And other delights greet you at every turn of your first trial trip.

Its Electromatic Drive, for example, is a revelation in simplified automatic driving. The clutch operates *itself* with uncanny skill, yet this is only *part* of the story. Electromatic Drive saves footwork . . . saves shifting . . . even saves gas, oil, and engine wear by letting the engine loaf. It's 1941's newest feature—and it makes driving a brand-new thrill!

Windows, in enclosed models of this distinctive One-Eighty, glide open—or shut—at the touch of a button. And available in *all* closed Packards, at extra cost, is a sensational new Packard "first"— *real, refrigerated* Air Conditioning!

The only thing that *isn't* surprising, in this surprising car, is that its long, rakish bonnet wears the most famous, best-loved face in motoring.

• • •

This superlative Packard Custom Super 8 One-Eighty is only *one* of many super cars Packard offers for 1941. We make no boast when we state that they represent the ultimate word in everything that a custom car should be. Packard has prepared a special brochure giving detailed information on these custom creations. It is yours for the asking.

*Delivered in Detroit, State taxes extra. Price also includes Electromatic Drive, installed at factory.

ASK THE MAN WHO OWNS ONE

The *Senior*

PACKARD

One-Sixty · One-Eighty

—THE CLASS OF '41—

A STAR IS BORN

1. One year ago, many a car-lover whistled enviously at the ad above. It pictured a long, swaggering, low-slung car —flight-lined as a trans-oceanic clipper. It was the custom-built Packard One-Eighty. Its price was $4570—and *up!*

2. Though the average man could only look and long, a fortunate few could—and *did*—look and act. A sprinkling of One-Eighties showed up at smart resorts. Wherever they went they stole the show. They became Palm Beach's favorite background for press photographers. They were, literally, the sensation of the fine car world.

3. Movie stars, no strangers to exotic cars, thrilled to the One-Eighty. A leading man, attending a premiere left his custom Packard parked by Grauman's Chinese Theater. Returning, he found it mobbed—not by just the usual admiring crowd—but by Hollywood's car-blasé celebrities.

4. From every quarter, Packard field scouts reported. "It's a sensation!" But the question furrowing Packard brows was this. Could this magnificent $4500 custom-made car be built to Packard's exacting standards and sold at a price most car-owners could afford?

5. Packard and three world-famous designers tackled the job. Result: a revolutionary new car that outshines even its custom-built "parent" —a car that brings fleet, modern clipper stream-lining down to earth in a new common-sense design. Packard proudly presents . . .

CONTINUED ON NEXT PAGE ➤

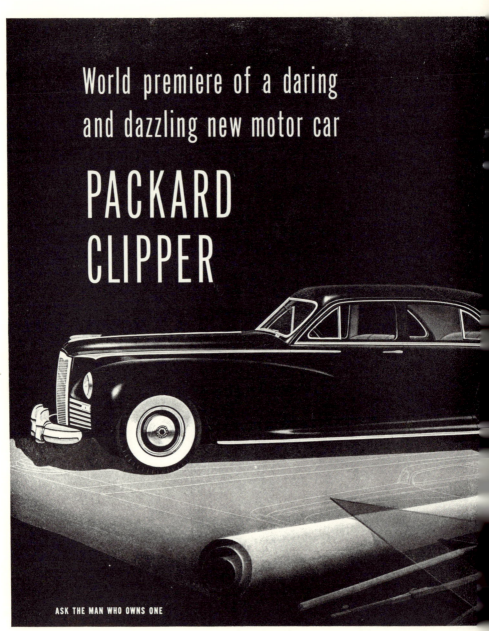

World premiere of a daring
and dazzling new motor car

PACKARD
CLIPPER

ASK THE MAN WHO OWNS ONE

Sensational addition *to the 1941 Packard line which now offers*
41 body styles in 6 different model series. The stunning Straight-

Eight Pa
(Not for

358

Low, wide, rakish—and the first car to bring common sense to modern design!

HERE, FOR THE FIRST TIME—in this glamorous new addition to the already-extensive 1941 Packard line—is a car of advanced streamlined design which recognizes that *beauty*—to be really modern—*must be functional . . . must serve some useful purpose.*

Thus, while the graceful and daring new PACKARD CLIPPER is a dazzling delight to your eye...everything about it adds in some way to your *comfort*, your *safety*, or your *convenience*. For instance . . .

WIDER THAN HIGH—by almost a foot! Widest body made, in fact—and a brand-new beauty line! Yet the Clipper's width is *inside the body* for "three-in-a-seat" comfort. And its overall width is no greater than that of ordinary cars.

LOWER—FOR SAFETY—The fact that the Clipper is low, racy, ground-hugging, makes it beautiful. But, because it has a lower center of gravity, it is a *safer* car to drive and ride in! And (though this is hard to believe) road clearance is actually *increased!*

6 lines of cars—41 body styles
$907 TO **$5550**

**Delivered in Detroit—white sidewall tires and State taxes extra.
Prices subject to change without notice.*

CONVENTIONAL STREAMLINED CAR   PACKARD CLIPPER

FULL HEADROOM IN THE REAR, TOO—Here is functional beauty strikingly demonstrated. For the Clipper—alone among the latest streamlined cars—has full headroom in *back* seat as well as front. No neck-bending. No hunching-over. No hat-hitting.

FADE-AWAY FENDERS—Notice that runningboards are concealed—until you open the door. Thus it is the most natural thing in the world for the front fender to "fade" into the door in a beautiful new treatment, and for even the *rear* fenders to blend smoothly into the body—no unsightly seams or joints.

A "Mid-Season Auto Show"!— THE CLIPPER, with its rugged, low-slung chassis, is a triumph in engineering as well as styling! We can only *hint*, in this limited space, at the 84 new improvements that await you. *For example:* The Clipper's sensational ELECTRO-MATIC DRIVE is the last word in simplified automatic driving . . . worth far more than its extra cost . . . well worth a visit to your Packard dealer just to try it!

This daring new Packard Clipper is an Auto Show all by itself! It's more than stunning! It's revolutionary. See it . . . and drive it . . . at your nearest Packard showroom!

National defense comes first with Packard!—Marine motors for the Navy, and Rolls Royce aviation engines for the Army, have a clear right-of-way. But Packard is big enough to handle defense assignments and car production—so important to employment and prosperity—at the same time.

...own above is priced at only $1375*
...ut for the 4-door sedan illustrated).

Above: Brilliant 1941 Packard addition, the straight-eight Clipper—a 4-door sedan—$1375*

PACKARD CLIPPER
—first streamlined car planned for "lookers" and riders!

LOOK AT THOSE LINES! Your eye telegraphs the news that this is no ordinary streamlined car!

But the real news is *this:* The beauty of this dazzling new Straight-Eight Clipper is truly modern *because it's functional!* Every feature adds in some way to your safety, your comfort, or your convenience.

Notice, for example, the long sweep of the Clipper's "Fade-Away" fenders . . . how they actually fade into the body. Result: the widest of bodies with the width *inside* where inches count!

Balance — And Beauty! That shapely, streamlined deck is big and sturdy, and you might expect it would be hard to raise. But one finger lifts it easily, because it's counter-balanced for your convenience. There's an abundance of storage space, of course.

Every new beauty line of the Clipper has an *inside* reason that means more comfort. Example: a low roof line—yet most rear-seat headroom of any car.

Wider Than High, by nearly a foot! The Clipper's low-slung breadth means more stunning appearance —also more comfort for "3-in-a-seat" occasions, and *safer* driving because of a lower center of gravity. Yet the Clipper is no wider overall than ordinary cars—and road clearance is actually *increased!*

A Revelation In Roominess — more modern, more luxurious interiors feature the Clipper. For smarter appearance, as well as ingeniously added leg room, Packard has double-recessed the back of the front

seat. Comfort and luxury are made uniquely complete by the Clipper's new Air-Glide Ride—that brings rear-seat passengers all the smoothness and softness of "front-seat" riding. A superb achievement of Packard engineering.

A New Angle On Smartness! The windshield is raked smartly back—49 degrees to be exact. And it's the widest windshield made—for unequalled visibility!

Your Packard dealer invites you to "skipper the Clipper." Try it! You'll find it the most revealing experience a motor car has ever provided!

ASK THE MAN WHO OWNS ONE

6 lines of cars—41 body styles

$907 TO $5550

*Delivered in Detroit—white side-wall tires and State taxes extra.

Prices subject to change without notice

Sensational addition to the 1941 Packard line—the stunning straight-eight Packard Clipper Sedan.

New beauty you'll appreciate with your eyes closed

PACKARD CLIPPER 4-DOOR SEDAN $1375*

ANYONE WITH half an eye can see that the daring, low-slung Packard Clipper is the handsomest thing that runs on rubber.

But, more important, it brings you a new *kind* of beauty—beauty you can appreciate, even *blindfolded!* This is *functional* beauty—beauty that serves a useful purpose in addition to delighting your eye.

Hence, you can ride in the Packard Clipper and realize, without having to look, that everything about it contributes, in some way, to your comfort, your safety, or your convenience.

Wider Than High by almost a foot! Sit in the spacious front seat and stretch your arms in the *widest* body made! Fade-away fenders make this possible, by "fading" into the front doors with a lovely new line. Yet this extra width is *inside*, where it means more

"3-in-a-seat" comfort, where it permits the concealed running boards to be wide and safe. Overall, the Clipper is no wider than ordinary cars.

Full Rear-Seat Headroom! Lean back in the roomy rear seat, and leave your hat on! The Clipper, alone among modern streamlined cars, provides full headroom in the *back seat* as well as in the front seat. This is real functional beauty—low, graceful streamlining that puts the passenger's comfort first!

New "Air Glide" Ride—Cradled in a newly-designed suspension, the Clipper gives you the first rear-seat ride with "front seat comfort," levels out the road with magic ease. Yet this is only one of 84 new ad-

vancements the Clipper will show you at your nearest Packard dealer's.

Lower—For Safety! Low-slung, rakish, yet the Clipper has *more* road clearance—and a lower center of gravity makes it *safer* and easier to handle. It's a new thrill to "skipper the Clipper"—try it today!

ASK THE MAN WHO OWNS ONE

6 lines of cars—41 body styles
PRICES BEGIN AT $907*

Delivered in Detroit—white side-wall tires and State taxes extra. Prices subject to change without notice.

361

HISTORIC HORSEPOWER

TODAY, with defense a national watchword, American engineering and production skill is a priceless asset. Packard speeds its defense assignments with an experience gained by designing and building practically *every* type of engine: land, marine, and aircraft—gasoline and Diesel—"V", parallel, "X", in-line, radial, inverted, single and opposed.

3. 124 miles per hour on the water! Gar Wood's famous "Miss America" packed the greatest concentration of power ever built into a speedboat—6400 horsepower! For years, these Packard engines have turned back all efforts of Europe's top engine designers to lift the coveted Harmsworth trophy.

1. Remember the famous Liberty motor? Packard co-designed it! Packard was also the first and largest builder of this sensational World War engine. Fast LePere fighter plane above (Packard-built and Packard-Liberty powered) set one-time world altitude record of 34,509 feet. And now, Packard has been entrusted with building—by the thousands—an equally-famous engine...the ultra-modern motor that powers today's battle-tested, history-making fighters—the Hurricane and Spitfire.

4. Water Wasps powered by Packard for the U. S. Navy! The trio of Packard motors in this sea-going "Elco" torpedo boat churn up 1350 horsepower each—4050 in all! Hundreds of these super-marine engines are needed for this new development, and Packard is proud to be responsible for this mammoth production assignment.

2. It has never mattered to Packard engineers whether the assignment calls for something that flies...floats...rolls...or crawls! For example, this U.S. Army tank—swift 23-ton predecessor of today's monsters—depended upon V-8 power specially designed and built by Packard.

5. What does all this mean to the man who is about to buy a motor car? *Just this:* You, as a Packard owner, will have a stake in this record of achievement. For in this superb 1941 Packard is the sum total of Packard's 42 years of experience. One glance will tell you that it is new from roof to road...completely re-styled inside and out for new smartness, new luxury. But to realize what its 64 brilliant new mechanical improvements mean, *you must drive this great Packard yourself.* Visit your nearest Packard dealer, check each of its exciting new features, and you'll be the next owner of a 1941 Packard! *$907* to *$5550*, delivered in Detroit, State taxes and white sidewall tires extra. Prices subject to change without notice.

ASK THE MAN WHO OWNS ONE

Horse Power for the Navy—Six of the Navy's new "Elco" patrol torpedo boats, streaking through coastal waters at close to a mile a minute. Each of these swift, hard-hitting Water Wasps is powered by a trio of 1350 horsepower Packard marine engines, churning up a total of 4050 horsepower!

Somewhere in England—A squadron of Spitfire fighting planes lined up for action. Packard, chosen to build—by the thousands—the famous aviation motors which have been so thoroughly battle-tested in the Spitfire and Hurricane fighters, recognizes this assignment as a tribute and a challenge to Packard precision production.

Packards for the Army—Just a part of a Packard fleet, over three blocks long, recently delivered to the Army for service as Staff cars. Land transport, too, must have swift, dependable performance—and these roomy, 160-horsepower Packard Super 8's answer all of those major requirements with plenty of power to spare.

Sisters under the skin

On LAND, sea, and in the air, Packard-built power plants are answering today's emphasis on the need for swift, powerful, and dependable performance.

Thanks to 42 years of experience—with almost every type of engine, for almost every type of mobile equipment—Packard has been ready and able to undertake assignments calling for superfine precision production.

Fortunately, too, Packard is big enough to fulfill its responsibilities to national employment and prosperity—to give defense clear right of way and carry on with regular car production at the same time.

All of Packard's traditional skill in engineering, production and craftsmanship are embodied in every new 1941 Packard that "rolls off the line". Once you enjoy the superb performance it combines with amazing dependability and all-round economy—you'll want a Packard for your own. $907 to $5550, delivered in Detroit, State taxes extra.

PACKARD

ASK THE MAN WHO OWNS ONE

Low, wide and swagger—with smart *functional* beauty—the first Packard Clipper was a sensation overnight! Prominent style-mark: Speed-lined "Fade-away" fenders, first featured by Packard. For 1942, Clipper styling is yours in even the lowest-priced Packards!

Choose your horsepower—for 1942—on the same wheelbase—you can have either a Clipper Six (105 H. P.) or an Eight (125 H. P.). Difference in price: only $55. Both motors are thrifty, fiery, precision-built marvels.

Save gas, oil, and engine wear with Packard's sensational Electromatic Drive. Eliminates clutch-pedal operation...banishes wasteful "slip"...reduces engine speed by 27.8%. An "extra"—but delighted owners say, "It pays for itself!"

For 1942, *new Clipper styling* - in

STUNNING NEW CLIPPERS JOIN FLEET—Above is shown the smart, new-styled 1942 Packard Six Club Sedan. Both Clipper Six and Eight are available as either Special or Custom models *and in three distinguished body styles.*

Beauty that pays off in dollars — The Clipper's super-slipstreamed design results in important gas economy! Precision meters prove the 1942 Clipper tops even last year's gas-thrifty Packard by as much as *18% more miles per gallon!*

Pedometers tell the story of the low-slung Clipper's "cradled" ride. Sensitive shock-recording meters show that on rough testing-roads the Clipper is at least 29% smoother-riding than its predecessor, a car famous for its Air-Glide ride.

You may have to keep your new car a long time. Will it see you through? Yes—if it's a Packard. Typical reason for long life: Clipper uses 44 ball and roller bearings (instead of far less costly bushings) — more than *any* competitive car.

even the lowest-priced Packards!

A FEW SHORT MONTHS AGO, Packard raised the curtain on a daring, brand-new kind of car . . . the Clipper . . . and the whole country joined in a roar of applause.

Today Packard brings *two new versions* of this sensationally-successful Clipper styling to *every* price class in the 1942 Packard line. Now, not only the more expensive Packards, but even the *lowest-priced* Packards, are stunning, super-streamlined Clippers!

Beauty that *works* for you!

These magnificent new Clippers, even more than before, recognize that beauty, to be keyed to the times, must be *functional*—must contribute to *economy, long life,* and *comfort.*

For example, the Clipper's flight-lined styling not only achieves dazzling new beauty, but cuts down air resistance to an almost unbelievable extent. Result: Tests conducted with scientific accuracy prove that these brilliant new 1942 Clippers knife through the air with an actual improvement in gasoline savings of 12% to 18% over even last year's thrift-champion Packards!

Dozens of dividends!

In addition to fuel savings, Clipper functional design pays welcome dividends in many more ways.

These dividends are yours in the form of 26% better visibility through the Clipper's wider, deeper, sharply-raked windshield . . . easier, safer handling—evidenced by 24% steadier "wind-steering" . . . 20% more quiet inside the car —for Clipper streamlining hushes the wind . . . a 14% step-up in acceleration—to give you the security of always having a lightning burst of passing speed on tap.

More power reserve!

And by cutting wind drag as it does, Clipper design combines with improved engine efficiency to provide sparkling performance with a gain in power reserve of 32%! This means less engine strain on hills— smoother operation at *all* times.

And for the man who buys a car today, the Clipper offers something else—even more important . . .

Built for the "long haul"

When you buy a Packard Clipper you *know* you have a car that's precision-built for lasting durability . . . with nothing skimped, no "substitutions" that impair quality . . . a car that will give you *extra* miles and *extra* years of service, long after ordinary cars have worn out—in looks and fact!

So drop around today or tomorrow to your nearest Packard dealer's. Skipper a Clipper just once— and you'll want to skipper one for keeps!

CLIPPER DIGEST FOR '42

Here's a quick review of still other high-spots you'll find in the new 1942 Clippers . . .

- Nearly a foot wider than high
- Full headroom front *and rear*
- *Integral* "Fade-away" fenders
- Even wider doors
- Phenomenal handling ease
- Wide-angle vision

ASK THE MAN WHO OWNS ONE

LOOKING AHEAD?

SKIPPER THE CLIPPER

One of two distinguished new versions of Clipper styling for 1942 — the smart Packard Clipper Touring Sedan. Both Clipper Six and Eight *(only $55 difference)* are available as either Special or Custom models.

How Clipper beauty pays off...
in more miles per gallon!

THOSE LONG, LOW, RACY LINES you admire so much do more than delight your eye.

They're also there because (among other benefits) they enable the Clipper to cut through the wind with phenomenally low resistance — *hence save you gas.*

Proving Ground tests provide exact figures on this new economy. For example: last year's Packard was a marvel of thrift (an economy champion, in fact). Yet, tested against the new Clipper, it lost out. The Clipper was not only better—but 12% to 18% better on gasoline mileage!

Yet the Clipper offers something even more important to the car buyer of today. *It is built to meet the times!*

These are times that put a new high premium on *quality.* Quality that pays out in *extra miles, extra years, extra value.*

So, if you want a car that's a "long haul" husky — combined with the fuel economy so important today — Skipper the Clipper! There's one waiting for you at your Packard dealer's. **ASK THE MAN WHO OWNS ONE**

1942 PACKARD CLIPPER

MEET THE NEW CHAMPION! — 1941 Packard was *thrifty.* But actual test shows how Clipper design steps up economy. Same amount of gas was put into both cars. True-scale diagram shows Clipper's margin.

FLIGHT-LINED FOR ECONOMY—Precision meters prove that Clipper streamlining cuts wind resistance; results in important gasoline-economies! The 1942 Clipper delivers up to *18% more miles* per gallon!

BRINGING SENSATIONAL CLIPPER STYLING to every Packard line permits lower Clipper prices. Even the 1942 Clipper 8 is substantially lower priced than '41 Clipper 8 —same power—same room—same comfort.

SLICE YOUR GAS BILL FURTHER . . . and enjoy automatic driving at its best . . . with Packard Electromatic Drive! Lets engine run slower . . . saves gas, oil, and engine wear. More than repays its extra cost.

One of the two new versions of sensational Clipper styling for 1942—the Clipper Special Club Sedan.
Both Clipper Special and Custom models offer your choice of 6 or 8 engine—only $55 difference.

How Clipper beauty adds up...
TO A 29% SMOOTHER RIDE!

LOOKING AHEAD?

SKIPPER THE CLIPPER

YOU'LL LOOK at this rakish 1942 Packard Clipper with kindling eyes! And you'll think, "More beautiful—*sure!* But what's beauty got to do with ride?"

Just this: The Clipper is exceptionally low-slung for greater beauty. But this *same* daring design also permits a better type of suspension, which smothers jolts . . . bounce . . . sidesway. It delivers, *naturally*, the smoothest ride you've ever enjoyed. Scientific shock-recording meters show that the Clipper rides *29% smoother!* (See test below.)

Another advantage of this advanced streamlining: it enables the Clipper to cut through the wind with far less drag—*and to save you gas*. Example:

Proving Ground tests show that the Clipper gives 12% to 18% better gasoline mileage than last year's economy-champion Packard!

But, perhaps even more important now is *long life*. The 1942 Clipper is a wise choice for your new car, because it's built for the "long haul" . . . with nothing skimped, no "substitutions" that impair quality. So, for *extra* miles and *extra* years, head for the nearest Packard dealer's and . . . Skipper a Clipper!   **ASK THE MAN WHO OWNS ONE**

1942 PACKARD CLIPPER

RIDE-RECORDERS reveal the Clipper's incredibly smooth "cradled" ride. Sensitive shock-recording meters prove the Clipper 29% smoother-riding than last year's ride-famed Packard!

TURN-AND-BANK indicator adds proof of improved Clipper ride. Measuring roll on turns, this device shows the Clipper to be 12% steadier than even last year's "solid-citizen" Packard.

NEWS! CLIPPER STYLING throughout the Packard line means lower '42 Clipper prices. Even the Clipper 8—same power, room and comfort as the '41 Clipper 8—actually costs less!

SAVES GAS, SAVES WEAR! Electromatic Drive is simplified automatic driving at its best! Eliminates gas-wasting "slip" . . . saves gas, oil and engine wear. Worth many times its extra cost.

367

ANNOUNCING A

Wartime Service Plan for Packard owners

Today, of course, Packard production is 100 per cent on war assignments.

But even though we are no longer building cars, we are not forgetting our responsibility to Packard owners. That is why we have set up a special Wartime Service Plan—a plan that will help conserve your transportation, and will save you expense and inconvenience.

See your Packard dealer for further information about the timely services described below:

1. A free inspection and "Car Health" analysis. Expert mechanics go over your car thoroughly—give you a complete "car health" analysis. If work is needed it is classified as (1) URGENT—do now; (2) IMPORTANT—do soon; or (3) DESIRABLE—but can wait. There is no charge or obligation. The rest is up to you. Chief purpose of the plan is to catch little troubles before they grow up.

2. Monthly Protective Service Contract. This contract entitles you to a substantial discount on certain essential services you *know* your car will need during the next 10,000 miles—such as chassis lubrication, oil change, wheel "toe-in," tire cross-switch, etc. Conserving your transportation is a patriotic duty. Your Packard dealer is best qualified and best equipped to help you. See him today.

PACKARD IS WORKING TO WIN!—building Rolls-Royce aircraft engines for the Army—Packard marine engines for the PT boats of the Navy.

PACKARD
ASK THE MAN WHO OWNS ONE

" THE AMERICAN MONSTER WITH THE FLAPPING WINGS ! "

WHEN Lt. John D. Bulkeley, U.S.N., returned from the Far East, he brought with him news of the Tokyo broadcast, that said:

"America has developed a secret weapon, a monster with flapping wings, which makes a lot of noise and fires torpedoes in all directions."

What "secret weapon" threw the Japs into this blind frenzy, dreaming up wings that just weren't there? It was the Navy's incredibly fast, highly versatile PT boats, powered by Packard. They're the boats that sank Jap transports in Subic Bay, that sent a Jap cruiser to the bottom, downed dive bombers, strafed troops on shore. One of them carried General Douglas MacArthur safely away from Corregidor.

You can get an idea of what we mean by *fast* when we tell you some of the history of the PT boats.

Powered By Packard

Ever since World War I, Packard has carried on research and development work in aircraft-type marine engines. Speedboats provided a natural proving ground and, year after year, famous craft powered by Packard engines outraced the best to be had in international competition.

When the Navy needed power for its PT boats, Packard was ready to roll with a super-charged marine engine perfectly suited to the job. Long before Pearl Harbor, the assembly line was sending an endless stream of these precision giants to boat builders here and abroad.

Precision Production

Packard wartime production is *precision* production—marine engines for the PT boats, Rolls-Royce engines for aircraft—both assignments of the most exacting kind.

Out of this experience are emerging new discoveries and advanced techniques that will be reflected in the Packards of the future.

ASK THE MAN WHO OWNS ONE

PHOTO COURTESY ELCO NAVAL DIVISION

PACKARD
FOR PRECISION POWER

The Navy "E"—awarded to Packard's Marine Engine Division "for Excellence and Achievement"

1. Without a single exception, Packard employees have gone all-out for the "Work to Win" program, have voluntarily pledged 60 full minutes of every working hour to speeding up production, proudly wear "Work to Win" pins, have changed the famous Packard slogan to "Ask the Man Who *Wears* One."

2. Teamwork! Packard president Geo. T. Christopher (center) and Union Local president Curt Murdock (left) show army air forces' Commanding General H. H. Arnold and Brig. Gen. B. E. Meyers (right) how Packard management and labor are striving together toward a common objective: Victory!

The kind of story Hitler hates

{ *What Packard is doing is the sort of thing* }
{ *Hitler thought couldn't happen in a democracy* }

RECENTLY, when Government first recognized the production efforts of U. S. factory workers, nine Packard employees stepped into the limelight to receive awards—the first ones given to workers in the automotive industry.

These awards were given for production shortcuts—fruit of a *continuing* plan of management-labor co-operation that recognizes employees on a man-to-man basis of fair treatment.

Birth of "Work to Win!"

Early in '42, Packard war production reached a new high in output of aircraft and marine engines. But Packard management was convinced it could go still higher . . . through a plan starting with a voluntary pledge from every worker to improve and increase war production by applying shop initiative and ability.

The idea was discussed with union leaders in Packard Local 190 UAW-CIO—men who shared the opinion that one way to win this war is to increase production.

Together, in a series of meetings, management and labor whipped the original plan into Packard's now-famed "Work to Win" program, a plan to speed up machines, not men.

Already, the plan is stepping-up production . . . is bringing a flood of workers' suggestions (8107 to date) . . . is carrying Packard's long-harmonious management-labor relations to new heights of understanding.

Workers give production ideas

Patriotic war-workers have already turned in 646 ideas which company engineers have put to use in increasing output . . . and hundreds more are under consideration for early adoption.

Some of the ideas have resulted in new, ingenious, time-saving tools. Others have enabled one machine to do the work which formerly tied up two. Still other suggestions have brought about entirely new methods and procedures, have greatly improved quality, stepped up efficiency.

Making records . . . then breaking them

As one result of the "Work to Win" program, Packard employees are consistently meeting tough WPB quotas on two of the most complicated and precise jobs in the entire U. S. war production effort.

And there is still another result—one which holds a promise for the *peacetime* era ahead. By helping to develop and perfect the skills and techniques of vast manpower, the "Work to Win" plan is also making a real contribution to the betterment of the industrial future.

But meanwhile, the entire Packard organization—spurred on by cheers from Washington—is out to break still *more* wartime records!

Secret of the new Curtiss (P-40F) Warhawk's spectacular performance is the terrific power of its Packard-built Rolls-Royce engine. Packard craftsmen tool these brute engines to the hairline accuracy of a fine jeweled watch. Pilots who've flown the P-40F say its power plant helps to make this ship a honey to fly—and a high-fightin' fool!

3. Joint Management-Labor Committee chosen respectively three from company (above left) and three from union (right) steers the program. Separate in function from usual shop committees, this impartial group scans every suggestion turned in, checks it as a workable idea, awards the war worker his coveted "Wings" pin.

4. Citation banners, merit awards, production scoreboards, plant posters, worker written shop slogans, all remind the Packard employee that every idea he contributes speeds up the war effort even more. In the "Work to Win!" program he finds an unusual chance for recognition and advancement.

5. These Packard Work-to-Winners' production shortcuts won them the first Government awards ever given war workers. Left to right: John Hook, Harry Gielniak, I. A. Clark, Fred Ospedale, Max S. Harris, Peter Cojei, William H. Switzer, George Smolarek, and (*absent*) David Fabert. **F-L-A-S-H!** Washington just advises 11 *more* have been similarly honored!

6. Another honor for Packard Workers. Stephen Kmieciak, veteran marine-engine builder, accepts Navy "E" button from Lt. Cmdr. A. R. Montgomery of an Atlantic PT-boat squadron, on behalf of his fellow workers. Kmieciak, with 38 years of continuous service, is third generation in his family to work for Packard. 531 Packard employees have served the company for 25 years or more.

PACKARD
PRECISION-BUILT POWER

★
Buy War Bonds and Stamps
★

OFFICIAL PHOTO—U.S. NAVY

Every Packard Worker is proud of the inspiring performance of the Navy's famous PT-boats. Powered by Packard super-marine engines, these swift, hard-hitting boats have seen plenty of action, have written glorious and heroic chapters in the naval history of the Allied Nations . . . from Subic Bay to the English Channel!

Ask the man who **FLIES** *one!*

1. *"I'll take this Warhawk* any time for combat flying," said one Curtiss test pilot after taking up this latest thing in pursuit ships, the P-40 F. Army pilots are now using the *Warhawk* against the enemy. Whisking "upstairs" in a hurry is its specialty.

2. **The Warhawk's terrific power** makes only short take-offs necessary. That was a comment of another test pilot. The *Warhawk* climbs fast— and its Packard-built Rolls-Royce engine is the source of the power back of that fast-climbing performance.

3. **It's a thrill** to see a trio of Warhawks swoop down on an objective, shoot upward and "blossom out"—but no more thrilling than it is to the pilots! Fliers say this combination of plane and power makes the P-40 F a wonder of maneuverability.

4. Loaded with terrific striking force, moving with bullet-like speed, the *Warhawk* is the newest member of the famous Curtiss P-40 family.

It is powered by a Packard-built Rolls-Royce engine—the same design that powers the versatile, battle-tested Spitfires and Hurricanes of Great Britain.

These precision engines, as they flow in great numbers off Packard's continuously moving production line, are like jeweled watch movements—so fine and so finished is their workmanship.

This isn't unusual at Packard. Since the last war Packard has precision-powered equipment that rolls, flies, caterpillars, and scoots through water: cars, planes, tanks, record-breaking speedboats—and now the hard-hitting, fast-moving PT boats you hear so much about.

When the war is over, Packard will be making cars again—better cars and finer cars. For many advances in making wartime motors can be translated into automotive improvements —and they'll be there in your future Packard!

ASK THE MAN WHO OWNS ONE

PACKARD

FOR PRECISION POWER

Back in "coffin corner" went Rommel's Axis divisions as U. S. Warhawks helped to pound them relentlessly. Packard workers heard the news with cheers, for they build the Rolls-Royce engines that power these planes.

"Streamline pile-drivers loaded with dynamite!" That's what men in Uncle Sam's famed Mosquito fleet call their PT Boats. The hit-and-run PT's, powered by Packard super-marine engines, are making a terrific dent in Axis tonnage.

Did you know this family secret?

You've read, in your daily newspaper, about the exploits of the fighting weapons shown here. The group ranges from the amazing PT Boats to four-engined bombers. Yet all of them are "sisters under the skin" . . . powered with precision built engines by Packard.

Too fast to catch! Swift DeHavilland mosquito bombers rely on pure speed to complete their missions unscathed. With two Packard-built Rolls-Royce engines to supply their power, these long-range streaks are giving the Luftwaffe plenty of headaches.

"Can openers" is the name they've given the Hurricane —equipped with 40 mm. guns—for its spectacular tank-busting feats in North Africa. Many a Packard-built Rolls-Royce engine has helped to write the fighting log of this deadly British fighter.

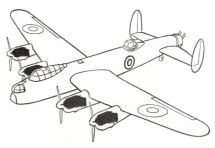

"To Berlin—with the compliments of Coventry" might well have been scrawled on the block-busters dropped by England's multi-ton Lancasters. These four-motored giants depend on Packard-built Rolls-Royce engines on their nightly sweeps over German targets.

Duration durability. Packard Clipper quality counts double today, for the craftsmen who once built these cars are "all out" on war work now. They're building *fighting* engines today—and storing up new precision experience that will produce even finer post-war Packard cars. Meanwhile, Packard dealers have ample parts and a special war-time "car health" plan to keep your car in A-1 running order.

PACKARD

Precision-built Power

•

ASK THE MAN WHO OWNS ONE

373

When life hangs on millionths of an inch

THIS INCIDENT HAPPENED WHEN the Allies were pounding Rommel's divisions back into "Coffin Corner"...

The engine of a Warhawk fighter plane, flown by an American pilot, was ripped by 20 mm. shell fire. Half-blind from leaking oil, the pilot refused to bail out. He streaked for home—and made it.

Later, he was reported* to have remarked, "I've been thinking about writing to the Packard people about the way their engine brought me over a mountain and kept me up for 45 minutes without any oil in it. But I probably won't get around to it."

It's not necessary for you to thank us, Lieutenant. A lot of the men and women at Packard who helped build that Rolls-Royce engine saw the dispatch. And many of them felt that they had *special* reasons for being both proud and thankful that you came back safely . . .

Sue Bramble, pictured at the right, for example.

It's her job to check surface finishes. She is one of many inspectors who made sure that vital parts of that precision engine you flew were finished down to *millionths* of an inch . . .

parts "jeweled" and polished so finely that they brought you home even with the precious lubricant leaking away.

Building engines like this has meant working to a degree of accuracy that was undreamed of by any automobile manufacturer in peacetime. Yet Packard craftsmen are turning out these superb Rolls-Royce engines in mass-production quantities, by modern mass-production methods.

Today, Packard-built Rolls-Royce engines

are going into twin-engine deHavilland Mosquito bombers, 4-motor Lancaster bombers, and Hurricane and Warhawk fighters—delivering the kind of performance that fighter pilots and bomber crews know they can depend on.

And in the Navy's famed PT boats, Packard super-marine engines are more than living up to the exacting and time-honored traditions of Packard craftsmanship.

Tomorrow, Packard's wartime lessons in precision manufacturing will bear fruit in immeasurably finer peacetime Packard cars.

Ask The Man Who Owns One

PACKARD
Precision-Built Power

* From a dispatch by Kenneth Crawford in the newspaper "PM", April 23rd issue

How soon

can <u>you</u> get a new car?

Perhaps, like so many other people, you're figuring on being able to get a new car in a matter of months.

If that's what you think, you're really an optimist!

And that's the reason for this message, published as a timely service to *all* motorists.

10 million people now need new cars

Yes, 10,000,000 people actually *need* new cars today. That's quite a waiting line!

And every year, several million more cars will wear out and need replacement.

Even when the car industry swings back into production, it will take quite a while to whittle down that waiting line.

Where do YOU stand in this line?

Maybe you will be able to get one of the first cars built.

But most people should plan on having to drive their present cars longer than they think.

If you can get one sooner, fine. But the wise course is to play safe—and take good care of your car.

Your "car of the future"

. . . may be the selfsame war-weary car you're driving today—for some time, at least.

But here's a cheering note. When the industry gets the "green light," it will re-convert to car production *fast*.

Packard's expansion program, mapped out long ago, calls for post-war car production double its best peace-time year. (And they will be finer, better Packards—well worth waiting for!)

So, pamper that car of yours!

Don't abandon the careful driving habits learned during the war!

Keep on driving carefully, to conserve your tires, your gas, and your car. See your dealer for a "check up" twice a year—and let him catch little troubles before they grow into big ones.

That's the way to make your car last. That's the way to keep it running right until you're *sure* you can trade it in on a new one!

A S K   T H E   M A N   W H O   O W N S   O N E

Packard-built Rolls-Royce Aircraft Engines

Packard PT Boat Marine Engines

PRECISION-BUILT POWER

375

The split second that brings 'em back <u>alive</u>

Marzean's <u>still in the fight</u>--
he just <u>changed</u> battlefronts!

Lae, New Guinea, Sept. 1943—The Jap planes came over at 2:00 P.M.

Then came waves of Jap bombers and torpedo planes.

Standing in the bow of his LST, Leo Marzean swiftly relayed orders from the bridge to the gun crews.

It took iron nerve to stand, a target for bullets and bombs, calmly passing along those vital orders. But the fate of his shipmates hung on Marzean's words.

Marzean came through—and so did the LST with its precious cargo and crew.

Detroit, Michigan, Oct. 1944—Leo Marzean didn't stop fighting when he came home with an honorable discharge.

Now he's one of the 41,000 workers manning Packard's production lines. Along with over 1,200 other veterans he's helping to turn out Packard marine engines for PT boats, and Packard-built Rolls-Royce engines for war planes.

These ex-servicemen know this is the time to bear down and finish off the Axis.

They don't want this war to last even one day longer than it has to—for every day costs more American lives that might have been spared.

Are, you too, doing everything you possibly can to help our fighting men shorten the war and come home again?

LET'S DO <u>MORE</u> IN '44!

PACKARD
PRECISION-BUILT POWER

ASK THE MAN WHO OWNS ONE

* **Leo Marzean,** now an aircraft gear machine operator at Packard, is a long way from New Guinea. But he's still in the fight—building the finest combat engines that can be made, vital parts to keep America's transportation system rolling. He's proud of the job he's doing, —and we're proud of men like him.

377

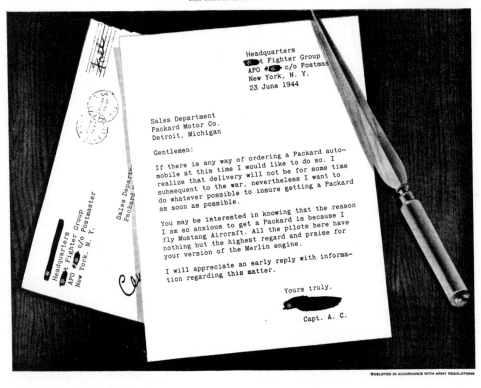

Headquarters
❋t Fighter Group
APO #❋ c/o Postmas
New York, N. Y.
23 June 1944

Sales Department
Packard Motor Co.
Detroit, Michigan

Gentlemen:

If there is any way of ordering a Packard automobile at this time I would like to do so. I
realize that delivery will not be for some time
subsequent to the war, nevertheless I want to
do whatever possible to insure getting a Packard
as soon as possible.

You may be interested in knowing that the reason
I am so anxious to get a Packard is because I
fly Mustang Aircraft. All the pilots here have
nothing but the highest regard and praise for
your version of the Merlin engine.

I will appreciate an early reply with information regarding this matter.

Yours truly,

❋

Capt. A. C.

❋DELETED IN ACCORDANCE WITH ARMY REGULATIONS

A letter we prize . . . from a Mustang pilot overseas

We're grateful to the pilot who took time out to write this letter.

For it's always welcome news to hear —right from the boys who fly 'em—that Packard-built Rolls-Royce engines are doing a good job in this war.

Today, we're concentrating on keeping these aircraft engines—and Packard marine engines for PT boats—flowing to the fighting front to help shorten the war.

But, as soon as the progress of the war permits, we'll swing back into car production again—and we have already told our pilot friend that he will get his Packard "as soon as possible."

He can be certain—and so can you—that it will be a car worth waiting for . . . built to the same high standards as that Packard-built Rolls-Royce engine he's flying today.

★ ASK THE MAN WHO OWNS ONE ★

Mustang
Fighter

Warhawk
Fighter

Hurricane
Fighter

Mosquito
Bomber

Lancaster
Bomber

Packard
PRECISION-BUILT POWER

Navy
PT Boats

Army
Rescue Boats

Built to Forget...that's why it will be long remembered

"Built for a pilot to forget!"

That, we believe, is the highest compliment that could be given an aircraft engine.

And that's the reputation the Packard-built Rolls-Royce engine has earned for itself—in famous planes like the Mustang, the Mosquito, and the Lancaster.

Behind the combat record of these Packard-built power-plants is Packard craftsmanship—the ability to turn out precision engines on a mass-production basis, at a rate the enemy never dreamed could be possible.

Packard takes pride in building an engine that pilots can "forget" while they're flying and fighting—but an engine whose role in this war will be long remembered.

ASK THE MAN WHO ~~OWNS~~ *FLIES* ONE

Strafing at ground level or fighting in the stratosphere, pilots bet their lives on Packard-built engines—and win!

MUSTANG
fighter

WARHAWK
fighter

HURRICANE
fighter

LANCASTER
bomber

PACKARD
PRECISION-BUILT POWER

MOSQUITO
fighter-bomber

NAVY
PT boat

ARMY
rescue boat

● When war progress permits, Packard cars will roll off assembly lines again. They will be cars worth waiting for—built by the same skills that have already produced more than 60,000 Rolls-Royce aircraft engines and Packard marine engines for PT boats.

Presenting a Patriotic Hoarder

1. Supporting the coming Victory Loan—and holding on to *all* your War Bonds—is one of the finest ways to be a patriot.

The boys who fought Germany and Japan did not let *us* down. We will never be able to repay our debt to them in full. But putting the Victory Loan over in record time will be some recognition of what they have done.

2. In addition to buying Victory Bonds, there's *another* way to serve your country—and to do *yourself* a service at the same time.

It's this. Be a car patriot!

Pamper your car—keep it rolling as part of the nation's vital transportation system. Make it l-a-s-t. Even with the war won, it may be a long time before you can buy a new one.

True, Packard is ready to build new cars, just as soon as materials become available. But like all other manufacturers, Packard can produce only a limited number. America's total output of new cars this year will be only a drop in the bucket toward meeting the tremendous pent-up demand.

So, we repeat—take good care of that car of yours. Whenever you need expert help, your Packard dealer is ready and eager to do his part.

ASK THE MAN WHO OWNS ONE

Packard
PRECISION-BUILT POWER

Nearly 70,000 Packard Marine engine and Packard-built Rolls-Royce aircraft engines—for the famous planes and boats at the right—have helped to speed victory over Germany and Japan.

Two ways to be a Patriot

1. **Giving your blood** to help save an American boy's life — that's one of the very finest ways to be a patriot. Won't you call up your nearest Blood Donor Center today and make an appointment?

★　★　★

2. **There's another way** to be a patriot, too. It's a way to do an important service to your country — and to yourself.

In short, be a Car patriot!

For, with cars heading for the junk pile at an alarming rate, America's transportation system is seriously threatened. And a breakdown in our transportation system would be a crippling blow to war production.

So, for your own sake, and your country's sake, do everything you can to keep *your* car rolling. Drive it carefully, and stretch out the mileage in your war-weary tires by staying under wartime speed limits.

Most important of all, go to your Packard dealer and have him check little mechanical troubles before they grow into big ones.

Remember — thousands of cars are joining the "ghost fleet" every week. Don't let yours be one of them!

ASK THE MAN WHO OWNS ONE

Packard

PRECISION-BUILT POWER

Over 65,000 combat engines — and still they come!

Packard-built Rolls-Royce aircraft engines for Mustangs, Mosquitoes, Lancasters, Warhawks and Hurricanes.

Packard Marine engines for PT boats and rescue craft.

Here's the last *PACKARD*
'Til we win the war—
It's "all out" on *ENGINES*
To even the score !

Since this picture was taken, Packard has completed more than 55,000 combat engines. Shown here escorting the last Packard from the lines are factory officials, including Pres. Geo. T. Christopher (right)

Don't make the mistake of forgetting this picture

HERE YOU SEE the last new Packard that rolled off the line— *more than three years ago.*

We're showing you this picture to remind you that your car— even if it's one of the last cars built in America—is now an *old* car.

So drive it carefully. Take good care of it. For it will be longer than you think before you can get a new one.

You can conserve your car, and prolong its life, by protective service. Take care of little troubles before they develop into major repairs. Don't let "hidden dangers," caused by wartime driving conditions, catch you by surprise.

Here at Packard, we've already built over 55,000 Packard marine engines and Rolls-Royce aircraft engines—and still they come. Someday, a new and finer Packard car will roll off our assembly lines. But until that day, remember this picture.

Its moral is: *take care of the car you've got!*

ASK THE MAN WHO OWNS ONE

| MUSTANG fighter | WARHAWK fighter | HURRICANE fighter | LANCASTER bomber |

PACKARD
PRECISION-BUILT POWER

| MOSQUITO fighter-bomber | NAVY PT boat | ARMY rescue boat |